IMAGINATION AND THE CONTEMPORARY NOVEL

Imagination and the Contemporary Novel examines the global pre-occupation with the imagination among literary authors with ties to former colonies of the British Empire since the 1960s. John Su draws on a wide range of authors including Peter Ackroyd, Monica Ali, Julian Barnes, André Brink, J. M. Coetzee, John Fowles, Amitav Ghosh, Nadine Gordimer, Hanif Kureishi, Salman Rushdie, and Zadie Smith. This study rehabilitates the category of imagination in order to understand a broad range of contemporary Anglophone literatures, whose responses to shifts in global capitalism have been misunderstood by the dominant categories of literary studies, the postmodern and the postcolonial. As both an insightful critique into the themes that drive a range of the best novelists writing today, and a bold restatement of what the imagination is and means for contemporary culture, this book breaks new ground in the study of twenty-first-century literature.

JOHN J. SU is Associate Professor of English at Marquette University.

IMAGINATION AND THE CONTEMPORARY NOVEL

JOHN J. SU

Marquette University

CAMBRIDGE
UNIVERSITY PRESS

CAMBRIDGE UNIVERSITY PRESS
Cambridge, New York, Melbourne, Madrid, Cape Town,
Singapore, São Paulo, Delhi, Mexico City

Cambridge University Press
32 Avenue of the Americas, New York NY 10013-2473, USA

www.cambridge.org
Information on this title: www.cambridge.org/9781107645974

First published 2011
First paperback edition 2013

A catalogue record for this publication is available from the British Library

Library of Congress Cataloguing in Publication Data
Su, John J.
Imagination and the contemporary novel / John J. Su.
p. cm.
Includes bibliographical references.
ISBN 978-1-107-00677-5 (hardback)
1. English fiction–20th century–History and criticism. 2. English
fiction–21st century–History and criticism. 3. Imagination in literature.
4. Literature and globalization. 5. Postcolonialism in literature. 6. English
fiction–English-speaking countries–History and criticism. I. Title.
PR881.S785 2011
823´.91409–dc22
2011002470

ISBN 978-1-107-00677-5 Hardback
ISBN 978-1-107-64597-4 Paperback

Contents

v

Preface and acknowledgments

This study is motivated by the desire to understand the global pre-occupation with the imagination since the 1960s, particularly among literary authors with ties to former colonies of the British Empire. The historical tendency of academic scholarship to couple the imagination and Western European Romanticism has meant that the preoccupation with the imagination in the fiction of authors from across the Anglophone world has gone largely unnoticed.[1] Yet its presence in the works of Amitav Ghosh, Nadine Gordimer, N. Scott Momaday, Salman Rushdie, and many others demands a critical re-examination. The categories of literary history that have dominated academic discourses – "postmodern" and "postcolonial" most prominently – have partitioned literary histories in ways that often efface the broader significance of phenomena such as the imagination. Because prevailing literary categories discourage, for example, comparative analysis of South African writer André Brink and British writer John Fowles, or even Fowles and fellow Briton Hanif Kureishi, scholars have largely failed to recognize the social significance they all attribute to the imagination. This study proposes to explore the possibilities and limitations of the imagination as a social practice and the extent to which a re-examination of imagining might offer insight into the resurgent interest in aesthetics in the humanities.

My central argument is that the emergence of the imagination as an explicit topic of discourse in contemporary fiction comes as a response to epistemological crises opened up by the perceived consolidation of an imperialist form of capitalism as the dominant world-system. Less a mimetic or creative power, the imagination increasingly becomes characterized in contemporary Anglophone literatures as a knowledge-producing faculty crucial to countering ideological mystification. The imagination accomplishes this task in somewhat different ways for the diverse authors in this study, but they all share a sense that current social, economic, and political conditions necessitate a reconsideration of the imaginative functions of the novel.

Although the imagination has a remarkable capacity to defy strict definition, it is a term we apparently cannot do without, now more than ever.[2] It continues to be considered the precondition of all literary production; no work of literature can be ascribed significant artistic value and at the same time be described as "unimaginative." More importantly, the imagination is identified as a social practice crucial to living in an age of globalized modernity. No longer relegated to the domain of Western European Romanticism, the imagination is, according to anthropologist Arjun Appadurai, "now central to all forms of agency, is itself a social fact, and is the key component of the new global order."[3] Philosopher Richard Kearney is far more pessimistic about the fate of the imagination, but he considers it no less essential to daily life. The "imminent demise of the imagination" that defines the postmodern condition, for Kearney, represents not the death of European humanism but of humanity itself.[4]

The repudiation of all things postmodern in the humanities and the rise of postcolonial studies has not rendered Kearney's anxiety moot. Whatever else the various theories of postmodernism were, they were responses to the same social and economic conditions that, for Appadurai, characterize the present moment: the ever-increasing flows of capital, information, and people across national boundaries; the ubiquitous and inescapable presence of electronic media in everyday life. If theories of postmodernism presented by Jean Baudrillard, Ihab Hassan, David Harvey, Linda Hutcheon, Andreas Huyssen, Fredric Jameson, Charles Jencks, Jean-François Lyotard, and others often failed to provide compelling accounts of the experiences of minorities in the United States and Western European nations – and majorities everywhere else – this does not necessarily imply that the theories asked the wrong questions. Indeed, fundamental questions formulated by these theorists remain unanswered, and the disappearance of postmodernism from academic discourses has meant that some of the questions that were central to writers since the 1960s linger: to what extent does ideology limit our capacity to acquire knowledge about our circumstances? To what extent can experiences be communicated? What, if any, epistemological significance does identity have?

The implosion of postmodern studies in the 1990s and the current crises facing postcolonial studies can easily give the impression that the questions taken up by literary studies are guided by taste or fashion rather than the production of knowledge. I wish to emphasize, however, that my study is made possible by the very theories of postmodernism and postcoloniality of which I am often critical. I will challenge their nearly unanimous dismissal of the imagination as elitist, Eurocentric, preoccupied with formalism to the exclusion of political concerns, and reproducing the very ideologies that enabled the rise of capitalism. But my efforts to explore the complex and conflicted appropriations of the imagination by contemporary Anglophone authors necessarily presupposes earlier critiques of Eurocentrism and its universalizing propensities. Indeed, theories of postmodernism and postcoloniality are crucial to understanding the historical function of the imagination, and my study builds on Saree Makdisi's argument that modern notions of imagination were central to the emergence of modernity itself.[5] From their inception, such notions represented a crucial means of registering dissent against industrial modernization in Western Europe and the basis for exploring alternatives to the universal history projected by modern forms of imperialism and capitalism. The reemerging interest in the imagination in contemporary Anglophone literatures since the 1960s, then, need not be read as a turn away from political concerns toward some rarefied formalism but rather as a mode of exploring possible forms of response to prevailing political, economic, and social conditions.

I would like to express my profound gratitude to friends and colleagues who have made this work possible. In particular, Tobin Siebers, Michael Patrick Gillespie, Tim Machan, Satya P. Mohanty, Linda Martín Alcoff, Michael Hames-García, and Jodi Melamed provided crucial advice and feedback – I have benefited immensely from their help. I would like to thank audiences at the University of Michigan, the University of Wisconsin, Cornell University, and Stanford University, who have attended talks drawn from this work; I appreciate the thoughtful and often critical responses I have received. Writing was facilitated by a year-long sabbatical fellowship, and I would like to thank Dean Michael McKinney for granting me leave time. I would also like to thank Ray Ryan and Maartje Scheltens at Cambridge University Press for their superb editorial guidance, and the anonymous readers of this manuscript for their helpful suggestions.

My greatest debts are to Cindy Petrites and Gabriel and Julian Su, who have supported me and brought me happiness.

An earlier version of chapter 5 was published as "Ghosts of Essentialism: Racial Memory as Epistemological Claim," in *American*

CHAPTER I

Introduction: globalization, imagination, and the novel

One of the greatest paradoxes of contemporary culture is that at a time when the image reigns supreme the very notion of a creative human imagination seems under mounting threat. We no longer appear to know who exactly produces or controls the images which condition our consciousness. We are at an impasse where the very rapport between *imagination* and *reality* seems not only inverted but subverted altogether. We cannot be sure which is which. And this very undecidability lends weight to the deepening suspicion that we may well be assisting at a wake of imagination.

Richard Kearney, *The Wake of Imagination*

The image, the imagined, the imaginary – these are all terms that direct us to something critical and new in global cultural processes: *the imagination as a social practice*. No longer mere fantasy (opium for the masses whose real work is elsewhere), no longer simple escape (from a world defined principally by more concrete purposes and structures), no longer elite pastime (thus not relevant to the lives of ordinary people), and no longer mere contemplation (irrelevant for new forms of desire and subjectivity), the imagination has become an organized field of social practices, a form of work (in the sense of both labor and culturally organized practice), and a form of negotiation between sites of agency (individuals) and globally defined fields of possibility. This unleashing of the imagination links the play of pastiche (in some settings) to the terror and coercion of states and their competitors. The imagination is now central to all forms of agency, is itself a social fact, and is the key component of the new global order.

Arjun Appadurai, *Modernity at Large*

The emergence of modern notions of imagination was inseparable from a longing to effect radical social change. Friedrich Schiller and Samuel Taylor Coleridge both argued that the rise of capitalism and the modern nation-state dissolved an essential bond of human nature, and they looked to the imagination to provide the basis for a more egalitarian state. Even as the European colonial powers subsumed ever greater spheres within their orbit, William Wordsworth and William Blake saw in the imagination the possibility of identifying and preserving images of what Saree Makdisi has called "sites of difference and otherness," thereby forestalling the worldwide assimilation of all cultures and histories within a single dominant narrative of modernity.[1] Such responses were often less a radical critique of capitalism than efforts to provide a tragic consolation for it,[2] but well into the twentieth century artists including T. S. Eliot, E. M. Forster, D. H. Lawrence, and Pablo Picasso saw what they took to be vestigial remnants of alternatives to modernity in the far-flung reaches of the European empires. Eliot, in particular, held out hope that the preservation of such remnants within the aesthetic sphere of art might lead one day to a "mass-conversion" that would fundamentally redefine social and political institutions.[3]

The apparent consolidation of capitalism as the dominant world-system in the final decades of the twentieth century has led to significant anxieties about the capacity of the imagination to aid utopian thinking. Russell Jacoby's *Picture Imperfect: Utopian Thought for an Anti-Utopian Age* (2005), for example, ponders whether the relentless barrage of electronic media images has not finally overwhelmed our capacity to imagine. Reiterating a line of thinking tracing through Fredric Jameson and Richard Kearney back to Herbert Marcuse's *One-Dimensional Man* (1964), Jacoby reads the imagination as a final frontier on the verge of incorporation.[4] His distinction between a now outdated "blue print tradition" and a still vital "iconoclastic tradition" of utopian thinking implies that the imagination – historically understood as an image-producing faculty – is no longer to be trusted.[5] In an "age of extreme visualization," the imagination itself has in large measure become unimaginative, reproducing commercial fantasies of limitless consumption.[6]

Intriguingly, the imagination reemerged as subject of explicit interest and meditation in a wide variety of contemporary Anglophone literatures written during the same era. It figures prominently in texts that have been categorized as postmodern, such as John Fowles's *Daniel Martin* (1977); it also figures in texts that have been categorized as postcolonial, such as Amitav Ghosh's *The Glass Palace* (2001). Indeed, despite their different backgrounds and social locations, both Fowles and Ghosh portray multinational capitalism as the dominant social, political, and economic formation in terms of which all conditions of life must be understood. Both Fowles and Ghosh claim that the novel enables its readers to engage in a unique form of imagining that is crucial to recovering and communicating alternative systems of knowledge. Their narratives repeatedly turn to questions of what can be known or not known, what can be verified, and what is considered authentic knowledge. To the extent that they posit spaces beyond the reach of global capital, *Daniel Martin* and *The Glass Palace* have a utopian quality. Neither seeks to provide a blueprint for the future, but they both explore the extent to which imagining enables individuals to recognize the current conditions in which they live, and the nature of the exploitation they endure and often promote.

The crucial role these authors assign to the imagination in recognizing and interpreting reality is one that it historically has not often had. The mystification of everyday life effected by capitalism and imperialism means that conceptions of the imagination as a mimetic faculty tracing back to Aristotle or a creative faculty tracing back to European Romantics have little purchase. Rather, the imagination is required to engage in what André Brink calls a "transgression" of the senses.[7] Imagining is not seen as a withdrawal from the world but an effort to interpret it more accurately, and thereby to enable a clearer recognition of the possible shared horizons for the future.[8] In other words, the relevance of the novel depends on a new attention to the epistemological significance of the imagination.

THE EPISTEMOLOGY OF THE IMAGINATION

As a field of philosophical inquiry into questions of how knowledge is acquired and verified, epistemology has tended to be understood in terms of the preoccupations established by René Descartes and developed by Immanuel Kant. Despite their differences, both philosophers understood the resolution to epistemological problems to lie in the pursuit of what has been called a "God's eye view" notion of objectivity. According to this idea, the cultural contexts, personal identifications, and philosophical commitments of an individual necessarily introduce distortions in perspective, the resolution to which demands temporarily bracketing these impediments to rational deliberation. This preoccupation with a transcendental point of view or transcendental self was rejected by both Hegel and Marx for its lack of historicity. Similar critiques were echoed throughout the twentieth century. In the Anglo-American academy, Richard Rorty provides perhaps the most well-known critique, declaring the impossibility and irrelevance of epistemology; critiques can also be found among thinkers influenced by hermeneutic traditions, including philosopher Hans-Georg Gadamer and historian F. R. Ankersmit.[9]

This study does not attempt to revive epistemology in its modern sense; however, I will argue that the conditions associated with late capitalism demand attention to epistemology of a certain kind. If Kearney is correct that capitalism has managed to effect a basic subversion of reality, such that it has become difficult to distinguish between reality and advertisement, then questions about where a person acquires knowledge and how he or she verifies truth become important. Such questions are central foci for the literary texts in this study. Ghosh, for example, explicitly addresses the importance of epistemology, declaring in an interview that "one of the essential topics of my writing is, what is it to know? ... In a world where everything is known, how do you become what is not known, how do you escape the omniscient gaze?"[10] Taking my lead from feminist philosophers Linda Martín Alcoff, Donna Haraway, and Sandra Harding, I argue that epistemology needs to be revised rather than rejected outright: to address questions of knowledge with respect to subjects who are located in history rather than universalized, whose biases are shaped by both the identities ascribed to them and those they fashion for themselves, and whose inescapable historicity is not only an impediment to but also a precondition of knowledge. Thought of in this way, epistemology – that often belittled field of inquiry – becomes vital to understanding the limits of ideology and the possibilities for experience to be communicated.

I will argue that one of the primary conditions of the post-1960s era is the extent to which the epistemological colonization, to borrow Gaurav Desai's term, of Africa, Southeast Asia, and Latin America is increasingly the fate of populations in the former colonial centers as well.[11] In contrast to theorists of postmodernism such as Brian McHale, who read postmodern literature in terms of ontology rather than epistemology, I will suggest throughout this study that authors who perceive capitalism to be a hegemonic world order tend to be preoccupied with epistemological issues. To anticipate later claims, the "free play" that is characteristic of the imagination in Western thinking since Kant – and the withdrawal or disengagement from the world of perception or action that it characterizes – becomes a necessary precondition for acquiring more objective knowledge about the world. If ideology involves conditioning the empirical senses to take certain images as more real than others, then the imagination's unique status as a mediator between the senses and cognition makes it crucial to recognition and understanding.[12]

This argument runs counter to the dominant strain of thinking in literary studies, within which the imagination is characterized as possessing minimal epistemological significance except insofar as the critical analysis of it yields knowledge of the workings of ideology. Since the pioneering work of Jerome McGann, Paul de Man, and others, the imagination has been read as inseparably bound to ideology. As Deborah Elise White more recently put it, "the imagination posits a structure of recognition that authorizes claims of interiority, autonomy, and subjectivity, but it does so in the service of an exteriority, heteronomy, and objectivity that it denies."[13] Implicated for ignoring or mystifying social inequities, the imagination cannot be rehabilitated according to this argument. At best, for Forest Pyle, it can help to identify how ideology conceals dissent and difference in the name of promoting social consensus. "The poetic failure of the imagination," Pyle writes, "like a sort of photographic negative, leaves an image of the 'nontotalizability' of the social."[14] His explicit rejection of Paul Ricoeur's optimistic reading of the imagination suggests that any genuine utopian project requires rejecting all efforts to envision utopia in a direct manner.[15]

Pyle's categorical rejection of the imagination as a "positive faculty" highlights the extent to which critiques of the imagination have been guided by anxieties similar to those that led contemporary Anglophone authors to appropriate it.[16] Both the deconstruction and Frankfurt School Critical Theory that undergird Pyle's argument for the "'nontotalizability' of the social" are themselves responses to the increasingly totalizing grip of capitalism. Emerging out of particular crises in European modernisms, these theories do not provide a neutral, disinterested backdrop against which to evaluate literary texts. Indeed, their guiding philosophical assumptions warrant scrutiny in light of the anti-imperial struggles that emerged across the globe in the decades since their initial formulations. Nontotalizability is an assertion, not a given, though it is often taken as such in Anglo-American academic discourses. Even were it to be true, its implications for utopian thinking are by no means a foregone conclusion. As we will see in subsequent chapters, the novelists in this study are keenly aware of the historical culpability of many utopian fantasies and Western conceptions of the imagination underlying them. What is striking is that authors from so many different cultural, ethnic, and social contexts would perceive the dominance of ideology to require them nonetheless to turn to the imagination as a resource to be critically appropriated and revised.

The argument in *Imagination and the Contemporary Novel* does not understand the imagination as a universal and unchanging phenomenon, but as something that is historically produced. From their emergence in the eighteenth century, modern notions of imagination took the forms that they did in Germany and Great Britain because of contemporaneous developments in modes of production, and the shift toward capitalist forms of industrialization. The idea of an individual, creative imagination could not have emerged without it. Yet the fundamental connection to the economic system it critiques does not inherently mean that the imagination reproduces the ideology of capitalism. Distinct from a notion of fantasy as an escape from reality, distinct from a notion of a creative imagination that depends on partitioning reality and art into distinct and autonomous spheres, and distinct even from a notion of a utopian imagination that constructs an idealized alternative world, the notion of the imagination proposed here understands it to be an epistemological faculty for interpreting reality – a task that is inseparable from the creation of a horizon of expectations that emerges from an individual's social location, cultural identity, and idiosyncratic aspirations.

The definition of imagination as an epistemological faculty for interpreting reality separate from rational reasoning has historical precedents, of course, but rarely has its epistemological significance been tied so directly to the demystification of everyday life. Prior to Kant, the imagination was considered crucial to the production of knowledge to the extent that it plays a mediating role between sensory perception and rational reasoning. Aristotle declares in *De Anima*, for example, that "Imagination is different from both perception and thought; imagination does not occur without perception and without imagination there can be no belief."[17] The imagination is indispensable, in other words, if only as a medium. Kant grants a more significant role to the imagination in the first edition of *The Critique of Pure Reason* (1781), arguing that it is "an indispensable function of the soul without which we should have no knowledge whatsoever, but of which we are scarcely ever conscious."[18] Yet Kant's significant diminishment of the power of the imagination in his second, revised edition (1787) represents a signal moment in the modern history of the imagination – a history in which the opposition between reason and imagination tends to limit the purview of imagination to aesthetic appreciation and artistic creativity.[19] This partitioning of the realms of mental experience, which was largely adopted by Western European Romantics, meant that the knowledge purportedly produced by the imagination historically did not concern the specific economic, social, and political conditions of a person's life. As Nigel Leask and many others have shown, Coleridge understood the imagination to provide a model for civil society; however, the model itself emerges from a highly abstract notion of an "organic" synthesis of soul and nature, subject and society, not from a sense that the imagination enables individuals to interpret the observable features of their world more accurately, as will consistently be the case for the authors in this study.[20]

The definition of the imagination used in this study is not meant to preclude or to minimize the considerable variations in how the word *imagination* is employed by the authors to be examined. Indeed, the variations in how the imagination is characterized in the following chapters provide a key to understanding the distinctive features of various localized responses to an apparently stable world-system. In other words, the differences between J. M. Coetzee's and N. Scott Momaday's conceptions (or even Coetzee's and fellow South African Nadine Gordimer's) illuminate the cultural contexts in which their ideas emerged and the different forms modernity has taken in their lives. And exploring how the imagination has been critically appropriated and translated to the specific situations in which authors write will be a core concern of this study.

While it has long been a truism within literary studies that the cultural institution of the novel endured well after the official end of European colonialism, how postcolonial authors inherited European notions of a creative imagination as the basis for literary production is less well recognized. As Simon Gikandi notes, after World War II, institutions of higher learning in Ghana, Kenya, Nigeria, Tanzania, and elsewhere throughout the British Empire systematized the study of English literature according to the Leavisite model of the "Great Tradition" of English literature.[21] The moral significance of imaginative literature was central to the education of early postcolonial writers such as Chinua Achebe and Ngũgĩ wa Thiong'o, and is apparent throughout their nonfiction writings. Ngũgĩ declares in *Decolonising the Mind* (1986) that "these great three [Matthew Arnold, T. S. Eliot, and F. R. Leavis] dominated our daily essays" in school.[22] Both Achebe and Ngũgĩ also discuss European Romantics and I. A. Richards, whose *Coleridge on Imagination* (1934) helped to reestablish the category of imagining as a central concern of literary studies. Perhaps Achebe's most famous pronouncement on the imagination occurs in an essay in which he discusses both Richards and Coleridge: "art is man's constant effort to create for himself a different order of reality from that which is given to him; an aspiration to provide himself with a second handle on existence *through his imagination*."[23]

The idea of a creative imagination was crucial to Achebe's project of validating African cultures and traditions as sources of genuine knowledge. His declaration that imagining enables individuals to acquire a "second handle on existence" implies that the conditions of everyday life are not immediately apparent, and may be obfuscated by what he calls the "malignant fictions" of racism and colonialism (143). To accomplish his oft-cited goal of "teach[ing] my readers that their past – with all its imperfections – was not one long night of savagery from which the first Europeans acting on God's behalf delivered them" (45), then, requires readers to engage in a mental activity that would require more than simply interpreting what they read based on their current standpoint, fitting unfamiliar stories and traditions in terms of their pre-existing categories of knowledge. The language of "imaginative sympathy" – and Leavis's insistence on aligning it with "moral discrimination" – provided Achebe with the vocabulary for describing such a process and the rationale for why readers should feel an imperative to engage in it.[24] Achebe characterizes the moral dimension of art in terms of its capacity to elicit "imaginative identification" (144) through which readers develop a vicarious experience of the world through literature.[25] The terminology of imagining is consistently invoked by Achebe when he asks his readers to engage in a hypothetical exercise of viewing the world through an alien standpoint. By reminding his readers of the European tradition of characterizing Africa as its alien other, Achebe not only makes the representation of Africa a central criterion for artistic achievement but also redefines the moral imperative of art: to engage with cultural traditions that have been demeaned and effaced by the colonial system of education. The imagination is invoked, in other words, to resolve problems introduced by European colonialism, which actively sought to attenuate sympathetic identifications with colonized populations. Recognizing that "it is even arguable whether we can truly *know* anything which we have not personally experienced," Achebe argues that the imagination gives us "the closest approximation to experience that we are ever likely to get" (145).

The conception of imagining as a mental activity directed toward sympathetic understanding helps to explain the relative unimportance attributed to it in literary scholarship on Achebe, which has tended to view him as an embodiment of what Abdul R. JanMohamed has called the "generation of realism."[26] According to this argument, African writers during the 1950s and 1960s countered a history of colonialist representations by recourse to a kind of Lukácsean critical realism; as JanMohamed puts it, "they overc[a]me the colonialist 'romance' of Africa by using metropolitan 'realism.'"[27] The opposition between romance and realism presupposes a set of aesthetic dichotomies that devalue imagination as fantasy, opposed to reality. Thus, the preoccupation among literary scholars with realism combined with the tendency toward anthropological readings of postcolonial literatures has meant that questions of aesthetics have been seen as tertiary, and the imagination has been relegated to a curiously minor role: the basis of artistic production, but not itself meriting significant analysis.

In the case of Ngũgĩ, the concept of a creative imagination was crucial to his theory of how art could intervene in ideological struggles against capitalism. As early as his first collection of nonfictional essays, *Homecoming* (1972), Ngũgĩ describes the mind of the writer as broken up into territories of rationality and imagination: "In a novel the writer is totally immersed in a world of imagination which is other than his conscious self. At his most intense and creative the writer is transfigured, he is possessed, he becomes a medium."[28] To assert that the creative imagination represents a territory separate from other faculties of the mind simultaneously situates Ngũgĩ with respect to a tradition of European writing whose cultural capital depended on a notion of an autonomous imagination and highlights the capacity of capitalism to penetrate all spheres of existence. "There is no area of our lives which has not been affected by the social, political and expansionist needs of European capitalism," Ngũgĩ declares only two paragraphs after his assertion of imaginative autonomy.[29] In subsequent collections of essays including *Writers in Politics* (1981; revised edition 1997), *Decolonising the Mind* (1986), *Penpoints, Gunpoints, and Dreams* (1998), and *Something Torn and New: An African Renaissance* (2009), Ngũgĩ continues to emphasize both points: the autonomy of the imagination and the limits placed on it by the social, political, and economic conditions in which writers are born and raised. The tension between the two points is highlighted in a lecture entitled "Art War with the State: Writers and Guardians of Post-colonial Society." On the one hand, Ngũgĩ insists on the imagination's autonomy and agency, declaring that writers simply follow the direction toward which their imaginations point: "In indulging and following their imagination wherever it leads them, even to the realms of what could be, writers do often stumble upon truths, to which they give the bodily form of words."[30] Later in the same lecture, however, Ngũgĩ suggests that the forms imagining takes are limited by ideological biases of which authors are not necessarily even aware: "Artists, after all, are products of social classes and ranks, and their imagination takes flight weighed down by ideological moorings consciously or unconsciously held" (28).

Ngũgĩ largely retains Achebe's conception of the imagination as a faculty for sympathetic identification even as he shifts focus toward an African bourgeoisie who sought to retain colonial structures of economic exploitation after independence. In "The Allegory of the Cave: Language, Democracy, and the New World Order," for example, Ngũgĩ follows Achebe's practice of explicitly invoking the imagination when he invites readers to engage in an exercise of hypothesizing how others might view the world: "Here we all need a leap of imagination to comprehend the enormity of a situation which we can't otherwise feel because we can all talk among ourselves. I want you to imagine a peasant or worker in a court of law accused, say, of murder" (*Penpoints*, 90). Ngũgĩ's point is that language shapes how individuals view the world, and that the continued usage of English among the African middle class in Kenya prevents them from identifying with their fellow countrymen. On this understanding, the idea of the imagination as a faculty of the mind possessing a certain degree of autonomy becomes the necessary precondition for overcoming the ideological biases associated with a particular language. Without the imagination, in other words, middle-class Africans would continue to endorse the economics of free market capitalism inherited from Europe and the United States: "For in its wilful narcissism, to use Fanon's phrase, this class sees itself as constituting the nation" (93).

Fanon's influence on Ngũgĩ's thought is crucial to understanding the latter's vision of the often antagonistic relationship between rational cognition and imagining – an antagonism that will figure centrally in the writings of so many contemporary Anglophone authors in this study. Whatever else narcissism involves, it short-circuits sympathy in such a way that the issues and concerns of other classes are understood to mirror those of the middle class. If this is genuinely the case, then the shift toward social realism that Gikandi and others have observed in Ngũgĩ's writing risks reaffirming rather than challenging middle-class ideological biases. In Ngũgĩ's first novel written in Gĩkũyũ rather than English, *Caitaani Mũtharaba-inĩ* (1980; English translation *Devil on the Cross*, 1982), he seeks to overcome the problem by shifting language. Yet the plot of the novel seems to imply that a language shift is insufficient, requiring a kind of mental activity often characterized in terms of the imagination. The transformation of the novel's protagonist, Warĩĩnga, from a self-loathing victim to a revolutionary is certainly facilitated by the workers and university students she encounters, but her most significant discovery occurs during a dream in which she converses with the Devil, the embodiment of capitalism. Only he can finally explain why so many Kenyans willingly embrace their own exploitation:

WARĨĩNGA: But won't the workers refuse to let their bodies be exploited like that? Won't they refuse to be robbed of their lives?

VOICE: Why have you never prevented your own body from being exploited? ... *Anyway*, the workers will never know what's being done to them. They'll never see or feel those machines and pipes in their bodies. And if they should ever chance to see them, they won't mind the burden ...

WARĪĪNGA: Why?

VOICE: Because the Kīmeendeeris of this world are not as foolish as you think they are. Kīmeendeeri will show them only two worlds, that of the eater and that of the eaten. So the workers will never learn the existence of a third world, the world of the revolutionary overthrow of the system of eating and being eaten. They will always assume that the two worlds of the eater and the eaten are eternal.[31]

The implication is that overcoming ideology requires something more than exposing false consciousness. Despite all of her conversations with workers and students, Warīīnga cannot overcome her view of class conflict in terms of "two worlds" prior to her dream. Put another way, ideology constitutes the very limits of the world as a totality, and as long as individuals are unable to recognize the possibility of a different kind of totality – one that would include the "third world" the Devil describes – the best they can hope for is to recognize themselves as exploited. Fundamental political change thus appears to require something like imagination, and, indeed, throughout *Penpoints* Ngũgĩ describes dreaming as a form of imagining, declaring: "Dreaming becomes a crime of thought and imagination" (20).

The critical and often revisionary appropriations of European notions of creative imagination by authors since Achebe have been haunted by the desire to disentangle the imagination from the cult of bourgeois individualism historically tied to it. The tension is acutely apparent in Achebe's 1984 lecture "The Writer and His Community." Achebe echoes the language he used in "The Truth of Fiction" to describe the function of the imagination in literary production: the artist "afford[s] himself through his imagination an alternative handle on reality" (*Hopes and Impediments*, 58). Yet Achebe can only arrive at this conclusion after a complex set of reflections in which he criticizes the individualism of the West (49) while insisting that the "Igbo are second to none in their respect of the individual personality" (57). Similar discomfort with Western notions of a personal imagination does not disappear among more recent authors, but my claim in subsequent chapters will be that it is often mitigated by linking the epistemological significance of the imagination to various notions of cultural identity. In contrast to most forms of poststructuralism and Frankfurt School Critical Theory, I will argue that identity does not necessarily represent an imposition that restricts individual desires, misinforms individuals regarding their needs, or disciplines who they can be. Rather, identities represent theoretical descriptions of social and economic forces that place individuals in positions of relative privilege or want. Such descriptions emerge out of an ongoing process of reconciling individual fantasies, cultural traditions, and social ascriptions attributed to a person. Thus, the imagination is not an autonomous, free-floating faculty producing images divorced from the contexts in which an individual lives; rather, the images produced by the imagination are shaped by a person's social location and, thereby, the systems of knowledge and belief to which the individual is exposed. According to this logic, even that great bugbear of critical thought, essentialism, may be understood more productively. Essence, I will argue in chapter 5, is not a static condition but something produced through repeated descriptions over time. Thus, explorations of essentialistic claims of racial memories can yield crucial knowledge about the history of exploitation and the systems of difference on which national identities are based.

AESTHETICS AND UTOPIA

My argument emerges from and critically responds to the aesthetic turn in the humanities in the past decade. Perhaps more than any other work, Terry Eagleton's *The Ideology of the Aesthetic* (1990) laid the groundwork for this tectonic shift in disciplinary methodologies, rehabilitating a category that had been dismissed as minor or even irrelevant to the ideological questions central to academic research in the humanities during the 1980s.[32] Eagleton famously argued that the autonomy claimed by aesthetic works does not represent a retreat from political questions into a rarefied sphere of formalism or aestheticism. Rather, the rise of modern notions of the aesthetic in the eighteenth century was crucial to the production of a class structure that would, in turn, sustain an ever-expanding capitalist economic system. The ideological underpinnings of capitalism, then, require an aesthetic that could also represent a challenge to it.[33] This latter point has been returned to again and again by scholars during the past decade: the possibility that certain forms of aesthetic analysis have a utopian dimension, if not more direct political relevance. Isobel Armstrong goes so far as to suggest that the play enabled by the aesthetic is the prerequisite of all political change.[34]

The absence of a concept of imagination in recent aesthetic theories is striking from an historical perspective, and has significant consequences for the kinds of utopian thinking that can be attributed to works of art.

The autonomy of the aesthetic, for Kant, presupposes the capacity of the imagination to engage in "free-play." The imagination gives aesthetic judgments their unique character, differing from rational judgments in that they defy the mind's capacity to establish rules or criteria of assessment. The role of the imagination is radically diminished, however, in Eagleton and in Theodor Adorno's posthumous *Aesthetic Theory* (1970), on which Eagleton draws.[35] Adorno's assertion that the form of art registers a claim that the "nonexistent" must be possible suggests a profound distrust of representation and, by extension, the imagination.[36] The imagination, understood as a faculty of image-making, is seen as co-opted by consumerist capitalism. Even his descriptions of beauty are noteworthy for the absence of the imagination as a relevant faculty. Adorno asserts that the idea of beauty does not involve something directly articulated but rather a vague melancholic sense that an alternative to the present might exist.[37] To actually represent it, however, would render it available to commodification and appropriation.

Adorno's claim that genuinely utopian fantasies can take only a negative form, positing a world that cannot be directly represented, continues to be hugely influential. Recent studies by Deepika Bahri and Nicholas Brown, among others, take for granted the notion that utopia is literally unimaginable.[38] As we will see more fully in chapter 6, so-called "positive utopias" – those whose defining characteristics can be imagined and described – are condemned for recycling a discredited liberal humanism and short-circuiting the capacity of individuals to recognize more radical alternatives. Only negative utopian thinking provides such a possibility.

From the perspective of this study, however, the opposition between positive and negative utopian thinking has the potential to collapse into the same reductive binaries that characterized many postmodern and poststructuralist theories. The binaries of subject/object, self/other, stasis/flux, Cartesian subjectivity/schizo-subjectivity, etc. – binaries which Jacques Derrida suggested were a fundamental part of the Western philosophical tradition – risk creating simplified choices of wholesale affirmation or rejection.[39] Language does not necessarily represent an imposition or act of violence, at least from the perspective of many hermeneutic approaches, and this suggests that utopian thinking can be broadened beyond the polarity of positive or negative utopias. I will suggest that for the novelists in this study the goal of utopian representations is neither to establish a roadmap nor to gesture toward traces of the "nonexistent" or the "nontotalizability of the social"; rather, efforts to imagine and articulate utopian possibilities concern the challenge of developing an increased capacity to understand the nature of disappointments that lead individuals to utopian fantasies in the first place. Put another way, the reality that utopias created within the aesthetic spheres of art do not transfer directly to everyday life does not necessarily invalidate the knowledge they provide. My focus, then, is on what conditions are necessary for individuals to acquire sufficient knowledge to recognize their needs and to envision alternatives to contemporary social conditions, alternatives that might address those needs.

The shift away from the negative utopianism that, for Adorno, was exemplified by the work of Samuel Beckett represents a crucial development in contemporary literary history. This shift can be observed even in the works of J. M. Coetzee, whose doctoral thesis was on Beckett. Beckett's anti-representationalist suspicions are everywhere apparent in Coetzee's thought, and these suspicions led Coetzee to follow the tradition of linking imagination to fantasy and madness in his early works, particularly in his Booker Prize-winning *Life & Times of Michael K* (1983).[40] As we will see in chapter 2, however, the South African State of Emergency drove Coetzee to revise his position with respect to what he terms a *sympathetic imagination*. The qualified rehabilitation of the imagination is necessitated, for Coetzee, by the pernicious effects of apartheid ideology. Like many of the authors in this study, Coetzee does not deny the dangers of the imagination and its complicity with ideology. To the contrary, the imagination proves fascinating precisely because of its complicated status. Coetzee never directly endorses the notion of sympathetic imagination, but always places the idea in the mouths of characters whose own sympathies are suspect, thereby emphasizing that the power of the imagination is never separable from its most pernicious tendencies. Coetzee respects the Beckett who in *Imagination Dead Imagine* sensed that a genuinely useful notion of imagining could emerge only after the death of notions inherited from Romantic artists and philosophers.

THE IMAGINATION AND THE NOVEL

The diverse range of authors to be explored in this study demands some rationale. Nicholas Brown's *Utopian Generations: The Political Horizon of Twentieth-Century Literature* (2005) makes a powerful case for reading across traditional lines of literary history. Brown argues that British modernism between the World Wars and African literature during the period of national independence cannot be understood in isolation from each other. The division of the globe between wealthy and poor nations establishes a rift whose existence can be fully appreciated only by reading texts that come from both sides of the divide. Ford Madox Ford is no less concerned with the global expansion of capitalism than Chinua Achebe, and when the boundaries between Western and non-Western cultures are bracketed, "the differential movement of capital emerges not as one kind of content among many," Brown writes, "but as the fundamental content of both modernism and African literature."[41]

This study extends Brown's logic, suggesting that beyond the rift he identifies there exists a series of *micro-rifts* within countries and ethnic or cultural groups that complicate the preoccupation with the dynamics of center and periphery that has dominated postcolonial criticism despite repeated calls to the contrary.[42] Each of the chapters in this study will approach literary traditions, constellations of authors, or single authors for whom the term *postcolonial* is an uncomfortable fit (although most of them have been described as postcolonial, and a few have even embraced the term). For example, the tradition of reading postcolonial literature in terms of a broader metanarrative of "the Empire writes back" has created an interpretation of the divide between Englishness and Britishness that identifies the former as a prop of imperial identity and the latter as a potentially inclusive, even multicultural notion. Chapter 3 will explore how such readings overlook the ways in which "English" authors including Peter Ackroyd, Julian Barnes, and John Fowles represent Englishness as embodying ideals critical of British imperialism. Likewise, debates over essentialism in the United States have tended to focus on the existence or nonexistence of ontological differences among ethnic groups; such debates overlook how Frank Chin deploys an essentialistic concept of identity as a means of responding to what he takes to be the relativism of other Asian American authors, particularly Maxine Hong Kingston. Without attention to such micro-rifts, the terms employed by postcolonial theories risk homogenizing a diverse range of histories. Conceptions of cultural hybridity, for example, take different forms in Great Britain than elsewhere; I will argue in chapter 4 that its emergence was inseparable from the enterprise culture promoted by Prime Minister Margaret Thatcher, which, in turn, shaped the kinds of utopian futures presented in contemporary British fiction.

The broadly comparative focus of this study is thus necessitated by the global aspirations of imperialism and capitalism, and the literary responses to them. Brown's assertion that global capitalism frames the interpretive possibilities available for any concrete cultural context might be overstated, but it is a compelling argument for understanding many of the contemporary Anglophone authors in this study. Put another way, to understand the specific investments in the imagination by literary authors requires reading them in terms of both the long, complex history of modern discourses on the imagination and the current cultural, political, and epistemological crises out of which their specific novels emerge.

The terminologies of postcolonial and postmodern, which have provided the dominant theoretical lenses for cross-cultural readings, will have a limited though indispensable use in the comparative analysis proposed here. This study will draw from theories associated with both discourses, though not in a homogenizing manner. Many of the authors to be discussed have been described at turns as postcolonial and postmodern, based on the theoretical vantage point of the scholar analyzing them. The authors themselves have utilized or responded to these taxonomies of literary history, appropriating key terms from academic discourses in both fictional and nonfictional writings. While we must be careful not to conflate the concerns of academics and novelists, then, the boundaries between the two are highly porous and unstable, inviting investigations drawing from both realms. Indeed, many of the authors in this study have been academics themselves or had posts in academic settings. The extent to which academic discourses and fiction are blurred in this study will depend in large part on the authors themselves: André Brink invites a high degree of blurring when he asserts that his work represents an example of a multifaceted international postmodernism; Caryl Phillips and Monica Ali invite somewhat less, though they explicitly employ the language of hybridity in their fictional works; N. Scott Momaday would probably be uncomfortable with my use of the language of essentialism to describe his concept of racial or blood memory. The risks of my approach in this study cannot be denied or minimized. The reward I hope that it offers will be the possibility of finding in novels not simply objects of analysis but also sources of knowledge that can help to resolve significant impasses that have stalled academic debates over issues such as postcoloniality, postmodernism, hybridity, essentialism, and aesthetics.

In chapter 2, I explore the struggles by white South African writers during the State of Emergency to redefine their aesthetic principles in light of increasing state violence. As Rob Nixon notes, the anti-apartheid struggle became more globalized than any other post-World War II struggle for decolonization, and played an indispensable role in binding unstable international organizations like the United Nations.[43] It also became a test case for the political relevance of postmodernism, and hence provides a useful starting place for this study. Focusing on the works of André

Brink, J. M. Coetzee, and Nadine Gordimer, I argue that the imagination became an explicit topic of discourse in order to address the epistemological problems caused by state propaganda. As a faculty uniquely situated between sensory perception and abstract cognition, the imagination is identified as possessing a unique though limited autonomy that enables individuals to, in the words of André Brink, "*imagine the real*."[44] The turn to the imagination, then, does not represent a flight from political engagement but a necessary, if fraught, precondition for it.

While my reading in chapter 2 challenges central features of theories of postmodernism and readings of white South African writers as postmodernists, I argue in chapter 3 that the general disappearance of postmodernism from academic discourses creates significant problems for the analysis of Anglophone literatures. In "The pastoral and the postmodern," I explore the implications of the disappearance of postmodernism for contemporary British literature. Whether or not a postmodern era ever existed, the notion of postmodernism provided novelists the possibility of defining their literary projects in terms of an international response to a globalized modernity. By focusing on postwar representations of Englishness by John Fowles, Peter Ackroyd, and Julian Barnes, I challenge the central categories of literary history that separate these authors from others residing in Great Britain characterized as postcolonial, such as David Dabydeen and Salman Rushdie. Ackroyd no less than Dabydeen is committed to a critical engagement with Englishness that reveals the dark side of the imperial project. Representations of pastoral Englishness have been central to this project since the eighteenth century; in the context of contemporary British literature, they provide a generic mode of identifying an alternative, anti-imperial history of Englishness that is meant to serve as the basis for a postimperial national identity.

The analysis of pastoralism points to a claim that will be explored in chapters 4 and 5: that cultural identities are inseparable from notions of what Paul Ricoeur has called social and cultural imaginations. Chapter 4, "Hybridity, enterprise culture, and the fiction of multicultural Britain," explores this claim with respect to perhaps the most explicitly utopian theory of identity to emerge in recent decades, hybridity. The term has circulated widely within both postmodern and postcolonial studies; indeed, its own mongrel genealogy has placed it at the center of the most intractable debates between so-called materialist and culturalist postcolonial scholars. Drawing from both "wings" of postcolonial scholarship, I argue that the characterization of postcolonial studies as a debate between culturalists and materialists limits how hybridity can be understood because the latter tend to concede the former's authority over literary texts. A more careful literary history reveals a very different genealogy for hybridity, one linked to specific cultural and political crises emerging in the 1980s. Although hybridity has precedents dating back to the eighteenth century, it gained purchase as Englishness became linked to a Thatcherite "enterprise culture" that saw cultural traditions as commodities. Beginning with a brief "prehistory" of hybridity in the writing of Sam Selvon and V. S. Naipaul, I argue that Salman Rushdie's writings definitively shaped the terms of hybridity and its relationship to enterprise culture. The chapter follows how the rise of Islamic fundamentalism in Great Britain gave an afterlife to hybridity long after Thatcher's tenure as Prime Minister, and I focus particularly on the fictional works of Hanif Kureishi, Monica Ali, and Zadie Smith. Ultimately, I argue that the limitations of hybridity as a utopian model highlight the problems with more recent efforts to move "beyond race"; the planetary humanism invoked by Paul Gilroy, for example, demonstrates the same dependence on the imagination to translate an aesthetic ideal into a viable political reality.

Whereas chapter 4 argues that the utopian potential ascribed to hybridity is often overstated, chapter 5 makes the contrary argument for essentialism. "Ghosts of essentialism: racial memory as epistemological claim" calls for a re-examination of essentialism in light of the resurging interest in identity and identity politics. Since the mid-1990s, poststructuralist dismissals of identity as "pernicious and metaphysically inaccurate" have increasingly been challenged by feminist philosophers and cultural critics, race theorists, and, most recently, "postpositivist realists." Yet academic scholarship continues to read essentialism in ontological terms, a tendency exemplified by Walter Benn Michaels. I argue that essentialism in contemporary Anglophone literatures is often best understood not through ontology but through epistemology, involving questions of how experiences can be communicated and the role of the imagination in creating collective experiences. Debates over essentialism often hinge on unstated assumptions about the extent to which the imagination can enable individuals to identify with the experiences of others. My analysis focuses on how racial memory in ethnic American and First Nations literary texts redefines cultural knowledge in terms of personal experience. Through a close analysis of works written by Frank Chin and N. Scott Momaday, I argue that essentialism does not necessarily imply the existence of static identities or common experiences that define a people; rather, it implies the possibility of certain personal experiences to yield reliable knowledge about broader social patterns of exploitation, which is seen as a necessary precondition for utopian thinking.

Chapter 6 explores the resurging interest in aesthetics as it relates to current crises facing postcolonial theory. Building on Deepika Bahri's argument that aesthetics can play a crucial role in utopian thinking, I argue that notions of aesthetic experience provide a necessary complement to the notion of an individual, subject-centered imagination. Put too finely, the aesthetic holds out the possibility for establishing a collective imagination that both preserves the notion of moral universalism and respects intractable cultural differences. Focusing particularly on the work of Amitav Ghosh, I explore how his shifting attitude toward the imagination reveals the possibilities and limitations of reading aesthetics as a mode of utopian thinking. My reading ultimately argues that postcolonial studies would benefit from bringing the Frankfurt School aesthetic theories employed by Bahri, Brown, Ato Quayson, and others into conversation with Kantian and hermeneutic traditions, which would provide a more sophisticated and historically grounded understanding of the utopianism present in contemporary Anglophone literatures.

Taken together, the novels in this study represent a crucial shift in literary history that has significant ramifications for debates in the humanities and humanistic social sciences. While the imagination has often been dismissed as personal fantasy or relegated to the realm of aesthetics, its centrality to literary and cultural discourses demands further analysis. Dipesh Chakrabarty's concern that the "imagination remains a curiously undiscussed category in social science writings on nationalism" continues to be pertinent well after the publication of his *Provincializing Europe* and well outside of the disciplinary boundaries that were his concern.[45] Whether or not the imagination is ultimately an identifiable mental faculty, it has had a central place in cultural histories of modernity. In these histories it has been inseparably tied to its perhaps most celebrated artifact, literature, and this remains true even now that many of the functions historically assigned to literature have been taken over by electronic media. Understanding the renewed importance of the imagination as a concept to authors across the Anglophone world is thus crucial to understanding the forms of response and dissent available.

CHAPTER 2

Aesthetic revolutions: white South African writing and the State of Emergency

The State of Emergency in South Africa, which lasted from 1985 to 1990, presented an unprecedented crisis for white dissident writers.[1] The brutal and systematic violence directed at perceived enemies of the state demonstrated the lengths to which the apartheid regime was willing to go to maintain itself, and made the idea of literature as a politically significant act seem ridiculous – a vestigial remnant of an outdated liberal humanism. Despite their public criticisms of liberal humanism, prominent white South African writers including André Brink, J. M. Coetzee, and Nadine Gordimer were themselves branded with this term. Their aesthetic interests were often seen as incompatible with political commitment, an attitude bolstered by Alan Paton's shift from fiction writing after *Cry, the Beloved Country* (1948) toward politics.[2] Even one of the most prominent black South African novelists, Zakes Mda, declared that the novel is a "luxury" of freedom, a genre better suited to the post-apartheid era than to the political immediacies dictated by the struggle against the apartheid regime.[3]

The crisis of relevance experienced by white South African writers became a significant topic for debate among Western European, American, and Canadian academics on postmodernism. Brink and Coetzee were identified as representative figures of a global postmodernism, and their literary works were championed for their purported political relevance. Linda Hutcheon, for instance, cites both authors in her argument that postmodern literature provides a "denaturalizing critique" of ideology.[4] Such critiques were dismissed by many Marxian academics, however, as elitist, rarefied, and irrelevant to the lives of the vast majority of people, for whom potable water, adequate nutrition, and physical safety were more pressing concerns than deconstruction. The readings of white South African authors undertaken by Paul Rich, Michael Vaughan, Richard Peck, and Elleke Boehmer resonated with broader critiques of postmodernity made by David Harvey, Terry Eagleton, and Perry Anderson.

Peck's description of the "morbid fascination" of white South African authors with politics – a fascination inseparable from a profound unwillingness to explore viable political solutions – echoed Eagleton's characterizations of postmodern artists and academics throughout *The Illusions of Postmodernism*. Likewise, Boehmer's condemnation of Brink, Coetzee, and Gordimer for their unwillingness to risk envisioning a utopian society was all the more damning when read against Fredric Jameson's assertion that since the 1960s utopian representations are all that is left of our ability to imagine political change.[5] In this light, the valorization of indeterminacy by postmodernists and white South African writers represented not a subversion of metanarratives or state propaganda but a profound failure to inspire hope that viable political alternatives exist.

The question facing readers of literature produced during the State of Emergency and its immediate aftermath, then, is whether the novel can have legitimacy in a situation of political crisis, when revolution is not a metaphor for personal transformation but a reality of everyday life for significant segments of a population. To begin to answer this question, it is important to recognize that critics of Brink, Coetzee, and Gordimer often failed to distinguish between the claims of political relevance made by the authors and their defenders. Brink, Coetzee, and Gordimer repeatedly declared their irrelevance to the daily struggles faced by black South Africans, and they were painfully aware of their dual lives: celebrated as anti-apartheid spokespeople abroad and dismissed by the majority of whites and blacks at home. Indeed, Brink notes that he and other novelists were permitted to continue publishing at a time when the work of so many journalists was censored only because literature was perceived as elitist and irrelevant by the South African government.[6]

Brink's comment suggests an intriguing possibility, that the perceived irrelevance of the novel may be crucial to its continued existence and vitality. At the heart of such a claim is the idea that the novel provides a unique form of imagining that does not promote withdrawal but rather some kind of political commitment.[7] While such a claim seemed dubious in the South African context after the rise of the Black Consciousness movement in the 1970s, the State of Emergency led to a reassessment of the relationship between aesthetics and politics. Albie Sachs's declaration to an ANC in-house seminar in 1989 that "our members should be banned from saying that culture is a weapon of struggle" was perhaps the most famous example of this shift.[8] But, in the same year, Njabulo S. Ndebele similarly rejected the simplistic form of realism underlying much protest literature, arguing instead for an expanded conception of literary relevance that recognized the role of the imagination in creating the conditions necessary to wage a successful revolution. "The challenge is to free the entire social imagination of the oppressed from the laws of perception that have characterized apartheid society," he declared.[9] The challenge thus revolves around epistemology as much as agency, and the imagination represents a mental faculty whose relative independence of sensory perceptions means that it might be somewhat resistant to state propaganda. It is striking that despite their significant differences in style and focus, Brink, Coetzee, and Gordimer were all drawn to Romantic notions of a creative imagination – specifically, the rhetoric of what Edward S. Casey calls its distinct, *thin autonomy*. This turn to the imagination occurs despite their awareness of both its historical tendency to create self-defeating oppositions between subject and society and the real possibility that transplanting European notions of the imagination might decontextualize their fiction from the sociopolitical conditions of late apartheid South Africa.

ANDRÉ BRINK: IMAGINING THE REAL

Although André Brink demonstrated the most dramatic shift in writing style among the three novelists, his guiding commitment to representing the objective "reality" of South Africa has remained consistent over his career. Since the 1960s, Brink has insisted on the writer's responsibility to make the oppressive conditions of the black majority an explicit subject for literary texts, and his *Kennis van die Aand* (1973, translated into English as *Looking on Darkness*) became the first Afrikaans novel to be banned.[10] His subsequent shift away from what Felicity Wood terms the "liberal realist tradition" in South African literature toward aesthetics associated with postmodernism, then, should not be read as a repudiation of the ideals guiding his earlier writing.[11] To the contrary, the shift in aesthetics apparent in *States of Emergency* (1988) is motivated by a sense that the increasing violence in South Africa necessitated a new mode of representation in order to accomplish the goal of "revealing to people *what is happening*: what they themselves allow to happen," which he outlined in his acceptance speech for the 1980 Martin Luther King Memorial Prize.[12]

Brink never endorsed a strawman notion of literary realism as mimeticism or simple reflection, but his arguments for the political relevance of literature during the 1970s did have some characteristically realist assumptions. The most significant and troubling assumption was that a radical experiential gap existed between dissident writers and the societies in which they live. In one of his most famous essays from the era, "Literature and Offence" (1976), Brink asserts that "all significant art is offensive" (121) because it exposes readers to experiences they had previously refused to acknowledge:

And essentially this offence is determined by the tension which exists between the writer's use of language and that of society: the difference, in other words, between the uniqueness of the experience of an individual (the writer), and his interpretation of the experience – and, on the other hand, society's acquiescence in traditional, conventional, stereotyped ways of looking, listening, thinking and experiencing. (120)

According to this account, "writers" and "society" are distinct and apparently stable categories, constituted by differing patterns of interpreting experience. The idiosyncratic and "offensive" language of the writer and the conventional language of society each produce a distinctive way of viewing the world. The "offensiveness" of literary fiction results from its capacity to make readers experience the world through a different language or interpretive lens, to force them to rethink their unselfconscious reproduction of racist social norms. The novel is not, then, realistic by virtue of replicating or imitating historical events; rather, the realism of the novel is linked to its capacity to force readers to reassess what they observe in their daily lives.

Brink's categorical opposition between the writer and society has been subjected to significant critique in subsequent years, and Brink himself was already beginning to question it in his most famous pre-Emergency novel, *A Dry White Season* (1979).[13] The novel traces the efforts of the unnamed writer-narrator to uncover the truth behind the mysterious deaths of Ben du Toit (a former university colleague), Gordon Ngubene (a black groundskeeper at the school where du Toit taught), and Gordon's son Jonathan. While the majority of the novel follows conventions associated with literary realism as the writer-narrator collects evidence and testimony, interviews witnesses, and combs through documents left to him by du Toit shortly before his death, Part Three engages in something closer to metafictional speculation on the limits of language to represent experience neutrally and objectively. The narrator finds among du Toit's documents a page expressing concern over his inability to convey the experiences of black South Africans without silencing them: "Every gesture I make, every act I commit in my efforts to help them makes it more difficult for them to define their real needs and discover for themselves their integrity and affirm their own dignity. How else could we hope to arrive beyond predator and prey, helper and helped, white and black, and find redemption?"[14] Such an assertion undermines the epistemic privilege that Brink claims for writers when he casts them in strict opposition to the societies in which they dwell.

The imagination became such an important concept in Brink's fictional and nonfictional writings beginning in the 1980s because it implies the possibility of bridging experiential gaps among South Africans. By 1981, Brink had shifted his description of literature, arguing that it enables readers to "*imagine the real*" (*Writing in a State of Siege*, 221). This revised conception concedes that dissident writers are unlikely to provide a corrective to state media in the minds of most white South Africans. So-called protest literature has limited usefulness, according to this account: even the most sophisticated techniques of imitation or *mimesis* do not challenge readers to alter how they perceive and interpret the world. The realist text may invite its readers to view the world from the perspective of others, but portrayals of state violence and the suffering caused by it fail to address the interpretive biases that shape how individuals will perceive "reality." The actual conditions of daily life, Brink suggests, are mystified to such a degree that individuals cannot recognize either their own misery or their culpability for the misery of others without recourse to some special cognitive process – a process that has historically been assigned to the imagination since the Western European Romantics. Indeed, the rhetoric of his essay "Imagining the Real" is filled with phrases familiar to readers of Romanticism, not least of which is his insistence that literature provides "one of the few remaining domains" where individuals can recognize "the unity of individual experience and the unity of human experience" (*Writing in a State of Siege*, 220).[15]

Brink's definition of the imagination is shaped by the assumption that experiential gaps persist among South Africans because state propaganda diminishes the capacity of individuals to interpret accurately the political and social conditions in which they live. His definition is most clearly articulated in a 1998 essay in which he declares that the process of imagining involves:

a transgression of the boundaries of an originary sensual perception, a recognition of Baudelairean "correspondences" between otherwise disparate objects or events, while simultaneously "making them strange" in the Russian-Formalist meaning of the phrase, infusing the ordinary with a sense of the extraordinary, the everyday with a sense of the fantastic, producing a result in which the whole is decidedly more than the sum of its parts.[16]

The characterization of imagining as an act of "transgression" implies that it involves the forbidden, even the criminal.[17] The imagination is

transgressive because its two intertwined tendencies lead to the production of images that conflict with data from the senses. The first tendency
Brink lists, the recognition of correspondences, gravitates against what
the narrator of *States of Emergency* calls the pathological desire of the
apartheid regime to define people and things "in terms of their exclusivity
rather than in terms of what they have in common."[18] The imagination's
tendency to establish correspondences encourages white South Africans
to identify themselves and their concerns in relation to black South
Africans. To effect such a transformation in perception, however, requires
individuals to overcome their internalized ideological biases by defamil-
iarizing existing representations of events or "making them strange." This
second tendency of the imagination challenges the perceived stability and
banality of "ordinary" life for white South Africans, revealing it to be a
product of a state ideology that works to conceal or, when necessary, nor-
malize violence against the majority black population. Both tendencies of
the imagination – toward correspondence and toward defamiliarization –
are understood to reveal precisely what the senses fail to convey because
of internalized ideological biases. Thus, mental activities associated with
imagining mirror the political activities Brink finds necessary to challenge the legitimacy of the apartheid regime.[19]

Postmodern aesthetic techniques such as self-reflexivity and collage are
particularly suited to cultivating the twin tendencies of the imagination,
for Brink, because literary genres function analogously to the ideological
biases that predispose individuals to certain interpretations over others.
Brink highlights this point by portraying the repeated failures of his
unnamed though highly autobiographical narrator in *States of Emergency*
to write a love story uncontaminated by the political situation surrounding him. The narrator may state his desire to give his female protagonist a
name that is nothing more than "a triad of syllables, pure sound" (15), but
this declaration only emphasizes that he cannot control the possible historical resonances associated with the names he chooses: Melissa Lotman
and Philip Malan. The dissonance between the novel's title and its first
line, "Notes toward a love story" (1), likewise highlights the impossibility of creating an aesthetic sphere partitioned from the political circumstances of late apartheid. Brink's portrayal of his narrator's failure to
remain faithful to conventions associated with romance enables Brink to
emphasize the twin tendencies he associates with the imagination. The
narrator's declaration that no love story is "exclusive, insular, unique"
highlights a series of correspondences among the novel, other romances,
poststructuralist theories, and current political events – correspondences

that emerge from the defamiliarization produced by disrupting generic expectations (103). The analogy to apartheid is clear, if simplistic: literary genres maintain their consistency by repressing the default tendencies of the imagination toward creative and political freedom. Telling a postmodern love story, then, represents an act of transgression against generic and ideological boundaries, a point emphasized by having the narrator use the same terminology of transgression that Brink uses in his definition of the imagination. The narrator declares that his efforts to write a love story are best understood through Jacques Derrida's notion of the *hymen*, a word that signifies both separation and unity, the "transgression of [a] boundary" (103).

Yet the tendency among literary scholars to characterize Brink's preoccupations in terms of postmodernism – a tendency he has encouraged – obfuscates the role he assigns to the imagination. *States of Emergency* makes repeated references to Derrida, Roland Barthes, and other thinkers associated with postmodernism; it employs terms such as transgression, which have had wide circulation within postmodern and poststructuralist discourses; Brink himself has in subsequent years repeatedly identified himself as a representative of an international postmodernism, and has often used the term in his nonfictional writings.[20] However, Hutcheon's notion of "denaturalizing critique" significantly fails to capture Brink's aspiration to make ideology critique not an end in itself but part of a process of overcoming the experiential gaps produced by apartheid. This becomes particularly apparent when *States of Emergency* invokes Hans-Georg Gadamer rather than Derrida to describe how the free play of the imagination creates the psychological conditions necessary for political activism. The narrator's reflections on Gadamer interrupt the romance narrative at the very moment when Philip is convinced by Melissa to provide financial assistance to Milton Thaya, a black South African who is smuggling people between townships. The narrator declares:

Gadamer paraphrased: … Changing the world through play implies the playful transformation of the self. And this transformation of the "I" demands a moment of alienation, a "losing" of the I in the text in order to find it: in this way appropriation also becomes divestiture. (75)

The jarring shift in discourse from fiction to philosophical speculation disrupts reader identification with Philip and Melissa, short-circuiting the emotional satisfaction readers might feel from vicariously identifying with dissident activity – an identification that is accompanied by none of the risks to which actual dissidents are exposed. Yet, if the formal structure of the text works to render visible the techniques it had previously employed to produce such vicarious identifications, the content of the narratorial interruption encourages readers to speculate on the conditions for a more encompassing understanding of the circumstances of life under late apartheid. Play, according to the narrator's gloss on Gadamer, is conceived as an intermediary stage to restore the humanity of the novel's readers, a humanity that has been perverted by state propaganda.[21] Something like denaturalizing critique is a necessary part of the process, which the narrator emphasizes by declaring that play involves alienation. The narrator asserts: "the reader, through the process of reading, is … first withdrawn from the world, transformed, and then restored" (75). Because individuals tend to view the world in terms of a stable set of prejudices, they preserve the status quo as long as they preserve their habitual identifications. Suspending these identifications, if only temporarily, enables individuals to perceive the world in different ways. Thus apartheid becomes, in Brink's work, an extreme example of a more general hermeneutical challenge: to create what Gadamer called a "fusion of horizons."[22]

This conception of politics was highly abstracted from the realities of daily life for the majority of black South Africans, and does not exonerate Brink from criticisms that his portrayals of state violence are opportunistic.[23] Even if these long-standing criticisms can be addressed, however, the imagination can have the political relevance Brink attributes to it only if his assumptions about its autonomy are correct. The autonomy of the imagination is often characterized in two interrelated ways: the imagination is, to use Casey's words, "both *free from* undue dependence on perception or thoughts and *free to* project pure possibilities that exceed the mere probabilities that obtain when imagining is considered a mere function of the organism or a product of social determinations."[24] The close alignment of Brink's twin tendencies of the imagination with the two senses of autonomy described by Casey underlines the necessary conditions for imagining to achieve the "transgression of boundaries." Defamiliarization is possible only if the imagination is not exclusively dependent upon sensory perception; likewise, unfamiliar correspondences can be established only if the imagination has the capacity to do more than replicate or imitate the images an individual has been socialized to have.

Philosophers who argue for the autonomy of imagining, however, tend to be uncomfortable making the strong claims for the political relevance of the imagination that Brink does. Casey, for example, asserts that imagining possesses a *thin* autonomy characterized by an indifference to the concrete concerns of everyday life. Casey writes: "The imaginer displays such an indifference inasmuch as he does not seek to change either the given structure of his life-world or his apprehension of that structure."[25] The images produced through imagining might differ significantly from what an individual perceives in the world around him or her, but they are largely disconnected from the world. The act of imagining does not physically change the world in which a person lives, nor does it change how the individual perceives that world. Imagining thus creates a kind of partitioning or segmentation of experience, so that individuals are likely to feel that their imaginations draw them away from the political realities in which they live. At best, the autonomy of imagining encourages utopian thinking, and this is apparent among Frankfurt School thinkers such as Herbert Marcuse and philosophers influenced by phenomenology including Casey, Richard Kearney, and Eva T. H. Brann. Indeed, Brann's encyclopedic *The World of the Imagination* is striking for insisting on the one hand that the imagination is "the deepest force of political life,"[26] yet concluding on the other hand that it ultimately provides "an intimation of paradise."[27] The final words of Brann's work suggest that imagining has relatively little relevance to daily political life.

To understand Brink thus requires a somewhat revised conception of autonomy. While Brink agrees with Casey that the imagination is not constrained to reproduce mental images of sensory perceptions, he rejects the contention that imagining is separate from how individuals apprehend the world. As early as his essay "Imagining the Real," Brink declares that "imagination brings reality into its own: only through rivers running with wine do we really perceive, as if for the first time, the running waters of the time we live in" (*Writing in a State of Siege*, 221). Brink had not developed, by this point in his career, the notion of imagination in terms of correspondence and defamiliarization, but he was already groping toward it with his claim that the imagination affects perception by leading individuals to reconsider familiar images with an intensity and concentration generally reserved for highly unfamiliar, incongruous objects. The initial sense impressions that constitute perception are shaped by a process of filtering, contextualizing, and highlighting them into comprehensible forms – a process that Brink calls imagining. The imagination is thus integral to perception, and its autonomy would be defined in terms of a capacity to contextualize sensory data in ways that are not socially sanctioned.

In *States of Emergency*, the capacity of an autonomous imagination to recontextualize initial sense impressions opens up the possibility for individuals to perceive within the circumstances of everyday life the rudimentary conditions for social change. The novel's male protagonist, Professor Philip Malan, initially perceives the State of Emergency in South Africa to be a repetition of what he lived through during his student days in Paris in the 1960s, and this perception leaves him feeling helpless. He finds his marriage unfulfilling, his job unsatisfying, and his government intolerable, yet his inability to perceive the possibility of changing any of these circumstances renders him passive. Every perception confirms for him the inevitability and stability of his current situation. Through his romantic affair with the theory-savvy graduate student Melissa Lotman, however, Philip slowly discovers his capacity to view his world in terms of a broader range of possibilities, and this changes how he perceives people around him, poststructuralism, and even the State of Emergency. Indeed, the novel portrays Philip's blossoming romance, his growing the-oretical sophistication, and his budding political activism as inseparably intertwined. Initially reluctant to join Melissa in a public rally against police incarcerations of dissidents, he slowly recognizes: "Of course. She's right," he thinks to himself. "There are times like that. This isn't Paris, 1968: these aren't a crowd of strangers in a distant city in Europe: this is here, now, today. This concerns *me*" (180). By breaking his initial impulse to view the current situation as a repetition of the past, Philip and, by extension, readers learn to be more sensitive to how historical events are not fated or determined in advance.

The narrative structure of *States of Emergency* is designed to disrupt further any sense of historical determinism or narrative closure. After evoking Frank Kermode's assertion that the distinguishing generic fea-ture of the novel is a "sense of an ending" that leads readers to interpret every scene or event with respect to a posited conclusion, Brink's narrator proceeds to unravel his own narrative's ending (203). The narrative thread concerning the romance between Philip and Melissa is broken off by the narrator's discovery that Milton Thaya (who is both the narrator's friend and a character in the Philip–Melissa romance plot) was murdered. This juxtaposition of various narrative threads with disruptions from the nar-rator's personal life highlights the extent to which a sense of closure is contingent upon a highly selective process of shaping an otherwise inco-herent jumble of life events. The novel proceeds to describe three frag-mentary, alternative endings for its love story, only to conclude that none of them is satisfactory. The future of the lovers and the future of South Africa remains unwritten and undetermined, possible only within "a story not yet written" (244).

Brink's conception of imagining suffers from a basic problem that has haunted Western theories of the imagination for more than two centuries: how are the insights about social oppression gained by an individual translated into collective political action? If discovery depends on an individual withdrawing himself or herself from a community, this would seem to establish a tension between the subject and society. Indeed, this has been a central anxiety of advocates of the imagination since the Romantic era. At least since Friedrich Schiller's *On the Aesthetic Education of Man* (1795), the imagination has been identified as providing an important contribution to social change because of its unique status as a mediating faculty between sensory perception and abstract cognition. The assumption has been that there is an analogous relationship between society and the individual, and that the imagination could mediate potential tensions between the two. But the cautions provided by scholars of Romanticism are relevant here, especially if Deborah Elise White is correct that postmodernism is its heir.[28] The various configurations of imagination in the eighteenth and early nineteenth centuries were all assigned the responsibility of making a linkage between people, a linkage that often served the ideological function of concealing the existence of social fissures rather than eliminating or transcending them.[29] One of the real dangers of not recognizing how the imagination is deployed within discourses of nationhood is that it creates the perception that social tensions can be alleviated merely by encouraging individuals to imagine an idealized community. Brink's allusions to a wide range of literary theorists and philosophers including Derrida, Gadamer, and Kermode reinforce this perception, and *States of Emergency* seems at moments to suggest that the heterosexual romantic couple provides a model for citizenship in South Africa.

The struggle to translate individual acts of imagining into programs for collective political or social change is central to Brink's post-apartheid novels such as *Imaginings of Sand* (1996). This novel portrays the return of expatriate Afrikaner Kristien Müller to South Africa in the run-up to the nation's first free elections in 1994. Over the course of the novel, Kristien becomes increasingly able to commit herself to working toward political change as she hears her dying grandmother, Ouma Kristina, tell stories of nine generations of women in her family. From the outset, readers are informed that these stories are explicit acts of imagining rather than an historical chronicle, and Ouma Kristina insists in the first paragraphs of the novel that "I can remember things that never happened."[30] According to her grandmother, Kristien's inability to commit herself politically or romantically results from her diminished capacity to imagine, which is characterized by her amnesia of the "memories" Ouma Kristina passed on to her as a child. Thus, Kristien's transformation in the final pages of the novel – marked most notably by her new assertion that she must be engaged in "more than a private act of commitment, a personal rebellion" (348) – is understood to have been made possible through her renewed efforts to engage her imagination.

Kristien's transformation points to a conception of imagination subtly different from that apparent in earlier works such as *States of Emergency*, one aimed at alleviating anxieties among white Afrikaners that they might have no place within a post-apartheid nation. This anxiety is apparent throughout *Imaginings of Sand*, perhaps nowhere more so than in a scene late in the novel in which Ouma Kristina's assertions about imagination are ratified by an exiled black leader, Thando Kumalo. After listening to Ouma Kristina, Kumalo declares: "We can't imagine the future by pretending to forget the past" (264); he goes on to insist that all South Africans are indebted to her. Such an insistence on solidarity through imagining is crucial to the project of the novel, which posits that the imagination provides the basis for white citizenship in post-apartheid South Africa. In a move that simultaneously establishes her right of tenure to the land and her separation from her racist parents, Kristien declares that she feels a connection to her imagination that her Calvinist parents suppressed. "But they have not denied, in the process," Kristien reflects, "precisely this surge of the imagination which links us to Africa … How sad – no, how dangerous – to have suppressed all this for so long" (97). The imagination provides the basis for claiming a common heritage among black and white South Africans as the nation transitions to a more genuine democracy, even as the imagination is also used as a means of distinguishing between racist and egalitarian Afrikaners.

The simultaneous healing of social tensions and differentiating racist from egalitarian white South Africans is apparent in the shifting relationships between Kristien and her sister Anna and brother-in-law Casper. Initially, there is a rift between Kristien and Anna, the latter considering herself part of a beleaguered minority whose way of life is rapidly disappearing with the prospect of a majority black government. Over the course of the novel, however, a realignment of relationships occurs, so that Casper remains the embodiment of white intransigence while Kristien and Anna heal the rift between them. The key turning point occurs when the two sisters discuss Ouma Kristina's imagined histories of their mother. As was the case in *States of Emergency*, acts of imagining lead to altered perceptions of real events. Even as the sisters doubt the veracity of Ouma Kristina's story, Kristien begins to view her mother in a more favorable light. Previously, she had condemned her mother for her decision to sacrifice her personal ambitions for the sake of the family, "But last night – Ouma suddenly made me realize that there was another side to it. She had a whole secret life of her own which we knew nothing about" (132). This willingness to alter her perceptions of the past gives Anna sufficient confidence to share her own experiences with her sister.

Brink's unwillingness or inability to conclude *Imaginings of Sand* with a more concrete portrayal of positive social change indicates the limits of the imagination in the post-apartheid era. Anna cannot sever her ties from Casper, and she shoots him, her children, and finally herself. Nor is the novel comfortable portraying the post-apartheid government. While the novel reaches a climax on election day, the final scene portrays Kristien alone at night communicating with her now dead grandmother. The ambiguity about the ontological status of Ouma Kristina is telling: is she the product of Kristien's imagination or is she "real"? The novel's repeated insistence on the importance of remembrance to creating the future requires Ouma Kristina's presence in the final scene. Answering the question about her status, however, would cause problems previously identified with imagining to reemerge. If Ouma Kristina is nothing more than an image in Kristien's mind, then once again the rift between the subject and society emerges, and Kristien's personal transformation fails to translate into a promise of social or political revolution. If Ouma Kristina is a real ghost, then this would seem to imply a reliance upon the supernatural that Brink himself has rejected since his own repudiation of Christianity. Thus, Kristien's grandmother remains at the end of the novel as a symbol of the tensions that Brink invoked the imagination to heal.

The indeterminacy is all too familiar to readers of various forms of postmodern literature, a point that is troubling because Brink saw in his appropriation of postmodern aesthetics the possibility of establishing the political relevance of art in late apartheid South Africa. In a 1982 interview, Brink declared that after he returned from Paris in 1968 he abandoned the idea of writing in a "general European cosmopolitan way" in favor of focusing on his experiences in South Africa.[31] Declaring that he could not compete with writers like John Fowles, Brink suggested that his particular experiences would enable him to write a unique kind of fiction. That *States of Emergency* and *Imaginings of Sand* both end with a deliberate kind of indeterminacy characteristic of the postmodernism associated with Fowles, however, indicates the limited extent to which he could translate stylistic features and techniques associated with Euro-American postmodernisms to the South African situation.

NADINE GORDIMER: IMAGINED REVOLUTIONS

The State of Emergency in South Africa also led Nadine Gordimer to attribute greater political significance to the imagination. In a 1986 address entitled "The Writer's Imagination and the Imagination of the State," Gordimer declares that "The State has no imagination."[32] A state engages instead in what she calls *projection*, a deliberate effort to engineer a social vision for its populace. Writers are encouraged and sometimes compelled to use their imaginations to reinforce a particular vision, but the imagination cannot be reliably controlled or programmed. The autonomy Gordimer claims for the imagination is apparent in her rhetoric throughout the essay, which characterizes the imagination as possessing its own unique agency. "The Writer is *put into service* by his imagination," Gordimer declares; "he or she writes at its dictate."[33] The tendency of the imagination not to conform to expectations makes it implicitly anti-hierarchical and even utopian, for Gordimer, and therefore the writer is always a potential threat to the state.

Yet, as was the case with Brink, Gordimer's writing is tinged with a melancholic sense that the promise of the imagination is indefinitely deferred. Gordimer suggests that imagining leads writers into conflict even with the most altruistic regimes. The state and the writer are opposed not simply because politicians tend to betray the ideals they espouse before they gain power. Gordimer's model writer also recognizes that revolution is a continuous process of forming and disbanding political organizations. Gordimer states:

The Writer himself knows that the only revolution is the permanent one – not in the Trotskyite sense, but in the sense of the imagination, in which no understanding is ever completed, but must keep breaking up and re-forming in different combinations if it is to spread and meet the terrible questions of human existence.[34]

Gordimer's turn to the imagination represents an intriguing shift in terminology. In her essays prior to the State of Emergency, many of which are collected in *The Essential Gesture* (1988), the imagination is rarely an explicit topic of discussion. Gordimer frequently discusses the duties of South African writers, and insists on what she calls the "writer's freedom" to produce aesthetically beautiful art rather than propaganda.[35] Her essays in the 1970s also recognize that writers will face opposition from progressive or revolutionary groups as well as from the apartheid regime, and that the writer must resist the "conformity to an orthodoxy of opposition" (106). Yet the imagination is not mentioned; much less is it portrayed in the personified terms used in her later work.

Understanding the logic behind Gordimer's terminological shift is crucial to interpreting the evolution of both her political and her aesthetic values. Beginning with her novel *The Late Bourgeois World* (1966), Gordimer shifts away from liberal humanism toward what she terms radicalism.[36] The shift away from literary realism, in contrast, is a more subtle process. In large part, this is because Gordimer's reading of Georg Lukács in the late 1960s provided her the theoretical foundation for a "critical realism" that appeared to be consistent with her increasingly radical politics.[37] According to this idea, the narratorial persona can provide an ideological orientation for readers to recognize the economic and social construction of reality in South Africa. The critical realist thereby challenges readers to re-examine the circumstances of their own lives in light of the systems of exploitation presented in the novel. Under such circumstances, the imagination, freighted as it is by associations with Romanticism, is unnecessary because the politically committed artist has the capacity to identify and represent the conditions of exploitation. Or, put more glibly, there is no need to "imagine the real" at this stage of Gordimer's career because the artist can simply describe it.

Within her fictional works, Gordimer presents the transformation of consciousness among white South Africans as an inevitability as late as *Burger's Daughter* (1979), though it is most strikingly presented in *The Conservationist* (1974). *Burger's Daughter* traces the radicalization of Rosa Burger, daughter of a jailed white South African dissident based on Bram Fischer; *The Conservationist* focuses on the failed efforts of a wealthy white South African named Mehring to establish himself as undisputed holder of a farm. While Mehring evinces a "hankering to make contact with the land," his efforts to establish a weekend pastoral existence for himself are repeatedly frustrated.[38] An unidentified black corpse found on Mehring's property early in the novel functions as a symbolic reminder of the psychic repression necessary for white South Africans to rationalize their claim to the land. While the body may be hurriedly buried on the land by the police, it resurfaces toward the end of the novel after a storm. As Stephen Clingman notes, political and psychic repression are intertwined in the novel, so that Mehring's hysterical flight from the farm after witnessing the body's reemergence from the soil suggests that the restoration of the land to black South Africans is an historical inevitability.[39] The reburial at the end of the novel by black workers on the farm provides the opportunity for the local community to certify their claim to the land: "They had put him away to rest, at last; he had come back. He took possession of this earth, theirs; one of them."[40]

The problem with Gordimer's theory of critical realism becomes apparent in her 1982 lecture "Living in the Interregnum." In this piece, Gordimer continues to assert that the apartheid regime sustains itself by suppressing alternative epistemologies. "We have to believe in our ability to find new perceptions," Gordimer asserts, "and our ability to judge their truth" (*The Essential Gesture*, 266). The tone of this assertion, however, suggests some loss of confidence on her part about the capacity of literary representations to convince readers of their abilities.[41] More significantly, Gordimer expands the scope of the problem, declaring "for apartheid is above all a habit; the unnatural seems natural … The segment of the white population to which I belong has become highly conscious of a dependency on distorted vision induced since childhood" (266). The problem is thus not purely epistemological. By the 1980s, white South Africans were by and large aware that sanctioned media were not providing accurate representations but, according to Gordimer, had nonetheless habituated themselves to trusting the regime. Under such circumstances, the assumptions guiding Gordimer's theory of critical realism are no longer tenable even to herself. The idea of critical realism inherited from Lukács presupposes that exploitative systems of governance exist because individuals neither recognize the oppression experienced by certain groups nor empathize with such experiences when they witness them. The underlying assumption is that human decisions are made by deliberate and rational calculation, so that once a person recognizes that his or her way of life is directly responsible for the suffering of others, he or she will change accordingly. But if actions are largely the product of habit, as Gordimer proposes, recognition and empathy are insufficient to cause changes in behavior. Indeed, Gordimer's increasingly sharp criticism of white South African liberals appears to be guided by this point. People may be well-intentioned and even believe that the oppression of the black majority is wrong, yet their actions will directly and indirectly support the continued existence of apartheid.

The contradictions between belief and behavior among white South African liberals have been repeatedly portrayed in Gordimer's fiction, even in post-apartheid novels such as *The House Gun* (1998). Harald and Claudia Lindgard are uncomfortable with their attitudes toward their black Senior Counsel Hamilton Motsamai, but they never fundamentally alter their behavior toward him, even at the end of the novel. More significantly, the Lindgards demonstrate that habitual patterns of interaction can lead to contradictory behaviors on macro- and micro-levels. The Lindgards articulate progressive attitudes toward black South Africans when it comes to issues on the national level, supporting the rights of blacks to form a majority government. Likewise, when they make decisions as a doctor and board member of a national insurance company – decisions that involve deliberate, rational calculation – they are not explicitly racist. Claudia sees black patients; Harald works to ensure that poor blacks can find housing and reasonable insurance. It is rather in their everyday, mundane activities that they reinforce racial difference: Claudia cannot bring herself to accept a dinner invitation from Motsamai; Harald is reluctant to have a black Senior Counsel representing their son, who has been accused of murder.

The novel that explores the social consequences of habit most fully is *July's People* (1981), the first novel-length work in which Gordimer envisions a successful revolution by the black majority population. As with *The House Gun, July's People* focuses on the relationship between a white liberal married couple and a black man. Maureen and Bamford Smales are taken to the village of their servant, whom they call July, after the cities become consumed by violence. In this new environment, each of the characters struggles to understand and redefine his or her relations with the others. Yet, for much of the novel, the characters maintain their pre-revolutionary social roles. According to Dominic Head, the dependence of both blacks and whites on the "terms of a commodity culture" limits the possibility for significant political transformation after the black majority gains power.[42] Even as Maureen and Bam increasingly depend on July for their existence, he preserves the terms of their relationship. "But I'm work for you," he tells Maureen. "Me, I'm your boy."[43] The power dynamics are indeed shifting; July is explaining to Maureen why he should keep the keys to their truck, one of the central symbols of their power and bourgeois status in the novel. But July resorts to the habitual terminology of their relationship, "boy," and not simply for exploitative reasons. He continues to shelter and care for his former masters well after it becomes necessary or even expedient to do so.

Gordimer does not attribute the incomplete revolution in *July's People* to a failure of imagination, as she will in essays written after the State of Emergency is declared. The direct references to imagination in the novel are relatively critical. Maureen finds that her imagination is insufficient as an epistemological tool to aid in comprehending her new situation. The narrator declares: "No fiction could compete with what she was finding she did not know, could not have imagined or discovered through imagination."[44] The other reference to imagination occurs at the very end of the novel, as Maureen blindly flees the village toward a landing helicopter. "The real fantasies of the bush delude more inventively than the romantic forests of Grimm and Disney," readers are told.[45] The problem appears to be the result of an inability to interpret and represent experience accurately, and the narrator follows the Aristotelian tradition of defining the imagination as a mediating faculty with no direct access to the world. The imagination is indexed against fictional works of Grimm and Disney, not "reality."[46]

The crucial shift in Gordimer's thinking during the State of the Emergency has to do with the capacity of the imagination to provide accurate knowledge about the world that cannot be accessed through sensory perceptions or abstract rational reasoning. In her 1995 book of essays *Writing and Being*, Gordimer declares:

Only in the prescient dimension of the imagination could I bring together what had been deliberately broken and fragmented; fit together the shapes of living experience, my own and that of others, without which a whole consciousness is not attainable.[47]

The emphasis placed on prescience suggests that hypothetical scenarios of a utopian future now represent more significant forms of knowledge than the revelation of exploitative social and economic conditions. Such hypothetical speculations were previously unnecessary and counterproductive because the framework of Lukácsean critical realism provided a clear conception of the future classless society. Indeed, for Lukács, the entire arc of history is a predetermined narrative of the growing maturation of the proletariat.[48] Gordimer's account of her own growth, however, belies the possibility of an eventual convergence of experiences into a single class, racial, or national consciousness. A "whole consciousness" depends on engagements with black South Africans; her growth, in other words, comes not from recognizing shared experiences but from learning about very different experiences from her own. To take these engagements seriously means that the vision of a genuinely egalitarian post-apartheid nation cannot be known in advance, and thus cannot be modeled by other nations or rationally deduced in advance by any single individual. In this context, the imagination can potentially produce knowledge that cannot be arrived at through sensory perceptions or abstract rational cognition because imagining involves establishing associations that have no necessary historical basis or precedent. Put another way, the prescience ascribed to the imagination results from its tendency to draw associations between images that are not necessarily indexed against reality. The great irony for Gordimer, then, is that the imagination is called upon to engage in precisely the kind of fantastic speculation for which it was condemned in *July's People*.[49]

In Gordimer's most significant novel written during the State of Emergency, *A Sport of Nature* (1987), the protagonist's inability to connect her personal experiences with those of black South Africans prevents her from developing a political consciousness. Well into adulthood, Hillela is apolitical or incidentally political, based on whom she is dating. Even after she is forced to flee the country, she demonstrates strikingly little interest in political activism, to the surprise and chagrin of her fellow expatriates. The novel suggests that her political apathy results from an epistemological problem. In a conversation with a member of the exile community named Arnold, she insists that she cannot know anything that she does not personally experience. "How can anyone know what hasn't happened to them," she declares. "You can describe what it was like, but I … I never, I don't really believe it's *all* it's like."[50] This solipsistic declaration could be read as motivated by a scrupulous caution about the limits of sympathy to enable a person to acquire knowledge vicariously. But such declarations also enable Hillela to rationalize her own ignorance and unwillingness to pursue the truth. This latter point is emphasized when the conversation is disrupted by the news of the assassination of an important West African leader, and Hillela continues to swim in water "tempered to the body of amniotic fluid" (164), confident that the news is irrelevant to her life.

Hillela's declaration about the epistemological limits of experience is particularly significant for its indictment of Gordimer's earlier realist aesthetics. As noted before, *July's People* reflected critically on the capacity of realist literature to enable readers to overcome their habitual patterns of acting and thinking. *A Sport of Nature* goes further in its insistence that realism fails to provide a rhetoric compelling enough to convince readers that the events described by a work are "real." In pre-Emergency essays such as "The Essential Gesture" (1984), Gordimer addresses Hillela's question by exploring the extent to which a writer can or should extrapolate experiences of suffering that are not personally felt and represent them in literary form. At this earlier stage in Gordimer's thinking, realist aesthetics was uniquely suited for the task. Citing Chekhov, Gordimer declares that the only way to fulfill the writer's duty to transform the experiences of his or her readers is "to describe a situation so truthfully ... that the reader can no longer evade it" (*The Essential Gesture*, 299). Hillela's disclaimer, however, foregrounds the problems with the assumptions guiding Gordimer's argument. Gordimer's declaration presupposes an account of human nature according to which sympathy is central to moral reasoning. In a fashion reminiscent of Adam Smith's *A Theory of Moral Sentiments*, individuals have an inherent tendency to sympathize with other people, and they tend to ameliorate the suffering of others as they recognize it.[51] Hence, a narratorial voice that is relatively familiar to readers in values, style, and class will be able to represent events in ways that are interpreted as "truthful" or "real." Such a truth-telling voice will be uniquely suited to elicit a sympathetic response from readers, who will then feel a responsibility to change the present regime. What Hillela reveals is that individuals can be so desensitized to or distrustful of their own capacity for sympathy that they will be likely to discount any representation as "real."

Gordimer's tendency to link sexuality and political activism makes a great deal of sense in this context.[52] Only within an intimate relationship are characters in her fictional works able to gain sufficient confidence in their capacity to identify with the experiences of others. Hillela modifies her attitude toward knowledge after she becomes involved with the black South African revolutionary Whaila. Their sexual encounters lead her to recognize that the universalist ideas she inherited from her liberal caregivers actually prevent her from feeling genuine sympathy for others. She confesses to Whaila that previously she assumed that his "blackness was a glove ... Underneath, you must be white like me ... because that's what I was told, when I was being taught not to be prejudiced: underneath they are all just like us. Nobody said we are just like *you*" (207). Such assumptions about a common humanity not only prevent explorations of significant differences between people but also tend to devalue cultural differences as irrelevant or distractions from an "essential humanity."

After Hillela begins to engage with the experiences and beliefs of others, she becomes increasingly able to imagine more egalitarian social roles. Her post-coital conversation with Whaila leads her to imagine a more egalitarian future for South Africa embodied in their unborn child. She declares that she wants the child to be "Our colour," which the narrator goes on to note is a "category that doesn't exist: she would invent it" (208). The narratorial voice demonstrates significant suspicion of Hillela's utopianism, and the assassination of Whaila puts an end to the vision of a "rainbow family" (360). Hillela may be able to imagine a shared future for whites and blacks in South Africa, but her vision still retains elements of the universalism that made her so provincial in her thinking earlier. Her phrase "our colour" presupposes a future in which cultural differences can be made less important than a shared sense of identity, and the violence directed against black South Africans makes this future seem untenable.

The utopian conclusion of the novel is made possible only after Hillela further redefines the function of imagining. Whereas the focus of her imagining during her marriage to Whaila consisted of finding ways to bring white and black South Africans together as equal partners, by the end of the novel Hillela focuses on imagining how she might contribute within a black-majority social structure. After her second marriage to a black revolutionary, Hillela manages to make herself indispensable as General Reuel liberates his country, becomes president, and initiates an immensely successful set of economic reforms. That Hillela conceives of herself as a revolutionary working within a black social structure rather than an equal partner is apparent in her desire to receive an African name from her husband. In contrast to white liberal politicians who saw themselves as liberators of black South Africans, Hillela is characterized as identifying a role within the revolution that complements black liberation movements without displacing anyone: "Hers is the non-matrilineal centre that no one resents because no one has known it could exist. She has invented it. This is not the rainbow family" (360). The rejection of Hillela's earlier utopian fantasy suggests that the task of the imagination is not to envision a future that creates equality by erasing racial differences and the history of racial oppression; put another way, *A Sport of Nature* cautions against an entirely autonomous imagination. Imagining is useful to revolutionary struggle when it creates images of the future that draw from existing social and cultural conditions.

Gordimer's portrayal of the narrator, however, suggests that Hillela's imagination should not be taken as a straightforward model for individuals committed to anti-apartheid struggle. The tone of the narrator toward Hillela is by no means unambiguously positive; indeed, Richard Peck reads hostility in the narrator's portrait of the protagonist.[53] Whether or not Peck is correct, the stance of the narrator is sufficiently unclear as to raise questions about the reliability of both Hillela and himself/herself. Dominic Head, for example, argues that Gordimer deliberately presents an inconsistent narrator in order to undercut "facile teleological prescriptions," suggesting that Hillela's imagination cannot be entirely successful.[54] To portray a character modeling the notion of imagination that Gordimer herself endorses would contradict her critique of realist aesthetics.

The unreliability of the narrator thus highlights a significant difference between Gordimer and Brink in terms of their attitude toward utopia. For all of his metafictional commentary, the narrator of *States of Emergency* is entirely reliable. His expressions of self-doubt represent techniques through which Brink negotiates with his readers what constitutes reality. By emphasizing that certain elements of the narrative are artifice, Brink implies that other elements are genuine – such as the narrator's feelings and experiences – and provide a reliable guide for a reader's interpretation. Gordimer's more rigorous rejection of the idea that any single person or worldview can provide an entirely reliable interpretation means that neither a narrator nor a character can escape scrutiny. A utopian world may be presented at the end of *A Sport of Nature*, but only in a manner such that it can be distrusted by readers.

Gordimer's final novel written during the State of Emergency, *My Son's Story* (1990), demonstrates even more significant suspicion about the capacity of literature to model utopian political systems. The novel focuses on the fragmentation of a colored family involved in the anti-apartheid struggle. The portrait is significant in Gordimer's oeuvre not only because it shows the factional infighting and less than virtuous motivations of members involved in the struggle; more significantly, *My Son's Story* rejects the connection between sexuality and utopian politics that has been a hallmark of her writing. Whereas Hillela's sexual exploration ultimately leads her to more significant political commitment, Sonny's affair with Hannah – a white woman involved in the movement – tears his family apart. As his involvement with the movement and his mistress intensifies, his family begin to redefine themselves without him. Nor does the novel make the case that Sonny discovers a more politically virtuous relationship with his mistress than he enjoyed with his family. When police open fire on a group of protesters, Sonny's primary motivation is to escape safely with Hannah. Indeed, both lovers become haunted by the memory of their flight and their refusal to help a fellow protester who had been shot. The man's T-shirt, which reads *"An Injury to One Is an Injury to All,"* provides an ironic reminder that romantic intimacy and political solidarity can be mutually exclusive.[55]

While *My Son's Story* does not endorse the utopian portrait of *A Sport of Nature*, it too utilizes a metafictional narrator to undercut the notion of a stable, transparent, and neutral perspective for viewing the political situation in South Africa. As with the earlier novel, *My Son's Story* portrays multiple narratorial perspectives. The novel is narrated at turns by the eponymous son and an apparently omniscient third-person narrator, who is revealed to be the son as well. In the final chapter, the son reveals that his decision to create a fictionalized narratorial voice to complement his own was motivated by the need to describe events he did not personally experience. "In our story, like all stories," he writes, "I've made up what I wasn't there to experience myself ... I've imagined, out of their deception, the frustration of my absence, the pain of knowing them too well, what others would be doing, saying and feeling in the gaps between my witness."[56] But Gordimer is careful to undercut the overly inflated claims the narrator makes for the imagination's capacity to render other people's experiences accurately. The narrator takes for granted that he can reconstruct his father's affair: "All the details about Sonny and his women? – oh, those I've taken from the women I've known."[57] The casual dismissiveness of the narrator encourages readers to be suspicious of his broader claims of being able to narrate the diverse perspectives of a family involved in the anti-apartheid struggle.

Undercutting her narrator in *My Son's Story* emphasizes Gordimer's cautiousness about historical connections among the imagination, aesthetics, and politics. Modern conceptions of imagination, as they developed in Western Europe in response to the rise of industrial modernization, promised the possibility of healing social divisions by enabling individuals to sympathize with the experiences of others. As *A Sport of Nature* indicates, Gordimer retains a modified commitment to realism because imagining appears to offer a mental activity that can enable accurate interpretation of the economic, social, and political forces that define the everyday lives of people.[58] At the same time, Gordimer's long experience with the stability of the apartheid regime and the challenges of forming solidarity among dissidents leads her to emphasize that the imagination is given an impossible task outside of the realm of aesthetics. While imagining can help individuals to interpret their experiences more accurately, it can also lead to self-deception. Gordimer marks this problem much in the same fashion that Brink did at the end of *States of Emergency*, emphasizing the impossibility of creating an artwork within an apartheid state. "I am a writer and this is my first book – that I can never publish," the narrator declares in the final sentence.[59]

J. M. COETZEE: THE SYMPATHETIC IMAGINATION

As was the case with Brink and Gordimer, J. M. Coetzee increasingly wrote about imagination during the State of Emergency. Coetzee ends his 1987 Jerusalem Prize acceptance speech, for example, with the declaration that apartheid perverts the capacity of citizens to imagine. "In South

Africa there is now too much truth for art to hold," he declares: "truth by the bucketful, truth that overwhelms and swamps every act of the imagination."[60] Coetzee does not elegize imagination as one more casualty of the South African conflict, however, but insists that it is the necessary faculty for articulating a vision of political freedom. Coetzee's first novel to reflect explicitly on contemporary conditions in South Africa, *The Age of Iron* (1990), focuses less on the revolutionary activities of anti-apartheid supporters than on the efforts by the dying white protagonist to imagine and articulate the conditions that cause human "unfreedom."[61]

Not surprisingly, Coetzee's more significant interest in the imagination did little to satisfy critics who felt that he demonstrates, in Gordimer's words, a "revulsion against all political and revolutionary solutions."[62] Gordimer's own evolution has led her to soften her stance, but her shift represents the exception rather than the rule.[63] Even after a significant body of scholarly work has defended Coetzee by emphasizing his focus on ethics rather than politics per se, he continues to be faulted for his purportedly anti-realist, postmodern stylistics that cater to elite Western European and American academics and fail to promote the cause of political freedom in South Africa.[64] The publication of his most controversial novel to date, *Disgrace* (1999), sparked critiques even from sources who would presumably be more sympathetic. Salman Rushdie, himself faulted for promoting a kind of postmodern cosmopolitanism, declared that Coetzee creates a "dystopic world" that "increases the sum of what it is possible for us to think," yet he fails to illuminate that world.[65]

Rushdie's critique highlights Coetzee's discomfort with attributing significant autonomy to imagining. When Rushdie asserts in his 1983 novel *Shame* that Pakistan's postcolonial political strife is due to the fact that the nation was "*insufficiently imagined*," he is suggesting that the problem results from an unwillingness rather than an inability of politicians to imagine a more egalitarian nation-state.[66] Indeed, the task of imagining does not involve some grand act of creating common principles or foundational beliefs and values; Rushdie is very clear that such principles already exist but Pakistan's leaders have consistently chosen greed and sectarianism. "The third option [for challenging Pakistan's leaders] is the substitution of a new myth for the old one," Rushdie's narrator declares. "Here are three such myths, all available from stock at short notice: liberty; equality; fraternity."[67] The task of imagining, then, involves translation, and the artist serves his or her nation by encouraging readers to identify less with the myth of "roots" and more with the myth of national solidarity.[68]

For Coetzee, in contrast, the problem facing South Africa is less an unwillingness than an inability of individuals to imagine a post-apartheid nation. In an interview with David Attwell, Coetzee declares that "freedom is another name for the unimaginable."[69] Drawing on Kant and Plato, Coetzee suggests that even under the best circumstances freedom can only be intimated, not represented directly.[70] The "myths" that Rushdie takes for granted are thus neither modeled by Western states nor readily available for appropriation by postcolonial communities. Apartheid further complicates the task of "get[ting] from our world of violent phantasms to a true living world," Coetzee asserts in his Jerusalem Prize acceptance speech, because it forces writers to become preoccupied with power and its abuses.[71] According to this logic, the images of violence that became part of daily life during the State of Emergency radically diminish the scope of mental images that can be created, in such a way that all relationships become defined by their potential to reproduce the violence of apartheid. Coetzee's fiction repeatedly portrays the frailty of imagining in the face of violence, from the imprisoned magistrate in *Waiting for the Barbarians* to the mutilated Friday in *Foe* and the terminally ill Mrs. Curren in *Age of Iron*. Put epigrammatically, the autonomy of imagining is limited by the materiality of the body, which can be disciplined, tortured, and destroyed by a repressive state.

Given his pessimism about the autonomy of imagining, it should not be altogether surprising that Coetzee's pre-Emergency writings tend to link the imagination to madness.[72] The flights of fantasy engaged in by the narrators of Coetzee's first two novels, *Dusklands* (1974) and *In the Heart of the Country* (1977), are primary symptoms of their madness. In both cases, the madness of the characters is understood as symptomatic of the pathological political attitudes of the states in which they reside: America's hysterical fear of communism and the Afrikaner repressive fantasy of occupying an uninhabited pastoral land granted by God. The madness of Coetzee's protagonists results from their inability to reconcile the realities they observe with the ideological assumptions they have internalized. While Coetzee presents a protagonist more capable of challenging internalized assumptions in *Waiting for the Barbarians* (1980), the Magistrate's acts of imagining often produce fantasies designed to help him escape the uncomfortable recognition of his complicity in state-sponsored violence. Near the end of the novel, waiting for the barbarians to invade his tiny frontier settlement, the Magistrate's fantasies take an explicitly escapist turn:

I lie on the bare mattress and concentrate on bringing into life the image of myself as a swimmer swimming with even, untiring strokes through the medium of time, a medium more inert than water, without ripples, pervasive, colourless, odourless, dry as paper.[73]

Waiting for the Barbarians nonetheless endorses a limited notion of autonomy for imagining. The Magistrate's fantasy is not guided by a deliberate desire to critique the Empire; it is born instead of frustration with the troops who have occupied the settlement for the majority of the novel in a fruitless effort to hunt down the barbarians. The fantasy evokes an earlier scene in which the Magistrate first recognizes how imperial ideology conceals the vulnerability of the Empire. "Empire has located its existence not in the smooth recurrent spinning time of the cycle of seasons but in the jagged time of rise and fall, of beginning and end, of catastrophe. Empire dooms itself to live in history and plot against history. One thought alone preoccupies the submerged mind of Empire: how not to end, how not to die, how to prolong its era" (133).[74] The Magistrate's ability to recognize that the purported inevitability and invulnerability of Empire are part of its own self-sustaining and self-justifying narrative suggests that he possesses at least a minimal degree of autonomy. More significantly, his identification of a "natural" experience of time with the barbarians suggests that the end of Empire is inevitable, prolonged only by increasingly violent and repressive measures. His own fantasy of escape at the end of the novel, then, leads to an identification with the barbarians precisely because they are identified with the "natural" medium of time in which he hopes to float.

Intriguingly, the Magistrate's acts of imagining become most threatening to Colonel Joll and his forces when they are not cast as overt acts of defiance. The Magistrate's efforts to imagine that wood slips with words in the barbarian language written on them represent a critique of the Empire are dismissed by Joll (112). But the Magistrate's efforts to imagine how the soldiers can live with themselves after torturing the barbarians spark a violent response from Joll's soldiers. "Do not misunderstand me, I am not blaming you or accusing you," the Magistrate declares to one of his guards; "I am trying to imagine how you breathe and eat and live from day to day. But I cannot! That is what troubles me!" (126). The soldier is so threatened by this line of thinking that he strikes the Magistrate and flees, suggesting that he, too, may be struggling with its implications.

The scene provides a glimpse of what Coetzee terms *sympathetic imagination* in later works such as *Disgrace* and *Elizabeth Costello*. Coetzee's characterization of a sympathetic imagination is clearly distinct from, but not entirely dismissive of, Adam Smith's theory of moral sentiments. The soldier's violent response to the Magistrate indicates that the imagination does not necessarily drive individuals to sympathize with the needs of others, yet it is not limited to simply reproducing sensory perceptions. Recalling the basic definition of autonomy – that imagining is an activity not entirely determined by individual perceptions and biases – *Waiting for the Barbarians* suggests that the imagination also postulates how others perceive the same events. Given that the imagination appears to produce these images without direction from the rational mind, even the most diehard advocate of Empire will on occasion imagine how the barbarians are perceiving their treatment. This is not to say that such moments produce sympathetic responses, according to Coetzee, but they at least necessitate the kind of repression that the guard engages in when faced with the Magistrate's probing.

Age of Iron addresses the question that *Waiting for the Barbarians* never fully answers: why more conscious and deliberate acts of imagining do not appear to represent a significant threat to a repressive regime. In this novel, the primary means of disseminating propaganda is the television, and even the retired lecturer in classics Mrs. Curren finds herself watching it. She repeatedly demonstrates contempt for the medium and the parade of politicians reiterating the message of the state. Mrs. Curren declares:

And their message stupidly unchanging, stupidly forever the same. Their feat, after years of etymological meditation on the word, to have raised stupidity to a virtue. To stupefy: to deprive of feeling; to benumb, deaden; to stun with amazement. Stupor: insensibility, apathy, torpor of the mind. Stupid: dulled in the faculties, indifferent, destitute of thought or feeling. From *stupere*, to be stunned, astounded. A gradient from *stupid* to *stunned* to *astonished*, to be turned to stone. The message: that the message never changes. A message that turns people to stone. (29)

According to this logic, propaganda works not because it manages to persuade or to inspire but simply because its endless repetitions prevent viewers from witnessing any contrary messages. Television bombards and overloads all sensory perceptions, and to the extent that the imagination is not entirely autonomous of sensory perception, it too can be affected. Deliberate acts of imagining require concentrated attention and opportunities for active reflection rather than passive reception of incoming stimuli. If sympathy requires an act of imaginative identification with the experiences of others, then this is what television prevents. Mrs. Curren herself is not immune to the stupefying effects of television, despite her protestations otherwise; immediately after her speech unraveling the etymology of stupidity, she falls asleep in front of the television (30).

The tracing of etymologies by Mrs. Curren appears to provide a model for a more deliberate form of imagining than was possible in *Waiting for the Barbarians*. As Curren's etymology of the word *stupidity* indicates, the act of uncovering the root meanings of a particular word involves a process of historicizing that counters the static temporality that Coetzee associates with apartheid propaganda. By tracing the twists and turns of a word over time, Curren highlights the dynamic nature of language. Etymology, in this context, is not an effort to claim an authoritative, fixed meaning; rather, it provides Mrs. Curren an opportunity to shift the source of authority away from any one institution or person, including herself. Shifting authority away from the self is crucial if the earlier point is true that deliberate reflection tends to reproduce existing biases. Mrs. Curren's exercises in etymology are imaginative acts because they do not seek to historicize language through the paradigm of a fixed, linear scheme of development; instead, her etymologies are guided by more associative connections, so that stupidity evokes not only a Latin root but also the image of white South Africans being turned to stone in front of their television sets.

While Curren's exercises in etymology are promoted as a crucial mode of imagining during the State of Emergency, the novel recognizes both their irrelevance to the majority of the population and their capacity to reinforce authoritarian hierarchies. The novel repeatedly highlights Mrs. Curren's irrelevance to the anti-apartheid struggle: she is dying, a white liberal humanist, and a retired lecturer in classics. And her etymological reconstructions are often undertaken with less than altruistic motives. In one of the first examples of her drawing out the etymology of a term, Mrs. Curren insists that the history of the word *charity* provides a rationale for why she does not need to be charitable to the vagrant Mr. Vercueil. In this instance, etymology is used by Mrs. Curren to establish her authority over Vercueil: she is university-educated and he is not. The text highlights the inappropriateness of Mrs. Curren's efforts by having her admit that the etymology she provides is false, that *charity* does not derive from *heart* but from *care*.

The scene nonetheless highlights an autonomy of imagining similar to that presented in *Waiting for the Barbarians*. Imagining represents an activity that is not entirely governed by rational reflection, and hence it always has the capacity to create images that were not initially intended or desired. The paragraph that begins with her rationalization for lying to

Mr. Vercueil ends with an implicit self-critique. "Care. The true root of charity," Mrs. Curren admits. "I look for him to care, and he does not. Because he is beyond caring. Beyond caring and beyond care" (22). The final recognition does not represent overt self-castigation, but it does suggest that Vercueil exists in an environment that does not promote his well-being. Previously, Mrs. Curren had insisted that his troubles and vagrancy were the result of his own laziness. To recognize that he is "beyond care," however, admits the failure of the social order to which she is committed although critical. She has rationalized her status as a beneficiary of a racist, oppressive state because she has convinced herself that the apartheid regime is an aberration that will be replaced by a more progressive state through the very political process that brought the National Party to power in 1948.

The tendency for imagining to be an associative process means that, for Coetzee, the imagination gains its highest degree of autonomy from state propaganda when individuals are engaged in genuine dialogue. As long as Mrs. Curren remains within the relatively safe confines of her home, the kinds of imaginative associations she is capable of are shaped by the beliefs and attitudes of the white South Africans around her and the classical literatures of Greece and Rome that she studied professionally. When Mr. Vercueil shows up in her alleyway, he introduces a new set of associations that create a crisis of confidence. But, as the scene above indicates, her recriminations are limited to vague expressions of liberal guilt. Only after she enters a space dominated by black South Africans and converses with them is she forced to question more profoundly her beliefs. Witnessing the squalor and violence that fills everyday life in the townships, Mrs. Curren is herself silenced. When pressed by Mr. Thabane, a former teacher living in the township, to declare that what she is witnessing is a "crime" (98), Mrs. Curren demurs. Yet by the end of the novel it is precisely this word that she uses in a conversation with Mr. Vercueil (164).[75] After being forced to recognize the authority of black South Africans like Mr. Thabane to describe experiences of which she has only limited knowledge, Mrs. Curren is finally able to articulate a notion of freedom that echoes Coetzee's earlier characterization:

I have no idea what freedom is, Mr. Vercueil. I am sure Bheki and his friend had no idea either. Perhaps freedom is always and only what is unimaginable. Nevertheless, we know unfreedom when we see it – don't we? (164)

Freedom is thus a conception that is unavailable to the senses, yet only through sensory perception can Mrs. Curren or anyone else begin to intimate it through recognizing moments in which freedom is lost, moments of "unfreedom."

Although freedom is still described as "unimaginable" in *Age of Iron*, the novel demonstrates a subtle shift away from the philosophical idealism of Coetzee's earlier writings.[76] Michael Marais provides one of the most articulate analyses of Coetzee's idealism, arguing that the presentations of sympathetic imagination in his fiction are designed to indicate how a genuinely ethical relationship requires an *ek-stasis* that can never be fully accomplished through imagining. The eighteenth-century model of sympathy associated with Adam Smith fails to go far enough, for Marais; the effort to identify from the subject position of another person inevitably defines the other person in terms comprehensible to the sympathizer, thereby limiting the possibility of genuine understanding or dialogue. Instead, Marais argues, "the imagination must ecstatically divest itself of all subject positions in language and culture … and, in so doing, construct for it a position that is precisely not a position, one that would therefore allow the self to be within the world while viewing it from nowhere within it."[77] Marais powerfully captures a sense in *The Master of Petersburg* and *Disgrace* that a genuine ethical relationship with other people continually eludes our capacity to imagine it. But the recognition of the failures of the imagination to effect the transformations it promises is taken as only the starting point of imagining. As indicated by the passage above, Mrs. Curren's recognition that she cannot successfully imagine a notion of freedom is immediately followed by efforts to approximate it. There is no long mourning process or melancholic lament on her part; one sentence conveys the impossibility of the task she nonetheless takes up. Nor does she accept that the goal of imagining should be to divorce herself from her body. Her assertion that "we know unfreedom when we see it" suggests quite the opposite, that it is precisely from our position as embodied beings with sensory perceptions shaped by a host of conscious and unconscious values that we should begin the process of imagining.

This last point is crucial to understanding the role of dialogue in the production of knowledge. Mrs. Curren's increasing knowledge about both the circumstances of the black majority and her participation in their exploitation certainly depends on her conversations with black characters; however, the novel refuses to endorse either the idea that knowledge represents a static, abstract object or the idea that a single perspective – even that of the oppressed – possesses an unquestionably objective view. For Coetzee, knowledge is inescapably the product of an individual's social location, his or her philosophical biases, political commitments, and language. Thus, whatever knowledge Mrs. Curren acquires over the course of the novel is shaped by the liberal humanism with which she was raised. This becomes apparent near the end of the novel, when Mrs. Curren witnesses the police breaking into her house to kill a young fugitive. Frustrated with her inability to protect "John," as the fugitive identifies himself, Mrs. Curren critically reflects on the vocabulary with which she had previously evaluated her life. "What I did not know, *what I did not know*," Mrs. Curren confesses to Mr. Vercueil, "… was that more might be called for than to be good. For there are plenty of good people in this country … What the times call for is quite different from goodness. The times call for heroism. A word that, as I speak it, sounds foreign to my lips" (165). The growth in knowledge here is measured by the shift in vocabulary. The vocabulary of goodness enabled Mrs. Curren to rationalize her inaction. Goodness is, at least in this context, a measure of a person's internal state of mind; one can be good, in other words, without influencing the external world. The vocabulary of heroism, in contrast, emphasizes the individual's efforts to transform his or her surroundings. According to this alternative description of herself, Mrs. Curren has fallen far short. Yet the vocabulary of heroism is not uncritically appropriated from Mr. Thabane or Mr. Vercueil or any of the younger generation of black revolutionaries. The novel keeps with its earlier dialogic spirit by presenting Mrs. Curren disagreeing with Mr. Thabane about the nature of comradeship in a phone conversation shortly before the police raid. To no small degree, Mrs. Curren's notion of heroism is constructed as a counterpoint to the "mystique of death" she observes among the young men and women committed to the anti-apartheid struggle (150). But the terminology itself is extrapolated from the ancient Greek and Roman models of heroism that she studied as a lecturer in classics.

The focus on Mrs. Curren's increasing capacity to interpret and describe accurately the events around her distinguishes *Age of Iron* not only from Coetzee's earlier work but also from certain poststructuralist conceptions of postmodernism to which Coetzee has been tied by his critics. According to this critique, Coetzee's obsession with textuality divorces his work from any historically grounded analysis of South Africa, leaving him to produce only abstract allegories. The same critique was directed at Jacques Derrida's essay on apartheid, "Racism's Last Word," which, according to Anne McClintock and Rob Nixon, "sever[ed] word from history."[78] Predictably, though perhaps somewhat unfairly, Derrida's argument is seen as part of a tendency by poststructuralist theorists toward a radical skepticism that rejects concrete affiliations and commitments. Coetzee himself demonstrates discomfort with what he sees as Derrida's "equanimity" about an "endlessly skeptical process of textualization."[79] Between the polarities of endless skepticism and unquestioning faith lie a range of possible attitudes toward the capacity of humans to know what constitutes freedom and how to promote it in everyday life. Mrs. Curren's declaration that individuals can identify "unfreedom" suggests that certain accounts can be more objectively reliable than others, even if the positivist dream of an absolutely objective account can never be realized. The "anti-illusionism" Coetzee associates with certain postmodernists and the Nouveau Roman is ultimately unsatisfying because there is nothing particularly revolutionary in revealing the artifice on which every attempt to represent reality depends.[80] For Coetzee, rather, political commitment depends on a calculated choice to commit to the most accurate account available to an individual at any given moment, a commitment that must be combined with sufficient humility to enable a person to revise based on knowledge gained from dialogues with others. Put more simply, *Age of Iron* may cautiously and provisionally endorse Mrs. Curren's eventual diagnosis of violent anti-apartheid movements, but she cannot arrive at this diagnosis without her conversation with Mr. Thabane.

Thus, the characterization of Coetzee as a postmodern author creates a misleading impression of his work and, more importantly, leads to a misunderstanding of trends in white South African fiction. The State of Emergency in South Africa and the failure of liberal white South Africans to effect significant political reforms led literary authors including Brink, Gordimer, and Coetzee to rethink their aesthetic and philosophical commitments; however, the shifts in their work were not entirely consistent. All three writers struggled with how literature might encourage epistemological investigations that would undermine state propaganda and trouble the complacency of the white minority, but to accomplish these goals Brink and Gordimer increasingly appropriated stylistics associated with postmodernism even as Coetzee appropriated elements associated with realism. Thus, the problem with the term *postmodern* is not simply the oft-bemoaned point that no one can agree on a common definition; more importantly, to use the term effaces the significantly different shifts occurring among writers who have been labeled by it – even among writers from the same country.[81] While the term has a certain usefulness, particularly since Brink and Coetzee have at various moments identified themselves with it, it diverts attention away from what does in fact unite these authors at a particular historical moment.

The notion of the postmodern as an historical moment has some use-fulness if attention is paid to how authors like Brink, Gordimer, and Coetzee help to constitute it rather than adhering to a nominalist position that would suggest that the term was simply imposed by academics on a broad set of political, social, and economic phenomena. The challenge of reconciling theoretical insights with political commitments was especially acute within the Anglo-American academy of the 1980s in part because of the issues raised by South African literature. Gayatri Spivak's notorious double reversal on the question of essentialism – endorsing a notion of strategic essentialism and then later repudiating it – represents only one of the most well-known examples of this struggle.[82] One could just as eas-ily speak of Derrida's "turn" to Marxism in *Specters of Marx* (1994). Seyla Benhabib wrestled with the recognition that the "infinitely skeptical and subversive attitude" of postmodernism was simultaneously refreshing and debilitating.[83] What is common to all of these thinkers and writers is the concern that theoretical insights into the artifice and potential violence of language would undercut the possibility of political solidarity and shared commitments. Indeed, Geoffrey Galt Harpham suggested that the enter-prise of reconciling theory and practice was ultimately impossible and unproductive, surrendering the political realm to forces guided by greed. His vision of finding the "center" was ultimately about learning to find acceptable compromises that would enable progressive intellectuals to participate in broader political coalitions.[84]

Coetzee has continued to struggle with this problem in his post-apartheid writings, and proposes a somewhat more refined answer in *Elizabeth Costello* (2003). As was the case in earlier writings, the ques-tion of the communicability of experience and the possibility of utopia are inseparable. In the novel's final "Lesson" (the novel is organized in terms of "lessons" rather than chapters), Elizabeth Costello finds herself apparently at the gate of Paradise and required by its guardian to provide a statement of her beliefs. The "Lesson" unfolds along fairly predictable anti-utopian lines. The transitionary world she occupies blends elements of Kafka and Nazi concentration camp; Costello is expected to provide a statement of concrete beliefs, and when she refuses she is brought before a tribunal to judge her case. Heaven itself (if Heaven it is) appears to be relatively disappointing as well. Granted a glimpse of the light on the other side of the gate, Costello is disheartened to discover that it does not exceed her capacities of imagining or representation: "But the light is not unimaginable at all. It is merely brilliant."[85] Following the allegory to this point, the straightforward interpretation is that utopia always disappoints, and collapses into totalitarianism. However, at the end of this section, Costello finds herself questioning the guardian about the uniqueness of her situation. The answer is surprising, if understated: the guardian declares that Costello's desire to refuse to provide a concrete statement of belief is not unique to a writer; nor is her situation in any other particular unusual. "We see people like you all the time," he declares, and with these words the section ends (225).

The declaration, while ironic on a number of levels, suggests that experiences are overlapping, whether or not they are directly communicable. To a modest degree Costello senses this point, and this recognition drives her to learn whether other people have been in her situation (224). At this moment, Costello is struggling to understand what her future might be, and she can only do this by means of the imagination: by attempting to relate her experiences from the perspective of others. The return to the imagination here, and throughout *Elizabeth Costello*, suggests that Coetzee cannot do without the imagination as a category, despite his reservations. The repeated references to the imagination throughout his fictional oeuvre, in other words, suggest that it does not exist simply to be transcended or deconstructed. As Marais and Durant have noted, the idea of a sympathetic imagination is fraught with dangers, and Coetzee repeatedly portrays instances in which the imagination and sympathy lead to something other than egalitarian community. However, in the final scene with Elizabeth Costello, the imagination also suggests a necessary sociality of humans. If a basic impulse of the imagination is to posit the world from the perspective of others, then the existence of the imagination implies an inextinguishable desire to reach out and share experiences with others. Elizabeth Costello's question is ultimately significant because it displaces earlier questions about whether or not a human being is required to have beliefs, and what it would mean to be committed to a set of beliefs. Ultimately, the question for Costello is not a question of belief but of community, and this appears to be the closest Coetzee can comfortably come to utopianism: the idea of an impulse toward recognizing and sharing experience.

Thus, the turn to the imagination in writings published during and after the State of Emergency in South Africa should not be read as a flight from politics or a refuge in aestheticism. Particularly Coetzee is painfully aware of the limitations of the imagination as a tool for political transformation. Yet these authors suggest that the enduring question of whether a revolution can ever succeed hinges less on political coalitions or identity politics than on more philosophical questions of the extent to which humans can indeed accomplish Gadamer's vision of a fusion of horizons, a vision that these authors suggest would require both a relatively accurate interpretation of experience and a minimal capacity to communicate it to others. The imagination is so crucial to white South African writers including Brink, Gordimer, and Coetzee because it provides a ground for preserving one of the few kinds of utopia that appear sustainable after the crisis of representation that is associated with postmodernism. The imagination, in other words, is no longer charged with the task given it by Romantic thinkers of dissolving differences between self and society. Rather, it has a more modest task of providing a mode of relating to others whose differences cannot be dissolved. The fantasy, as Kearney so succinctly puts it, is to see differences as converging without fusing.[86]

CHAPTER 3

The pastoral and the postmodern

While the disappearance of postmodernism from academic discourses may be cause for relief, if not celebration, in many circles, it has left a theoretical vacuum for the analysis of many contemporary literary texts and broader shifts in literary history. In its numerous incarnations, postmodernism was identified as an historical period, a transhistorical phenomenon, an epistemic condition, a phase of late capitalism, an extension or culmination of modernism. The values associated with postmodernism were likewise various, from elitist Western intellectualism to crass popular culture. Despite the inability of academics ever to arrive at a common, coherent definition, the immense popularity of the term in academic and mainstream discourses suggests that it nonetheless conveyed a compelling, if not always consistent, set of concerns and questions. André Brink and, to a lesser extent, J. M. Coetzee both understood their work in terms of an international postmodernism; indeed, the supposedly international character of postmodernism, more than any specific tenet associated with it, was crucial to Brink's hope that literature might effect political transformation in South Africa. Thus, if the movement among Anglo-American academics in the 1980s–90s to apply the term *postmodernism* to everything from *Beowulf* to *Beloved* was a mistake that stalled more complex investigations, the current marginalization of the term and authors associated with it also risks foreclosing significant and unfinished explorations into questions of epistemology, identity, and ethics.

The challenge is to read postmodernism as an international phenomenon that manifests in significantly different ways in different localities. The tendency to theorize a transhistorical, homogeneous phenomenon has led to often misleading and simplistic characterizations. This problem is nowhere more apparent than in the context of British literature, where postmodernism has been characterized as a critical response to Victorian values and mores generally, and a naïve realist literary aesthetic specifically. According to this now familiar account, postmodern fiction "plays" with Victorian literary conventions, demonstrating the impossibility of transparent language, objectivity, and liberal humanist fantasies of progress. Scholarship on Victorian literature since the 1990s, however, undermines this version of literary history by providing a more nuanced account of realism.[2] George Levine, for example, makes a powerful case that the paragon of Victorian realism, George Eliot, was highly sensitive to the epistemological challenges facing a realist narrative. According to Levine's account, Eliot's realism was motivated not by naïveté but by an ethical imperative to resist "the corrosive power of individualism."[3] Eliot anticipates the complex engagement with epistemological skepticism that characterizes postmodern fiction, belying what Suzy Anger calls the "strange either/or logic to many poststructuralist arguments on knowledge," which maintain that representations either transparently replicate reality or are entirely arbitrary and self-referential.[4]

The more sophisticated accounts of Victorian realism invite a critical return to so-called postmodern literary texts with greater sensitivity to moments in which they resist their own epistemological skepticism. Why, for example, does the most recognized British postmodern novelist, John Fowles, open *Daniel Martin* (1977) with a narrator who pines for an objective, omniscient point of view: "Whole sight; or all the rest is desolation" (1)? The line is striking when contrasted with the declaration by the narrator of Fowles's earlier and more famous *The French Lieutenant's Woman* (1969) that he cannot even determine the thoughts of his own characters. Why does Peter Ackroyd, who early in his career lamented the decline of national culture in Britain and railed against the unwillingness of the British to engage with the ideas of Lacan and Derrida, open *English Music* (1992) with an assertion that the past in its entirety may be reconstructed: "One day is changed into another, yet nothing is lost."[5] And why do pastoral images and scenes so consistently appear in the works of British authors who are characterized as postmodern, from Fowles and Ackroyd to Julian Barnes, A. S. Byatt, Graham Swift, and Tom Stoppard?

Exploring the pastoralism in contemporary British literature is crucial to understanding the historicity of postmodernism as an international phenomenon that has materialized multilaterally and multihistorically. Theories of postmodernism have tended to encourage readings of literary works that discount immediate historical contexts, with the result that so many authorial choices concerning genre, tone, and setting appear arbitrary. Charles Jencks is certainly right to identify the importance of pastiche in contemporary art and architecture, but his notion of postmodernism fails to explain the consistent patterns of pastiche among Fowles, Ackroyd, Barnes, and other contemporary British writers. Fredric Jameson is certainly right to historicize postmodernism with respect to global late capitalism, but such characterizations occlude the local traditions out of which generic forms such as the pastoral emerge and which predate capitalism.[6] The inescapable limitations of theories of postmodernism, however, should not dismiss the concerns its theorists raise. The epistemological skepticism sensed by Linda Hutcheon, for example, is indeed central to the concerns of contemporary British authors and necessary to understand the forms pastiche has taken in postwar fiction. By reading these concerns in light of historical uses of pastoral tropes in British literature, we can recognize that contemporary authors are engaged not in abstract philosophical speculation but in an effort to reposition Great Britain in the aftermath of the Empire's decline and the new dominance of the United States.

Restoring the historicity of postmodernism, in turn, invites a critical reconsideration of contemporary forms of pastoralism in British literature and culture. The sweeping condemnation of the postwar preoccupation with representations of the English countryside and heritage more generally made by Robert Hewison's *The Heritage Industry: Britain in a Climate of Decline* (1987) remains the default response in many scholarly discussions. In perhaps its most powerful recent formulation, Paul Gilroy condemns what he calls the "postcolonial melancholia" infecting Great Britain: a profound inability to mourn the loss of Empire and to confront present problems masked by a seemingly obsessive fascination with rural Englishness. The preoccupation with "Albion" – exemplified by Jeremy Paxman's *The English* (2000), Peter Ackroyd's *Albion* (2002), and Roger Scruton's *England: An Elegy* (2000) – represents a conservative backlash against postwar immigration, multicultural Britain, and the European Union. Despite the overall usefulness of Gilroy's account, however, his generalizations profoundly distort the complex appropriation and revision of Englishness undertaken by contemporary British writers. By rereading the so-called postmodern elements in their literary works, we can move beyond the reductive polarity of conservative apologists of Englishness and supposedly radical postcolonial critiques.

JOHN FOWLES: REALISM IN A LATE CAPITALIST WORLD

The tendency among scholars to read Fowles as the paradigmatic British postmodern author makes it difficult to interpret the pastoral imagery that suffuses *Daniel Martin* as anything other than parody or the kind of reactionary regression that Gilroy decries. Hutcheon's emphasis on post-modern literature "playing" with generic and social conventions implies that works of art that do not self-consciously identify their conventions are either naïve or propagandistic. Put another way, the meaning of a work or the historical knowledge it provides arises from the moments when it breaks the codes it establishes for itself. Fowles's earlier novels appear exemplary in this regard, and *The French Lieutenant's Woman* has been characterized as the seminal work of postmodern British fiction. The novel opens with a description of Lyme Bay that demonstrates a kind of pastoral tranquility, but the description serves to emphasize the naïveté of the Victorian world that will be disrupted shortly thereafter as the narrator repeatedly breaks from the conventions of Victorian literary realism. *Daniel Martin* is puzzling in the contrast it draws: the opening description of a wheat harvest is disrupted by the appearance of a German bomber, signaling to readers that this scene exists against a wartime back-drop; however, the novel immediately returns to generic codes associated with pastoral writing, and the bomber is replaced by four ravens play-fully flying. Indeed, the bomber only serves to heighten the convention of portraying simple country life sealed away from the quotidian present. Readers discover that the first chapter represents the opening of an auto-biographical novel to be written by the eponymous narrator, but the novel provides no obvious signals that readers should demonstrate contempt for Daniel's attachment to the innocent rural life of his youth. His cur-rent situation as a successful, middle-aged English screenwriter living in Hollywood with a screen actress half his age is instead seen as both less fulfilling and less "real."

Daniel Martin demonstrates numerous stylistic elements and the-matic concerns that were by the late 1970s already being characterized as postmodern, yet Fowles employs them for very un-postmodern ends. Metafictional commentaries, narratorial perspectives that shift from first to third person, self-conscious appropriations of cinematic language and convention, and at least some degree of pastiche are all apparent in the novel. It also demonstrates a preoccupation with the cultural impact of electronic media, explores the potential solipsism of representation, and struggles with the apparently inevitable complicity of the disaffected with the systems of power that dominate everyday life. For Daniel, the ques-tion of complicity with American hegemony is tied up with problems of representation. Initially drawn to screenwriting because of a sense that cinematic images convey an immediacy and realism that the stylized language of the novel cannot, Daniel increasingly finds that film is part of a culture industry that spurs consumption and contains disaffection. His growing disenchantment with film sets up the central opposition in the novel between word and image:

> Images are inherently fascistic because they overstamp the truth, however dim and blurred, of the real past experience ... The word is the most imprecise of signs. Only a science-obsessed age could fail to comprehend that this is its great virtue, not its defect ... I would murder my past if I tried to evoke it on camera; and it is precisely because I can't really invoke it in words, can only hope to awaken some analogous experience in other memories and sensitivities, that it must be written. (90)

To characterize representation as an act of violence is, of course, a familiar move to readers of various theories of postmodernism (from Baudrillard's to Hutcheon's) and theorists associated with postmodernity (such as Derrida and the duo Gilles Deleuze and Félix Guattari). The inadequacy of the sign, however, is not only taken as grounds for suspicion of the ideological subtext of any particular representation. It also holds the possibility for enabling the communication of experience with a fidelity or "realism" not possible through the conventions of film or the literary realism Fowles associates with Victorian fiction.[7] Fowles's preoccupation with the notion of "analogous experience" represents a willingness to surrender the possibility of realism in the sense of *mimesis* or imitation in order to reject solipsism; put more glibly, Fowles rejects realism to defend the existence of a nondiscursive reality.

The suggestion that pastoral tropes and imagery might be crucial to the representation of reality seems contrary not only to theories of postmodernism but also to the conventions of the English pastoral. Novels that employ pastoral conventions – including Thomas Hardy's *The Woodlanders* (1887), William Morris's *News from Nowhere* (1890), E. M. Forster's *Howard's End* (1910), and D. H. Lawrence's *The Rainbow* (1915) – have been read as critiques of industrialization in Britain, but neither the works themselves nor theorists of the pastoral identify such critiques in terms of a realist aesthetics. To the contrary, Terry Gifford characterizes the pastoral as a discourse that is fundamentally different from realism.[8] While it is certainly possible that a pastoral work could undertake to represent reality without using the conventions of literary realism (i.e., a commitment to philosophical realism does not necessarily presuppose a commitment to literary realism), the tendency among scholars of the pastoral has been to assume that the absence of the latter implies a lack of interest in the former. For Raymond Williams, this is the danger of viewing pastoral works as social critique. Williams recognizes that the plots of "neo-pastoral" English novels from the eighteenth century onward dramatize a struggle between "economic advantage and other ideas of value."[9] Yet such works risk creating a myth of modern England that conceals the economic and political forces that led to social suffering. By characterizing the present as an inevitable fall from an innocent agrarian life, the pastoral exonerates capitalism. Indeed, such mystification arguably represents the ideological function of the pastoral.

Contrary to what Williams's analysis might predict, *Daniel Martin* is more explicitly sympathetic to socialism than any of Fowles's previous fictional works or his book of philosophical musings, *The Aristos* (1964).[10] The epigraph to *The French Lieutenant's Woman*, "Every emancipation is a restoration of the human world and of human relationships to man himself," is drawn from Marx, but the novel's understanding of emancipation is shaped far more by Sartrean existentialism than by Marxism. In *The French Lieutenant's Woman*, the stultifying Victorian social conventions that limit human freedom have no basis in an economic system, nor does the novel have an explanation for their historical emergence or continued existence. In *Daniel Martin*, by contrast, the primary restraint on human freedom is internalized ideological biases that lead individuals to perceive the world in reified terms. The novel defines everything from Daniel's midlife crisis to the decline of Great Britain in terms of a quasi-Marxian narrative, and characters pepper their conversations with references to Georg Lukács, Antonio Gramsci, and Herbert Marcuse. Fowles himself cites Lukács and Gramsci in his acknowledgments; Jane, the female protagonist of the novel, summarizes the Gramscean notion of ideological hegemony as a gloss on contemporary British society (417–18). Even Daniel's decision to write a novel is characterized as a "supremely socialist" declaration, though he recognizes that it will not be recognized as such by most socialists (431).

Fowles's loose appropriations of Marxian theories suggest that pastoral imagery might play a crucial role in the representation of reality by providing a counterpoint to the dominant electronic media images in circulation. The opening declaration, "Whole sight; or all the rest is desolation," can be read as an allusion to Lukács, for whom reification has meant the lost capacity to perceive social life as a totality. Fowles makes repeated references to a sense of alienation and fragmentation among his characters, who long for a "totality of consciousness that fragmented modern man has completely lost" (353; see also 13, 417). The cultural and economic dominance of American hegemony is established in the first pages of the novel: Daniel is an Englishman living in Hollywood, writing unmemorable movie scripts that recycle popular commercial scenarios. If Lukács insists that the novel serves revolutionary causes by portraying "the concrete *historical genesis* of their time" that reveals how social, political, and economic forces created the conditions for the present catastrophe,[11] this is precisely what film preempts, and why it is "fascistic." Pastoral images in the novel do not represent an "historical genesis" directly, but they do emphasize the effects of reification by contrasting an idealized past with a disappointing present.[12] The longing to attribute "wholeness" and "totality" to the past reveals the extent to which fragmentation has become part of modern daily life.

The pastoral, then, is not a concessionary narrative, although it portrays the move from the past to the present in deterministic terms. In the first chapter, for example, the pastoral narrative ends at the moment when young Daniel etches his initials and the date on a beech tree – trapping his experience of being "[w]ithout past or future, purged of tenses" within a historical narrative (10). Taken in isolation, chapter 1 presents the deterministic narrative of pastoral simplicity forever sealed away in a world before the emergence of modern linear, progressive time. Taken in the context of the novel as a whole, however, chapter 1 emphasizes how the past haunts the present at every moment, threatening to unravel the very determinism it seemingly acknowledges. Long after he has rejected his life as a hack screenwriter, left America, and broken away from his actress girlfriend, Daniel continues to find himself drawn to the memory of his rural English childhood. In terms of the chronology of the novel, Daniel does not begin writing chapter 1 until the final pages. The memory of that harvest day refuses to be sealed off from the present or quarantined within some rarefied aesthetic sphere. Far from conceding the inevitability of late capitalism, pastoralism in the novel highlights its contingency by enabling Fowles to characterize determinism as an ideological projection designed to legitimize the current economic system and to contain any sense of dissatisfaction with it.

Recalling that the primary impediment to human freedom in *Daniel Martin* is internalized ideological biases, the capacity of literary language to identify multiple proposals for understanding the past gravitates against the perception that individuals have no choice. Hence, realism in the novel is not linked to the capacity to replicate accurately particular empirical features of everyday life but instead to the ability to narrate in a coherent form a narrative that resists the sense that the present is determined and inevitable.[13] The opposition of past and present that characterizes pastoral thus does not serve the purpose of establishing separate spheres – cordoning off the past in order to preserve its putative purity – but to undercut deterministic portrayals of history which suggest that the present was an inevitability. The "dialectical fluidity of dichotomous oppositions" that historically has characterized the pastoral, for Michael McKeon, functions here to identify the limits of the totalizing grip of capitalism.[14]

Fowles's purported postmodernism thus needs to be read in light of the literary history of the British novel and its role in the construction and maintenance of national identity. Fowles has on numerous occasions accepted the moniker of "postmodern author," but his discussions of postmodernism tend to involve piecemeal appropriations of a select group of thinkers (Derrida and Kristeva in particular), and such appropriations often come in the context of reflections on the current political and cultural climate in Great Britain or his relationship to earlier novelists, particularly D. H. Lawrence and Thomas Hardy. To some degree, Fowles's position evolves. The artistic credo of the narrator of *The French Lieutenant's Woman* – "*we wish to create worlds as real as, but other than the world that is*" – comes in the context of his declaration of Sarah Woodruff's existential free will, but it only implicitly endorses a set of values specific to Great Britain.[15] The reformulation of this credo in *Daniel Martin*, by contrast, is explicitly linked to Fowles's historical reconstruction of Englishness. Noting that authors "desire to create imaginary worlds other than the world that is the case" (288), Daniel suggests that the worlds an artist creates are inevitably shaped by memory and experience, and for him the desire to create alternative worlds is "a dominant mental characteristic, an essential behavior, an archetypal *movement* (akin to certain major vowel-shifts in the language itself) of the English imagination" (288–89). In other words, the commitment to creating alternative worlds is not shaped by an abstract postmodern sensibility celebrating the fluidity of language but arises out of a specific national tradition to which Fowles is responding.

Theories of postmodernism – even those most critical of its complicity with late capitalism – almost universally understand it as as a phenomenon uninterested in, if not antithetical to, conceptions of national identity. The focus on Fowles's postmodernism thus significantly distorts the rationale for the stylistic and aesthetic choices he makes, and underplays his preoccupation with Englishness. In Fowles's nonfiction, the pastoral functions as the dominant narrative form for understanding the genesis of modern Britain. In his early and perhaps most famous essay, "On

Being English and Not British" (1964), Fowles establishes an opposition between "Green England" and "Red-White-and-Blue Britain," terms which Daniel Martin uses.[16] Fowles's opposition magnifies and abstracts pastoralism beyond the traditional contrast between rural and urban, but the basic dialectical relationship remains: England signifies a past realm viewed from the vantage point of modern Britain, a realm which nonetheless defines the central characteristics of the latter. Indeed, Englishness is at once omnipresent and sealed away in a premodern past. Like the forests that have steadily disappeared since 1600, Fowles informs his readers, Englishness now resides in the traces of memory: "What we have done is to transfer the England of the trees to our minds."[17] According to this account, true Englishness was eclipsed by the notion of Britain as the Empire took form and appropriated Englishness as an ideological prop. And the process only accelerated as Great Britain became the dominant industrial power. According to a later essay written as an introduction to *Thomas Hardy's England* (1984), the "old rural past" was annihilated by the transition to an industrialized economy, resulting in nothing less than a "painful (and ever-growing) dissociation of humanity from the land."[18] Yet even as the topography associated with Englishness disappears, the generic codes of pastoral provide the means through which Englishness can endure as a spirit or essence, accessible through the imagination.

Extending R. Clifton Spargo's argument that the pastoral represents a mode of recollecting history that no individual person or poet could otherwise remember, I would like to argue that pastoral portraits of Englishness are crucial to Fowles's project of envisioning an alternative to the history of imperial Britain.[19] The pastoral opposition between past and present enables Fowles to unhinge the historical linkage between Englishness and Great Britain. Daniel declares: "Empire was the great disease … *aut Caesar, aut nullus*; and profoundly un-English. The whole nineteenth century was a disease, a delusion called Britain" (450–51). True Englishness was submerged and repressed; however, like the memories of pastoral childhood to which Daniel returns in middle age, this alternative England cannot be purged entirely. Even the most absolutely British figures, such as Lord Kitchener, turn out to have had English elements that can be identified retrospectively through the pastoral. Daniel discovers this in the process of writing a screenplay on Kitchener, declaring "This Englishness was even, in retrospect, immanent in archetypal red-white-and-blue Britons like Kitchener" (451). The pastoral genre enables Fowles to acknowledge the historical uses to which Englishness has been put while simultaneously asserting that it has always represented an implicit critique of the very Empire it has been called upon to endorse.

The resonance Fowles's notion of Green England has had for historians such as Jeremy Paxman arises from his ability to use pastoral conventions to provide the basis for a postimperial national identity.[20] McKeon notes that one of the reasons for the enduring popularity of the pastoral was its capacity to help regulate the contradictory sense of national and imperial identities as Britain became a world empire. The images of "England's ruins" figured as the enduring sign of national permanence, perpetuating the notion of a homogeneous identity that is sufficiently vague to remain relatively inclusive and fluid as the Empire attempted to incorporate ever more territories within itself.[21] Fowles's opposition between Green England and Red-White-and-Blue Britain enables him to disentangle Englishness from a history of imperial exploitation of colonial holdings. Indeed, Englishness is a "subversive ideal" that values justice over power, an ideal that outlives the rise and fall of the Empire itself.[22] This notion of an immaterial or even spectral Englishness means that it can be simultaneously inclusive and essentialistic. Fowles can readily declare that Englishness is defined in rather vague and arbitrary terms, and he can nonetheless confidently refer to "we" English. Crucially, the basis for solidarity has nothing to do with the political arrangements and history of Empire, so that a postimperial Britain may assert its independence from its own colonial past and imperial America. In the terminology of *Daniel Martin*, Englishness itself becomes the "analogous experience" that might provide the basis for national solidarity.

Fowles's work thus counters the central assumption of Gilroy's theory of postcolonial melancholia: that representations of the past serve to conceal postimperial realities. For Fowles, the creation of a viable postimperial nation depends on a critical and selective historical reconstruction of an alternative narrative of Englishness, one that undermines the monolithic characterization of imperial Britain. To this extent, Fowles utilizes many techniques that have come to be associated with postcolonial literatures and their responses to the colonial center. This is not to deny the potential culpability of Fowles's project: Simon Gikandi, Ian Baucom, and Gilroy himself have pointed to the intimate connections between Englishness and Empire, troubling the notion that England could represent an anti-imperial ideal.[23] More problematic from the perspective of the argument presented here is the tendency in *Daniel Martin* to circumscribe the world within the sphere of Englishness. Otherness is pastness in the novel, and this is readily apparent in the fact that race is never addressed as a contemporary issue.[24] But simply to dismiss Fowles as a "Little-Englander" or to quarantine him within the confines of "postmodern literature" significantly misunderstands the complex and conflicted dynamics to which he responds.

PETER ACKROYD: LATENT HISTORIES OF THE PASTORAL

Peter Ackroyd also envisions a postimperial national identity that draws heavily on pastoral conventions and images. In his most controversial works, the novel *English Music* (1992) and the literary history cum cultural study *Albion: The Origins of the English Imagination* (2002), Ackroyd portrays Englishness as a spirit that is simultaneously omnipresent and absent – evoked everywhere by the country landscapes, yet buried beneath modern imperial Britain. The title *Albion* itself signals Ackroyd's project of reclaiming what he perceives to be an enduring though effaced identity; Albion is an ancient word for England, a word now invoked to describe a world isolated from the present. Ackroyd declares: "Today, like those fading memorials, Albion is not so much a name as the echo of a name."[25] Yet, like Fowles, Ackroyd insists that an attenuated connection to this world remains within the realm of the imagination. Echoing Fowles's assertion that "Green England is green literally, in our landscapes … We are condemned to be green; and in all ways green,"[26] Ackroyd insists that "the English imagination is forever green" (418).

While Fowles and Ackroyd both invoke images of a Green England and employ pastoral conventions to place their ancestral homes within a realm that can be accessed through the mediation of literature, the actual characteristics of their Englands differ significantly regarding the importance of Catholicism and the emphasis on cultural hybridity. For Ackroyd, Englishness has been tied to Catholicism since Augustine's mission to England (*Albion*, xx); harking back to T. S. Eliot and Evelyn Waugh, Ackroyd declares, "I have always thought and believed that there is still in England a buried but scarcely concealed Catholic culture."[27] Fowles's archetypal figure of Englishness, Robin Hood, has no religious associations. Just as significant a difference, however, is the emphasis placed on cultural hybridity. While Fowles readily admits that few can claim a "purely English ancestry," Englishness is defined first and foremost in biological terms.[28] Ackroyd, in contrast, follows Ford Madox Ford in rejecting the notion of an English race in favor of an idea of a spirit "born of the environment" (*Albion*, xxi). Indeed, Ackroyd has repeatedly emphasized the diversity and hybridity of Englishness (see, for example, *The Collection*, 339; *Albion*, 36, 448).[29]

As was the case with Fowles, the tendency of scholars to read Ackroyd's early writings as postmodern has shaped the reception of all his subsequent works, and has fueled the often stinging responses to his portraits of Englishness. Michael Levenson's characterization of Ackroyd as a "Tory postmodernist" indicates the bemusement of scholars in the face of Ackroyd's apparently contradictory sentiments about the stability of the English canon and the fluidity of Englishness.[30] Readers of Ackroyd's early diatribe against English culture and letters, *Notes for a New Culture* (1976), are likely to be surprised by declarations in *Albion* and *English Music* that "there is no progress in English writing but, rather, a perpetual return to the original sources of inspiration" (*Albion*, 23; cf. *English Music*, 171).[31] Barry Lewis's assessment of Ackroyd as "culturally conservative, someone who is proud to uphold the virtue and integrity of the dead white English male"[32] seems consistent with John Lucas's assertion that the pastoral is a fundamentally conservative genre.[33] But it fails to recognize that the pastoral imagery apparent everywhere in *English Music* is largely absent from Ackroyd's earlier fiction, appearing only in the immediately preceding novel, *First Light* (1989).[34]

The tendency to read Ackroyd as postmodern creates a somewhat different problem than it did for Fowles. For Fowles, the problem was that prevalent theories of postmodernism articulated by Hutcheon, Brian McHale, Fredric Jameson, and others employ a critical vocabulary that effaces his commitment to realism. For Ackroyd, in contrast, the problem is that the critical vocabulary fits too neatly, diminishing the significance of local historical and cultural contexts from which his work draws.[35] Pastiche is one of the defining techniques of postmodernism, and Ackroyd clearly employs pastiche from his first novel, *The Great Fire of London* (1982), onward. Yet Ackroyd himself has insisted that the mixing and mimicry of styles found in English architecture and literature is not postmodern but a characteristically English trait, coming out of a nation that has embraced hybridity from its ancient beginnings (*The Collection*, 333). This sensibility is everywhere apparent in *English Music*: the even-numbered chapters represent visions experienced by the narrator Timothy Harcombe, each of which is written in the style of an author who fits in Ackroyd's English literary tradition. But there is no indication that the pastiche of Blake, Bunyan, Carroll, Defoe, Dickens, Doyle, Malory, and others involves an effort to reveal the ideological subtexts of these authors, as Hutcheon's theory would predict. If such an effort does motivate the portrayal of Timothy, as Jeremy Gibson and Julian Wolfreys sug/ novel does little to signal that it uses pastiche in such radically dinc. ways.[36]

Pastiche in Ackroyd's writing represents not a subversion of generic codes but a technique of historical reconstruction that demonstrates his affiliation with a tradition of English literature. The crucial figure shaping Ackroyd's thinking during this period is T. S. Eliot, one of the few English authors receiving sympathetic treatment in *Notes for a New Culture* and the subject of Ackroyd's second biography (1984). Ackroyd singles out Eliot's "Tradition and the Individual Talent" for its critique of selfhood, and Ackroyd has subsequently described himself as a "medium," echoing Eliot's term.[37] According to this understanding, pastiche represents a mode of reproducing the past or, more precisely, it enables a literary work to create the impression of simultaneity between the present and the past. An artist who immerses himself or herself in the literary and cultural artifacts of a past era can reproduce the cultural sensibilities of that era through literary imitation.[38] Put another way, Ackroyd claims that writers can adopt temporarily the ideological biases and cultural contexts of another writer with sufficient fidelity that their own biases and contexts provide relatively little distortion. This notion of the simultaneity or continuity of history lies at the heart of Ackroyd's early novels such as *Hawksmoor* and *Chatterton*, which, according to Lewis, repeatedly allude to Eliot.[39] Both of these novels are structured in terms of interwoven timelines in which characters living in the present unconsciously repeat words and actions of characters living in the past.

Pastoral conventions and imagery are absent in Ackroyd's fiction prior to *Chatterton* because historical knowledge is not a significant epistemological problem, as it was for Fowles. As discussed in the last section, Fowles considered a person's capacity for knowledge to be limited by language itself, which inevitably distorts reality. Film may represent a particularly pernicious medium, but even the novel codes reality in terms of the author's ideological biases. For Ackroyd, in contrast, language is precisely what preserves history. Ackroyd insists, for example, that Celtic culture continues to endure on the British Isles in everyday language usage, even though no public architecture built by the tribes remains. Ackroyd declares: "the presence of a thousand years can never wholly die; it lingers still in the words that spring most easily and fluently to the lips" (*Albion*, 9). Given that everyday language usage is rarely governed by deliberate selection based on intimate knowledge of the etymologies of words, Ackroyd appears to suggest that the cultural beliefs of the Celts or the authors he imitates are coded in the language itself. Traditional conceptions of the pastoral are incompatible with such a belief. Even in the bucolic poetry of Theocritus and Virgil, which provided the basis for what would come to be known as pastoral, one of the basic premises is a separation between past and present that is not simply temporal but also epistemological. As Paul de Man notes, the most basic pastoral convention is defined as the eternal separation between a mind that distinguishes and the original simplicity of the natural.[40]

The introduction of pastoral elements in *First Light*, then, implies the emergence of a crisis in Ackroyd's thinking about epistemology and the capacity of language to provide historical knowledge. Notably, three consecutive fictional works – *Chatterton*, *First Light*, and *English Music* – all present a scene in which characters experience a sense of continuity with the past after the death of a father figure. In *Chatterton*, the family of the dead protagonist Charles Wychwood perceives his presence "suspended in the air" of his room.[41] This discovery occurs only pages after another scene in which a forged painting of Chatterton – the initial discovery of which by Charles launches the action of the novel – is accidentally destroyed and, in the process, reveals itself to be not a single portrait but a palimpsest of faces:

The face of the sitter dissolved, becoming two faces, one old and one young.[42]

The analogous scenes are more intimately tied in *First Light* and *English Music*. In *First Light*, orphan Joey Hanover opens the coffin of an ancient ancestor:

And in this old face, now, he sees other faces … He sees in this face, too, the faces of all those who had come before him. And the faces of all those he has known.[43]

Two pages later, everyone who witnesses the body burning experiences a similar sensation.[44] Finally, in *English Music*, Timothy looks on the face of his dying father:

Yet as he looked upon the face of his father he saw it changing in wondrous wise, and taking on the lineaments of other faces which he knew. For he thought he saw his grandparents thereupon, and other yet more ancient faces.[45]

A page later, Timothy will hear the voice of his father asserting: "The old order changes, yielding place to the new, but I am eternal for I am Albion" (393). In each of these three novels, then, the most intimate experience of historical continuity occurs after the people or material traces associated with it die or are destroyed. As a result, the past becomes a spiritual presence rather than something coded in language, as was the case in Ackroyd's early novels.

In the case of *Chatterton*, the shift in Ackroyd's conception of the past is motivated by new anxieties about what motivates individuals to appropriate/copy/forge/pastiche the past. Curiously, Ackroyd's use of the word "forgery" to describe Thomas Chatterton's verse divorces the term from any economic motivations. In his essay "Forging a Language," for example, Chatterton is portrayed as motivated by antiquarianism rather than the desire for fame or material gain. Indeed, Ackroyd has repeatedly praised Chatterton's "Rowley" poems, declaring Chatterton to be "the one great genius of historical restoration and renewal in this country" (*The Collection*, 393; see also *Albion*, 421–32). In *Chatterton*, however, forgeries often are motivated by more familiar, criminal purposes. The forged painting of a middle-aged Chatterton and the accompanying personal papers that Charles discovers at the beginning of the novel were created for the purpose of ruining Chatterton's reputation. Charles's interest in the documents is altruistic, but the same cannot be said of the other characters, who see the economic potential in the "discovery" that Chatterton's suicide was faked. The novel struggles to distinguish between forgeries motivated by aesthetic/antiquarian concerns and those motivated by more selfish reasons. The accidental destruction of the painting by professional counterfeiter Stewart Merk provides just such an opportunity, but the novel cannot provide a convincing explanation for why Merk's act of forgery causes destruction while the initial act of forgery does not. Merk's effort to touch up the forged painting leads to a radical rupture with history, as the painting disintegrates; Charles's son Edward, in contrast, stares at Henry Wallis's *Death of Chatterton* (which is itself a forgery in the sense that the model was George Meredith and not Chatterton) and experiences a sense of historical continuity never previously felt: "He had seen his father again. He would always be here, in the painting. He would never wholly die" (230).

The use of pastoral conventions in *First Light* enables Ackroyd to raise the kinds of epistemological questions suggested by *Chatterton* without ceding his foundational premises about historical continuity. The first and last chapters of *First Light* are titled "Uncertainty Principle," and the allusion to Heisenberg initiates a set of reflections about quantum mechanics, chaos theory, and astronomy that have become a familiar staple to readers of postmodern works from Thomas Pynchon to Tom Stoppard. The first two chapters establish the basic pastoral opposition of simple past/complex present. In chapter 1, astronomer Damian Fall laments that the stars once appeared as "creatures of light leaping across the firmament" but now have no heavenly organization beyond that imposed by the stargazer.[46] In chapter 2, archaeologist Mark Clare laments the disappearance of forests in the English countryside, and a lost sense of sacredness.[47] Ackroyd further emphasizes the pastoral quality of the countryside that Mark's team will disrupt by locating the ancient burial mound they will excavate on the border of Devon and Dorset, in the heart of Hardy's preindustrial rural Wessex. But the growing epistemological skepticism felt by Damian and Mark never infects the local farmers, Farmer Mint and his son Boy Mint. They never shed a kind of rural "simplicity"; even after their mock pastoral simplicity is revealed to be a ruse to conceal the secret beneath the burial mound (the corpse of the original Mint dating back to prehistoric times), they are governed by a single-minded determination to preserve their rural way of life and a sense of historical continuity to a time that predates England. Damian will suffer a nervous breakdown after he confronts the possibility that his research demonstrates the impossibility of knowing anything: "Their own theories and inventions had lasted only for the briefest periods but, if all knowledge was a story, what did it really signify? Perhaps there were no stars and no planets, no nebulae and no constellations; perhaps they merely came into existence in recognition of our wishes or demands."[48] But the novel does not unambiguously support Damian's uncertainty. The hidden network of tunnels beneath the burial mound and the elaborate precautions taken by the Mints for thousands of years to preserve their heritage exceeds all the expectations of the archaeologists.

Damian's solipsism ironically provides the grounds for claiming the existence of an enduring Englishness. Damian is repeatedly presented in the novel arguing that quantum physics not only rejects the positivist dream of objective knowledge but also leaves individuals incapable of discerning the relative accuracy among competing accounts. His insistence that "Science is like fiction" dissolves the rigid dichotomy between the complex empirical present and the simplistic pastoral past with which the novel began. By implication, a pastoral narrative of the past would not be inherently more inaccurate than any other historical account; indeed, if knowledge is not progressive but simply a product of whichever story is employed at any given moment, then the pastoral could theoretically provide knowledge that other modes of writing could not. Such an argument would be consistent with the notion presented by theorists of the pastoral including Lawrence Buell that pastoral narratives are something that Western cultures cannot do without.[49] The alternatives to modernity coded within pastoral narratives are not simply fanciful delusions but perhaps intimations of a more integrated human existence within the natural world – intimations that emerge only as industrialization takes hold. *First Light* goes further in its epistemological claims for the pastoral, however. When Mark presents Damian with an image of a star map located inside the burial mound, they discover that it required a highly sophisticated understanding of astronomy. Indeed, Damian concedes that the builders of the tomb were able to forecast the movement of the stars as accurately as he can with the aid of computer models. The ancestral Mints, then, were not only able to view the stars in the poetic terms that the contemporary astronomer Damian cannot; they were also able to view the stars with the scientific rigor that Damian employs more than 4,000 years later.

The notion of reclaiming a buried history remains central to *English Music*, the novel that embraces pastoral imagery and conventions with the least irony. In the 1992 preface, Ackroyd declares that his "one central purpose" is "to restore the true face of the contemporary world by considering all the latent forces within it" (*The Collection*, 384). Within the novel itself, the past has been largely erased by institutions of late capitalism: chain stores and supermarkets have replaced family shops and the Chemical Theatre, where Timothy's father Clement once performed séances and healings. The interest in latency emerges in the novel's first pages: an aging Timothy Harcombe is portrayed as still able to see the outlines of the old buildings in his mind as he wanders the streets of London where he grew up some seventy years earlier. Readers soon discover that Clement devoted his life to recovering the latent: as a medium, he enabled Londoners living amid the squalor of Brick Lane to reconnect with the spirits of their lost loved ones. Set against a backdrop of 1920s London, the novel portrays such spirits as everywhere to be found, lurking reminders of Great Britain's imperial ventures and costly wars.

Ackroyd's portrait of post-World War I London suggests some response to critics who have argued that his conception of English history conceals the centrality of imperialism and capitalism. Terry Eagleton captures this sentiment: "Ackroyd's England is a Chestertonian realm of monks, mystics and morris dancers, not of slave traders, colonial adventures and industrial manufacturers."[50] Such criticism aligns Ackroyd with a heritage industry that has repackaged Englishness for consumption, portraying a rural Englishness divorced from the history of imperial exploitation and oppression across the globe. Yet Ackroyd's implicit references to this history, combined with his explicitly Dickensian portrait of poverty in

London, suggest neither ignorance nor a desire to sanitize history. Rather, his emphasis on the "latent" elements of history means that his focus will be on precisely those who envisioned alternatives to the dominant history of Britain. Ackroyd's obsession with "Cockney visionaries," as he calls them, concedes Eagleton's point that the nation was heavily invested in its imperial enterprises. Much as William Blake's Albion could exist as an alternative to imperialism only in his visionary verse, Ackroyd's Albion exists only in the visions of Timothy Harcombe.[51] Indeed, the pastiche of Blake's *Jerusalem* explicitly informs Ackroyd's vision of pastoral Englishness (see esp. *English Music*, chapter 16).

The formal structure of *English Music* emphasizes Ackroyd's revised conception of history in terms of latent forces. Whereas *Hawksmoor* and *Chatterton* were organized in terms of chapters that alternate between distinct timelines, *English Music* is organized in terms of chapters that alternate between the everyday life of Timothy and his visionary experiences, which take the form of pastiche of the writing style of canonical English authors. The historical continuity projected by the formal structure of the earlier novels is significantly attenuated in *English Music* because the visions occur within the same timeline as the other chapters. The separation of everyday life and visionary experiences underlines a sense of historical discontinuity, for Timothy's primary experience of the past is through his visions. The characters that Timothy meets in his visions repeatedly insist on the continuity of English history, which Clement refers to as "English music." But English music is a tune that characters in Timothy's everyday life rarely hear. Indeed, the visionary chapters simultaneously construct Englishness as an enduring, atavistic presence and as something unavailable to the majority of the English. At the end of the first vision, the novel notes that Timothy heard music as "a continuous presence," but "there were some who never heard the music, and for them there would be nothing to remember" (47).

The construction of a "latent" Englishness – one that is coherent, enduring, and separate from imperial Britain – relies heavily on pastoral tropes and images, which appear with increasing frequency later in the novel. In chapter 5, Timothy is taken away from London and his father by his maternal grandfather, William Sinclair, and is brought to live in a country farmhouse in Wiltshire where his mother grew up. After his initial despair at being separated from his father, Timothy increasingly looks to the forests around him as a "refuge" and an "enchanted place (109, 110); country landscapes will repeatedly be associated with Englishness. Evoking one of the oldest pastoral tropes, Timothy will be instructed in music by old masters, each of whom will insist that his music is part of a tradition that is grounded in the countryside (209–10). The final paragraphs end with a blatant evocation of pastoral elegy that is hard to read without either crediting Wolfrey and Gibson's suggestion of ironic pastiche or dismissing it as clumsy. On the lawn outside the Wiltshire farmhouse, a now ancient Timothy comforts the granddaughter of his best friend Edward Campion as they bury a small dead bird. After assuring her that "It's safe now. Its soul has flown away," Timothy observes another bird landing nearby, who immediately begins to "fill the white lane with its song" (400).

The probable irony of the final scene does not undercut the basic separation between past and present that is crucial to Ackroyd's project. Pastoral works have used irony and satire since Virgil's *Eclogues*, and irony does not preclude a commitment to the ideals subject to scrutiny. Recalling de Man's definition of pastoral, irony provides a means by which an author can signal the separation between the "simple" natural worldview and the "complex" worldview of the present, which cannot sympathize with or even entirely credit simplicity. In the final scene of the novel, an ironic tone would only confirm Timothy's assertion that the spirit of the bird exists separately from the dead body, and indeed comes into existence as a spirit precisely because it no longer exists as a material object. The scene thereby confirms the move in Ackroyd's prior two novels to claim the existence of the past as an essence that can be accessed only through the mediation of the imagination, which is guided by the literary text. This sentiment is underlined in the final sentences of the novel, where Timothy reiterates his initial assertion that "nothing is lost" by declaring that he no longer needs to open the "old books" handed down to him by his father because they exist within him. "Yes, I have inherited the past because I have acknowledged it at last … So you see, as I explained to you before, I no longer need to open the old books. I have heard the music" (399, 400).

The separation between the everyday present and the visionary past invites charges of conservatism, and it is not hard to read *English Music* as endorsing a parochial, nationalist version of Eliot's tradition, something that must be acquired through "much labour."[32] It can also be seen, however, in light of his increasing epistemological skepticism, a skepticism that emerges from an awareness that late capitalism seeks to preclude the existence of any genuine alternatives to itself. The anxieties about encroaching capital are expressed implicitly in *English Music*, but the novel emerges after a decade in which Ackroyd became far more explicit about such concerns in his nonfictional essays. In "The English Novel Now" (1981), for example, Ackroyd sees the emergence of a new English literature as a direct response to American imperialism and cultural hegemony. The prose of contemporary American writers mirrors the arrogance and moral poverty of its government, for Ackroyd, who sees the emergence of the new realism as an aesthetic explicitly associated with Englishness. "Their language becomes an imperialist syntax, co-opting all available realities and transforming them into the same bland shape. The prose of contemporary American novelists is like a veneer upon a painting, so thick that the human figures are distorted and unrecognizable beneath" (*The Collection*, 325–26). The urge to write a novel that proposes multiple realities and prioritizes latent forces or alternative visionary experiences, then, is neither parochial nor a flight from reality – as postmodernism is often accused of being. Instead, it can be understood as a process of recovering a sense of agency by discovering the contingency of historical events.

The pastoral is crucial to Ackroyd's "new realism," then, because it provides a mode for understanding historical events that is not overdetermined by American "imperialist syntax." If Hayden White is correct that every genre proposes a mode of making history into a meaningful narrative, then the possibility exists that certain modes might be more realistic than others. While the theories that historians use to interpret the past are not self-evidently present in the archival material or other material traces of the past themselves, the theories themselves are not historical abstractions but arise from particular historical contexts. Particularly when broad tropes or genres are viewed in the context of more localized literary traditions, their endurance suggests that they provide a set of values that have some compelling reason for their continued existence. The use of pastoral imagery within the British novel might provide one such mode. William Empson's suggestion that proletarian literature takes a pastoral form, for example, implies that it provides a mode of reading the past in an anti-capitalist light that is congenial with Ackroyd's sense that the rise of American dominance poses epistemological problems.[53] Certain modes might yield better historical accounts because they are shaped by repeated historical usage, and the fact that the pastoral continues to appear in British novels suggests that it in fact arises out of values held in the past rather than represents a simple imposition on it.[54]

JULIAN BARNES: PASTORAL HISTORIES

Perhaps the most significant indicator of the enduring power of the pastoral to provide a mode of recasting Englishness is the repeated efforts by immigrant writers to appropriate images of the English countryside. V. S. Naipaul's *The Enigma of Arrival* (1987), Kazuo Ishiguro's *The Remains of the Day* (1989), David Dabydeen's *Disappearance* (1993), Meera Syal's *Anita and Me* (1996), and Ben Okri's *In Arcadia* (2002) all explore the notion of a pastoral Englishness in light of postimperial decline, and the extent to which immigrants from the colonial peripheries might lay claim to Englishness. If the pastoral historically functioned to consolidate a British identity against a colonial Other and, more recently, to consolidate an English identity against a multicultural Britishness, it also provides a mode for immigrant authors to lay claim to Englishness. McKeon's suggestion that the pastoral tests the "dialectical fluidity of dichotomous oppositions" provides a crucial clue for understanding the plot of Dabydeen's *Disappearance*. The novel follows the efforts by the unnamed narrator to build a sea-wall to protect Dunsmere Cliffs from erosion. As was the case with earlier pastoral novels, *Disappearance* portrays Englishness as something fading away. However, Englishness is not accessed via nostalgic reminiscences, as is the case with Evelyn Waugh's *Brideshead Revisited* (1944) and Naipaul's *The Enigma of Arrival*.[55] Nor are the fragments of Englishness shored up by the English: the narrator is an engineer from Guyana. His proleptic fantasies at the end the novel about how his sea-wall will be viewed by the rural inhabitants seek to revise historical conceptions of Englishness. The narrator declares: "Future generations would see the wall as something that was always there, a quintessentially English monument; the efforts of Christie [an Irishman] and myself would be erased by ignorance or national sentiment. Was it not always thus in England: the drift into a deliberate unconsciousness; any awakening being a jolt of patriotic sentiment?"[56] The history of pastoral Englishness becomes viewed as an ideological effort to erase all traces of dependence on the colonies for labor and raw materials. Dabydeen confirms Raymond Williams's sense that pastoral representations of a fading Englishness provide a way for the contemporary English to disentangle themselves from a history of exploitation.

It would be a mistake, however, to endorse simplistic oppositions between English apologists and immigrant postcolonial critics. This has been the tendency within literary and cultural studies. Iain Chambers, for example, declares that there are two versions of Britishness, one that is "Anglo-centric, frequently conservative, backward-looking, and increasingly located in a frozen and largely stereotyped idea of the national, that is English, culture. The other is ex-centric, open-ended and multiethnic."[57] Such declarations disregard Ackroyd's simultaneously conservative and open-ended notion of hybrid Englishness. They also disregard the significant investment by immigrant authors from Naipaul to Dabydeen in the idea of Englishness. Dabydeen is certainly more critical than Naipaul of the value of English civilization, and *Disappearance* has been read as a critical response to *The Enigma of Arrival*. But Dabydeen's novel ends with a tantalizing, if fragile, hope for a more genuinely multicultural Great Britain that blends both versions of national identity identified by Chambers. In the final paragraph, the narrator discovers in his pocket a dried flower that might disappear with the slightest movement. It is a flower that he picked on his first day at Dunsmere Cliffs, and evokes a scene earlier in the novel when the narrator was reflecting on the possibility of being accepted in rural England. "It would take centuries for me to grow into the landscape, as it took centuries for a hybrid flower to evolve, slowly transformed by pollen from the east brought back by Crusaders and merchant venturers."[58] The final scene provides a reminder that his work to preserve the cliffs is part of this transformation.

The explorations of cultural hybridity undertaken by immigrant and multiethnic writers will be the central focus of the next chapter. The more immediate point is to elaborate on the fluidity between apologetics for Englishness and postcolonial satire that pastoral tropes enable. Dabydeen's novel ends with a kind of apologia despite itself, and similarly complex attitudes emerge, for example, in Julian Barnes's *England, England* (1998). Barnes creates two different versions of the pastoral in his novel. In the first and more explicitly satirical version, entrepreneur Sir Jack Pitman decides to take the heritage industry to its logical conclusion: to create a theme park island that contains all of the quintessential heritage objects, from the Tower of London to the royal family themselves. "England, England," as the renamed Isle of Wight is called, is an icon of late capitalism more than an effort to preserve a pure national identity. As Sir Jack's consultant puts it, "We are the new pioneers. We must sell our past to other nations as their future."[59]

The second version of pastoral in the novel occurs in the third and final section. Here, England collapses economically as national wealth and industries are shifted to England, England. After deindustrializing, England renames itself Anglia, removes itself from the European Union, and becomes a preindustrial enclave as cities and modern technologies are abandoned. Amid the shambles of the nation that was once England, a pastoral world emerges:

Chemicals drained from the land, the colours grew gentler, and the light untainted; the moon, with less competition, now rose more dominantly. In the enlarged countryside, wildlife bred freely … Common land was reestablished …

Meateating became popular again, as did poaching. Children were sei
rooming in the woods, and the bolder fell stupefied from a tentativ
others dug esoteric roots, or smoked dried-fern roll-ups and pretended
cinate. (264)

As the final lines indicate, the restored precapitalist world is by no means
portrayed unambiguously or without irony. Yet, as Dominic Head notes,
the novel seems fascinated by the artificial worlds it creates.[60] The ironic
portrait of the village reinstituting a "traditional" Fête does not undercut the longing for the kinds of lifestyles that have been annihilated by
capitalism.

As was the case with Fowles and Ackroyd, Barnes engages in a set of
reflections on Englishness that promote epistemological questions that
can be resolved only through pastoral tropes and imagery. Each of the
three sections of *England, England* begins with a question provoked by
the instability of personal and national memory. In the first, brief section of the novel, Martha Cochrane puzzles over the question "What's
your first memory?" (3). The question takes on increasing urgency for
her as she recognizes that each "first" memory turns out to have been
either preceded by other memories or revised over time. Her fantasy of
recovering a "true, unprocessed memory" leads to a set of painful reflections about how she and her mother were abandoned by her father. In the
second and by far the longest section of the novel, Sir Jack asks "What is
real?" (32). His musings lead him to the England, England project, which
freely blends reality and artifice, originals and replicas. The novel emphasizes the stakes of Sir Jack's project by introducing a French philosopher
modeled on Baudrillard, who insists that reality has been abolished by
simulacra. In the third section of the novel, Martha Cochrane is exiled to
Anglia, and finds herself questioning the authenticity of the traditions to
which her fellow villagers adhere.

Epistemological questions are apparent in Barnes's earlier writings,
though they were never posed with the urgency that haunts *England,
England*. Both of his most celebrated novels, *Flaubert's Parrot* (1984)
and *A History of the World in 10½ Chapters* (1989), explore the extent to
which the past can be known and written about accurately. The conceit
of *Flaubert's Parrot* is built around the search for the stuffed parrot that
was on Flaubert's work-table during the writing of *Un Cœur Simple*. After
chapters exploring a variety of different historical writing styles, the novel
ends with an almost blithe admission that the authentic past is impossible
to verify. Standing in a small museum room and staring at three identical
stuffed parrots (forty-seven others did not survive), the narrator Geoffrey

Braithwaite declares in the last line of the novel: "Perhaps it was one of them."[61] In the "half chapter" of *A History of the World in 10½ Chapters*, a character named Julian Barnes is more insistent on the importance of verifying truth, and he makes an impassioned plea against relativism:

> We all know objective truth is not attainable … But while we know this, we must still believe that objective truth is obtainable; or we must believe that it is 99 per cent obtainable; or if we can't believe this we must believe that 43 per cent objective truth is better than 41 per cent. We must do so, because if we don't we're lost, we fall into beguiling relativity … we admit that the victor has the right not just to the spoils but also to the truth.[62]

The first chapter of the novel appears to model this advice, portraying the biblical story of the Ark from the perspective of the woodworm, who "corrects" the authoritative and authoritarian account given by Noah. However, the novel never provides a clear rationale for why readers should believe that the woodworm's account is more accurate than the one presented in the book of Genesis. Each of the subsequent chapters provides a putatively historical account of an event from a perspective that has been lost in the histories written by the victors. But these accounts are written in an often deliberately fantastical manner that undercuts their purported truth value. Readers "know" that woodworms do not write histories, and the novel's final chapter presents a scenario whose accuracy is impossible to verify: the experience of someone in Heaven. These deliberate fabulations, to use the novel's own term, allow the novel to avoid having to provide readers with a model for discerning the objective truth among competing accounts. Even the plea for objectivity by the character "Julian Barnes" occurs only in parenthesis: the "half chapter" of the novel is entitled "parenthesis."

 (In the case of *England, England*, the question of objective truth is more unavoidable. In the final paragraph of the novel, Martha leaves the Fête and observes a rabbit, "fearless and quietly confident of its territory" (275). Earlier in the novel, Dr. Max, official historian of the England, England project, declares that reality is like a rabbit, something that people want tamed. "If you gave them the real thing," he declares, "something wild that bit, and, if you'll pardon me, shat, they wouldn't know what to do with it. Except strangle it and cook it" (136). The return of the rabbit in the final paragraph, then, baits readers: does the rabbit signify reality, implying that the pastoral representation of England in the "Anglia" section is somehow more real than the heritage theme park of England, England? This is the conclusion of Sara Henstra, who argues that the rabbit signifies the triumph of reality over image.[63] But the final paragraph does not explicitly evoke Dr. Max's simile. To refashion the famous phrase, sometimes a rabbit is simply a rabbit. Even if Henstra is correct, the novel can present the return of the real only as an image, which might lead readers back to the conclusion of *Flaubert's Parrot*: perhaps one of the Englands in the novel is real, but it is impossible to verify.

England, England thus provides an ironic gloss on the rise of the heritage industry in the 1970s, and the extent to which it destabilized notions of British history and identity. Jeremy Paxman argues that historically English identity has not been explicitly defined, in large part because the term was never under crisis (23).[64] While this assertion is by no means uncontestable, the rise of the heritage industry intensified underlying crises by commodifying culture into heritage objects whose market value depends in large part upon their perceived authenticity. The requirement of authenticity not only raises issues about what constitutes English/ British history and who gets to authenticate the past, but also means that Englishness can potentially be purchased, traded, or transferred. Barnes raises these issues explicitly in his 1990 essay "Fake!", which addresses a number of examples of the identity crisis produced by heritage. Reflecting on the British talent for the invention of tradition, Barnes suggests that the heritage industry forces Britons to recognize that national identity is a construction with a material history rather than an atavistic given. The battle over Harrods waged by the German-born Roland Rowland and the Egyptian-born Mohamed Al-Fayed, for Barnes, may provide a model for Britain's financial stability, but it forces Britons to reflect on assumptions about national identity. As is the case in *England, England*, questions about national history become inseparable from epistemology: "if we can't believe *that*, what can we believe," Barnes rhetorically asks. "And since individual identity depends in part upon national identity, what happens when those symbolic props to national identity turn out to be no more authentic or probable than a furbearing trout?"[65]

Barnes never directly answers his own question, and significantly reformulates how it is posed in *England, England*. In the paragraphs immediately preceding the reappearance of the rabbit, Martha observes how the reactions of children to a "dressing-up competition" differ from her own (273). She reflects:

What held her attention now were the children's faces, which expressed such a willing yet complex trust in reality. As she saw it, they had not yet reached the age of incredulity, only of wonder; so that even when they disbelieved, they also believed … They saw all too easily that Queen Victoria was no more than

Ray Stout with a red face and a scarf round his head, yet they believed in both Queen Victoria and Ray Stout at the same time ... she, Martha, could no longer do that. All she could see was Ray Stout making a happy fool of himself.

Could you reinvent innocence? Or was it always constructed, grafted onto the old disbelief? (273–74)

While this passage reinvokes the epistemological question of how reality can be verified, the question shifts by the end of the passage to the issue of what can be believed. Martha's epistemological doubts now appear to be the result of an unwillingness or inability to accept particular foundational assumptions or perspectives. The model here appears to be a kind of Derridean version of double consciousness: to accept that any given person's reality is a construction based on his or her guiding assumptions, but that at any given moment people need to believe in some notion of reality in order to act at all. A self-conscious acceptance of reality as shaped by a set of contingent assumptions appears to be the adequate compromise for Barnes.

By implication, Britons presumably should accept that traditions are invented, and use them anyway as a means of establishing unity while accepting that such traditions are subject to change. The final pastoral section of the novel provides a number of examples of this attitude. The fabulations of Jez Harris (an American lawyer from Milwaukee) about the rituals and histories of rural English life are endorsed by the narrator, if ironically. Martha, a lifelong atheist, becomes a devout churchgoer not because she believes in God but because it provides a sense of "seriousness" (244), a sufficiently vague commitment that anyone could theoretically affirm it. Indeed, for all of the restoration that occurs in the final pastoral section of the novel, Barnes is very clear that religious belief will not be making a comeback. Reverend Coleman is emphatically discouraged against any "moralizing sermons" or theology that would endorse universal or timeless truths (271).

The pastoral imagery of the final section enables Barnes to present his vision of double consciousness, to view ironically a "seriousness" that he nonetheless wishes to exist. Indeed, *England, England* suggests that the "pastoral revolution" described by McKeon may in fact be a definitive feature of what has come to be known as postmodernism in Britain.[66] For McKeon, the pastoral survived its eighteenth-century dismissal by Samuel Johnson and others by transforming itself into a more generalized view of the world that becomes crucial to Romanticism. To the extent that Romanticism is, as Saree Makdisi suggests, a response to modernization and an effort to articulate an alternative to an ever-encroaching capitalism at the moment when alternatives are beginning to disappear, postmodernism might be best understood as a response to a late capitalism that has effectively annihilated viable alternatives to itself. The pastoral mode characteristic of both Barnes and Dabydeen enables the representation of alternatives by accepting the basic premise that they may be expressed only ironically. Such a suggestion can be found in Martha's embrace of religiosity without religious belief and her avid interest in restoring the use of the English system of measurements. "This was hardly nostalgia, since most of these measures have been abolished before she was sentient," the narrator notes. "Or perhaps it was, and nostalgia of a truer kind: not for what you knew, or thought you had known, as a child, but for what you could never have known" (270).

Pastoral writing in so-called postmodern British literature, then, can be seen in light of R. Radhakrishnan's call for redefining postmodernism. Radhakrishnan argues that the epistemological claims associated with postmodernism can be usefully understood only if postmodernity is historicized rather than seen as an abstract universal. "Postmodernism, to be deserving of global attention, has to learn to historicize itself multilaterally, and multi-historically," Radhakrishnan writes. "If postmodernism is an epistemological condition, such a condition as 'universal' claim cannot be unilateral: it has to bear the burden of multiple and uneven histories before it can be legislated."[67] A crucial part of recovering the multiple and uneven histories of postmodernism is to divorce developments in British literature and culture from a vague and undifferentiated notion of "The West." As the writings of Fowles, Ackroyd, and Barnes attest, so-called English writers have struggled to understand Englishness and its complex relations to the histories of imperialism. All three authors characterize Britain in terms of a flexible, international system of capitalism that exploits all available markets. Their interest in epistemology, then, is not an abstract philosophical point, but addresses cultural and political struggles for how Britain can be envisioned in the postimperial era. Postcolonial scholars have demonstrated how immigrants have redefined Britain, and the challenge now is to understand more precisely how English authors have responded in complex ways that defy characterizations of them as conservative and xenophobic.

CHAPTER 4

Hybridity, enterprise culture, and the fiction of multicultural Britain

The breeding of millions of half-caste children would merely produce a generation of misfits and create national tensions.
Duncan Sandys

That Het'rogeneous Thing, an Englishman
Daniel Defoe

The preoccupation with pastoral images observed in the last chapter among both so-called English and immigrant authors living in Britain suggests a collective dimension to the imagination rarely apparent in the white South African fiction discussed in chapter 2. As we saw earlier, Brink, Coetzee, and Gordimer sought in the imagination an epistemological faculty that could counter the mystification of reality produced by state propaganda, thereby enabling individuals to feel sympathy with others. Yet all three authors were highly conscious of the dangers in claiming that they or their readers could vicariously experience what it meant to be black in South Africa. All three understood the necessity for the imagination to function as a social practice rather than an individual pursuit divorced from everyday life, even though the notion of the imagination bridging social divides or healing social tensions remained a heuristic rather than a genuine possibility in their fictional works. In contrast, the contemporary British authors discussed in chapter 3 repeatedly sought in a revised notion of Englishness the possibility of bridging ethnic, racial, and cultural divides. Rejecting the notion of cultural identity as a fixed set of categories or traits, these authors assigned the imagination a crucial role in the production, revision, and negotiation of Englishness.

The next two chapters in this study will explore two poles of cultural identity – hybridity and essentialism – in order to understand more fully how the imagination functions as a social practice and not simply an individual activity. While the tendency in Western thinking since Aristotle has been to view identity as a set of attributes, it can also be understood as a set of overlapping though not necessarily homogeneous experiences – experiences that shape and inform without determining an individual's worldview. From this perspective, identity can be seen as negotiated and ongoing rather than a static phenomenon. The notion of identity as produced through imagining is consistent, we will see in chapter 5, with even essentialistic claims of racial memory when we shift our focus away from interpreting identity as an ontological claim toward seeing it as an epistemological one.

Examining hybridity is particularly useful for this study because of its mongrel genealogy – the concept emerges from the intersections of theories of postmodernism and postcoloniality. Cultural hybridity, like the discourses from which it emerges, has multilateral histories that defy easy summary or efforts to articulate a single, coherent definition. There have certainly been crucial interventions, such as Homi Bhabha's, which have had significant and wide-ranging implications for various forms of hybridity. The interventions themselves have been appropriated and revised in different contexts, however, so that Bhabha's theory suggests a notion of "cutting and mixing" cultural traditions to some of his interlocutors and a notion of moving beyond identity categories altogether to others. This does not mean that the term itself is meaningless, but rather that engaging with it requires exploring its permutations within particular contexts before addressing the concept at an abstract level. Indeed, protean terms such as *hybridity* tend to take on more significant meaning in light of particular crises, and gain a richness and philosophical complexity that is, in many cases, apparent neither before nor afterwards. In the case of hybridity, perhaps its most crucial moment of transformation occurred not in a colonial setting but in the former imperial center, as Britons struggled in the 1970s–80s to redefine what would constitute a postimperial Britain. As will become apparent later, Bhabha's own contribution to debates on hybridity was heavily influenced by these events. Theories of cultural hybridity that have gained widespread academic prominence, in other words, were often shaped by responses to the profound political and economic changes occurring in Great Britain, changes that have often been attributed to the election of Margaret Thatcher as Prime Minister in 1979. Thus, to understand the forms hybridity has taken requires an analysis that views the phenomenon in light of Thatcher's efforts to radically redefine the postwar consensus and the welfare state which was at its center – efforts that valorized market-driven policies, privatization, and individual enterprise.

The rise of what has been termed "enterprise culture" in the 1980s promised new opportunities for populations previously relegated to the margins of British society.[1] The hierarchies of class and race would, at least according to the rhetoric of the day, be replaced by a marketplace that offered equal opportunities to all. Englishness itself would become another commodity, and the purchase of Harrods by the Egyptian-born Mohamed Al-Fayed in 1985 seemed to provide spectacular evidence of the new era. Literary characters from the same mold became prominent, and provided a sharp critique of the identity politics of the previous two decades. Nowhere is this attitude more apparent than in the rhetoric of the Pakistani immigrant Nasser in Hanif Kureishi's screenplay *My Beautiful Laundrette* (1985). Valorizing entrepreneurial individualism over ethnic affiliation, Nasser asserts that "we're professional businessmen. Not professional Pakistanis. There's no race question in the new enterprise culture."[2]

That enterprise culture failed to eliminate racism is now a matter of historical record, and the misfortunes Nasser suffers should surprise no one familiar with Kureishi's work or opinions about Thatcherism. But to dismiss Nasser simply as an ideological strawman would overlook the more profound challenge he and other literary characters born of the era of enterprise culture present to more progressive visions of multiculturalism. While Nasser's credo is crass and materialistic, it differs more in rhetoric than in substance from the ideas of Kureishi's protagonists and many postmodern and postcolonial theorists. Nasser's assertion that "[i]n this damn country which we hate and love, you can get anything you want … You just have to know how to squeeze the tits of the system" suggests that advancement requires learning to imitate, appropriate, and ultimately manipulate the social and cultural codes of white Britain.[3] Identity is conceived here as a performance involving mimicry and hybridity, much as it has been in the thinking of Homi Bhabha, Judith Butler, Iain Chambers, Stuart Hall, and others. Yet Nasser fails on all counts: he loses his money gambling; his white mistress breaks off their relationship; and, in one of the final scenes of the movie, his daughter leaves home. The usefulness of mimicry and hybridity is rendered even more questionable when it is recognized that Nasser has relatively modest social aspirations. His claim to be a businessman rather than a Pakistani represents an attempt implicitly to declare his Britishness, but he never risks making such a declaration explicit.

The repeated failures of cultural chameleons like Nasser invite a reassessment of cultural hybridity as an ideal and its capacity to provide a model for multicultural Britain. Hybridity continues to be a widely invoked term in the humanities and social sciences despite criticisms that it perpetuates nineteenth-century ideas of racial purity; portrays the history of colonial violence as inevitable; and conceals the ongoing effects of this history on economically and politically oppressed populations.[4] In many cases, theories of hybridity are grounded in literary works, and Homi Bhabha's repeated references to Salman Rushdie's novels are only the most well-known example. An exploration of how hybridity has been characterized in British fiction dating back to the *Empire Windrush* generation of the 1950s could provide a more historically grounded conception that would also help to explain the continuing preoccupation with Englishness among Afro-Caribbean and Asian authors in Britain despite obvious signs of national decline and the loss of international cultural prestige in the past five decades.[5] My argument involves three interrelated claims: first, cultural hybridity becomes a prominent ideal for writers in the 1980s seeking an alternative to existing conceptions of multiculturalism; second, the viability of hybridity as an alternative is rendered questionable because it is so easily appropriated within enterprise culture; third, the idea of hybridity remains a preoccupation among novelists because more fundamental political transformations are seen as infeasible.

The literary genealogy provided by this chapter invites a reassessment of debates surrounding hybridity and more recent efforts simply to move beyond them. Although the debates began in the late 1980s, even in recent works such as Ashley Dawson's 2007 *Mongrel Nation: Diasporic Culture and the Making of Postcolonial Britain*, the debate continues to be characterized as an argument between elite cosmopolitan culturalists and radical materialists. Dawson's admirable effort to recuperate what she describes as the "radical critique of racial capitalism developed by black British activists and theorists" is necessitated, in her mind, by the fact that so-called "celebrations of Britain's hybridity tend to highlight the cultural impact of black and Asian Britons while ignoring the enduring obstacles they face."[6] The intimate connections between the emergence of enterprise culture and conceptions of cultural hybridity that this chapter will trace, however, belie such an easy opposition. Visions of hybridity in contemporary British fiction have been acutely shaped by material conditions, and this is apparent in some of the most surprising forms hybridity has taken. As we will see, the essentialistic form of cultural hybridity advocated in Salman Rushdie's *The Satanic Verses*, for example, comes in direct response to concerns about consumerist notions of identity. Even the most utopian conceptions of hybridity that will appear in works such as Zadie Smith's *White Teeth* are not entirely divorced from material conditions, but are committed to envisioning a future that is not determined by them.

THE RISE OF HYBRIDITY

The more celebratory accounts of hybridity are based largely on readings of literary texts published since the 1980s. In particular, Salman Rushdie's *The Satanic Verses* (1988), Hanif Kureishi's *The Buddha of Suburbia* (1990), and Zadie Smith's *White Teeth* (2000) have been read as manifestos for a liberatory hybridity that promises to transform Britain into a more genuinely multicultural society.[7] These literary works have been championed for their purported rejection of ideas of multiculturalism circulating in the early 1980s that focused on the promotion of cultural diversity. The problem with promoting cultural diversity, according to Bhabha, is that it enabled white Britons to continue to take their norms for granted as transparent and universal. Cultural differences were seldom viewed as opportunities for engagement and education but rather potential threats to national cohesion.[8] Bhabha's conception of hybridity, in contrast, endorses an idea of national identity that emerges from an ongoing negotiation of cultural differences without seeking a single universal framework. Such a negotiation creates what he calls a "third space" from which entirely new identities might emerge. Bhabha claims: "This third space displaces the histories that constitute it, and sets up new structures of authority, new political initiatives, which are inadequately understood through received wisdom."[9]

While the characterization of hybridity in terms of a "third space" has significant problems, it nonetheless provides a useful starting point for this chapter.[10] Bhabha's conception has been so inspiring and infuriating to scholars in no small part because of its implicit utopianism.[11] As his spatial metaphors indicate, hybridity emerges only when individuals distance themselves from existing cultural and political identities. In Great Britain, for example, genuine social transformations have been inhibited by widespread attachments both to a notion of Englishness inseparable from the imperial past and to the political categories of right and left that permeate every sphere of daily life. To accept the idea of hybridity as a "third space," then, involves far more than a rejection of notions of fixed and pure identity; nor is Bhabha satisfied with the vision of hybridity as a harmonious blending of cultural traditions. As the quotation from the previous paragraph indicates, Bhabha is primarily concerned with the creation of radically new identities, ones that are not bound by the traditions from which they emerged. And literature plays such a significant role in the process of hybridizing only because social processes mirror textual practices, as Bhabha's critics sometimes caricature him to believe; post-colonial artists and scholars "open up space," for Bhabha, because their works insist upon the possibility of alternatives to the dominant beliefs circulating in a culture at a given time. A generous reading of Bhabha would thus see in his evocative, if nebulous, characterization a sense that no single, strict definition could encompass or even predict the forms hybridity might take.[12]

Even a cursory reading of fiction written by immigrants from the Caribbean, Africa, and Asia prior to the 1980s, however, reveals substantial problems with generalizing Bhabha's theory. Novels such as *The Satanic Verses* might substantiate sweeping declarations that all cultures are in a continuous process of hybridizing,[13] but Jean Rhys's *Voyage in the Dark* (1934) paints a very different picture. Rhys portrays England as inhospitable in climate and culture, and the tendency by the English characters to identify the immigrant protagonist Anna Morgan with black West Indians limits the kinds of interactions they are willing to have with her. Similar experiences are portrayed in the writings produced during the first waves of large-scale immigration from the colonies in the 1950s, including George Lamming's *The Emigrants* (1954), V. S. Naipaul's *The Mimic Men* (1967), and Sam Selvon's *The Lonely Londoners* (1956). Selvon's West Indian immigrants may walk the streets of London on a Sunday dressed "like Englishmen, with bowler hats and umbrella and the *Times* sticking out of the jacket pocket so the name would show," but they remain a foreign and unwelcome presence.[14] Nor does the novel suggest that its characters somehow destabilize Englishness; their efforts to mimic the habits and patterns of dress of the English display deep admiration. To the extent that the novel is read as an effort to engage with the challenges facing Afro-Caribbean immigrants in Britain, Bhabha's vision of a third space does not appear to be even a remote possibility. Selvon's generation appears less interested in the radical transformation of British society than in the more modest goals of integration and peaceful coexistence.

Even when Selvon portrays instances of what Bhabha would call "cultural mimicry," he does not attach similar political significance to them. Bhabha envisions mimicry as a strategy that can produce hybridity by destabilizing colonial authority and identity: "The effect of mimicry on the authority of colonial discourse is profound and disturbing. For in 'normalizing' the colonial state or subject, the dream of post-Enlightenment civility alienates its own language of liberty and produces another knowledge of its norms."[15] Selvon's sequel to *The Lonely Londoners*, *Moses Ascending* (1975), would seem to be a perfect text for demonstrating Bhabha's thesis. In this novel, Moses Aloetta mimics English middle-class civility: purchasing a home, stocking a liquor cabinet for guests, and, in an ironic reversal of *Robinson Crusoe*, hiring an illiterate white named Bob to be "my man Friday" and perform services as batman and manager of his rental property.[16] Yet Moses' mimicry of English middle-class life does not appear to challenge colonial authorities so much as to satirize the aspirations of black immigrants. Moses' rapid fall from landlord living in an attic "penthouse" to resident in his own basement indicates the futility of his effort to join the middle class.

The narrator of Naipaul's *The Mimic Men* comes closer than perhaps any other character produced by the *Empire Windrush* generation to articulating a vision of cultural hybridity; however, it is consistently undercut by the narrative he tells. From the first pages of his story, Ralph Singh characterizes himself as deliberately constructing his identity. On arriving in London, he declares, "It was up to me to choose my character, and I chose the character that was easiest and most attractive."[17] His subsequent narrative reveals that he has been engaged in a process of selectively appropriating cultural traditions ever since he was a child on the West Indian island of Isabella. Elements drawn from the West Indies, India, and England enabled Ranjit Kripalsingh to become Ralph Singh, and even after he is forced at the age of forty to return to England as an exile, he declares in the final pages of the novel that he is a "free man."[18] However, the novel establishes a pattern whereby such assertions are followed by suggestions that his identity is determined variously by birthplace, cultural tradition, and other people. He admits that the character he "chose" in London was created by the housekeeper of his boarding-house, Lieni;[19] after his final assertion of freedom, he worries whether or not he will be "reengaged in that cycle from which I have freed myself."[20] Indeed, cyclicity is the dominant metaphor for describing time in the novel, undercutting his claims to be fashioning an identity for himself.

After hybridity becomes a term widely circulating within the Anglo-American academies in the late 1980s, it continues to be dismissed by novelists including Joan Riley (*The Unbelonging*, 1985), David Dabydeen (*The Intended*, 1991; *Disappearance*, 1993), and Caryl Phillips (*The Final Passage*, 1985; *Cambridge*, 1991). What is particularly striking in Phillips's work is that even when both immigrants and the English demonstrate a desire for cultural interaction, nothing like Bhabha's vision of a "third space" emerges. In the case of *The Final Passage*, West Indian immigrant

Leila Preston breaks off her friendship with a white neighbor because she begins to associate all white women with her husband's mistress.[21] The novel does recognize hybridity to be an inevitability in ways that many novels of previous decades did not; when Leila fantasizes about returning to the West Indies and burns all of the objects and garments that remind her of England, she nonetheless has a premonition that her two children will return to England when they grow up. But hybridity does not represent an unambiguously desirable reality. Phillips underscores this perception in *Cambridge* by recalling the racist history of the terminology of hybridity within nineteenth-century pseudo-scientific discourses.[22] Set on a West Indian plantation in the nineteenth century, the novel portrays the slaves' physician, Mr. McDonald, declaring that "the clearest evidence of West Indian moral turpitude was to be found in the social evil of miscegenation, a practice contrary to the Anglo-Saxon nature, and one that gave rise to a sub-species of hybrid."[23] The novel's female protagonist, Emily Cartwright, later echoes these sentiments despite her putatively enlightened views,[24] and her own prejudices prevent her from engaging in any real conversation with the English-educated slave Cambridge. The structure of the novel emphasizes the impossibility of achieving Bhabha's notion of cultural hybridity; Emily's and Cambridge's narratives are physically separated into distinct sections, and their representations of each other are relatively superficial. There is literally no "third space" in the novel in which they might interact.[25]

The seeming impossibility of cultural dialogue untainted by racist systems of power and prestige highlights the dependency of Bhabha's "third space" on a conception of history defined in psychoanalytic terms. While Benita Parry's characterization of the third space as an "ideology-free zone" is an overstatement in that Bhabha never stipulates that people must abandon their ideologies,[26] she is correct that Bhabha describes an almost utopian scenario in which all parties involved can, to a large degree, entertain the possibility that the perspectives of others might be legitimate. The implication, for Parry, is that the interaction Bhabha envisions to occur in the third space represents "a conversation scripted by the critic, and is remote from what could properly be described as a dialogue, where a minimum prerequisite is surely that each party perceives the other as an agent of knowledge."[27] Bhabha's argument is rescued from such a charge only as long as his premise about the psychoanalytic nature of colonial history is accurate. According to this idea, colonial ideology is best understood as the national equivalent of psychic repression, utilized by Britons attempting to erase the memory of events that would contradict portrayals of the Empire and its benefits.[28] In a conversation in which his premise holds, every representation that mystifies or conceals such events requires an act of repression, the content of which will haunt the speaker even if it is not directly voiced by the other parties in the conversation. Hence, in Bhabha's conception, a kind of intercultural dialogue will inevitably, though often belatedly, occur between colonizers and the colonized. And the waves of immigration from the 1950s through the 1970s could be perceived as the literal manifestations of what Freud termed the return of the repressed.[29]

Bhabha's theory is unsatisfactory for literary historians, however, less for its questionable political analysis than for its failure to provide a rationale for why the "return of the colonial repressed" is not a central theme of immigrant fiction written in the 1950s–70s. Even in the works of Kazuo Ishiguro, whose first three novels appear in the 1980s and portray the unraveling of official narratives by repressed memories, historical shifts are characterized in terms more materialist than psychoanalytical. In his masterpiece of English mimicry, *The Remains of the Day* (1989), Ishiguro portrays the destabilization of Englishness as the result of globalization and the infusion of American capital. The country house, a central symbol of Englishness for three centuries and one of the most identifiable icons of postwar British heritage, has been purchased by an American, Mr. Farraday, as a trophy to impress his friends.[30] What is striking in Ishiguro's portrayal is the disappearance of any unquestionable authority to verify the genuineness of heritage. When his American friend Mrs. Wakefield declares the seventeenth-century architecture of Darlington Hall to be fake, "Very skilful, but mock,"[31] Mr. Farraday is at a loss as to how to defend the authenticity of his purchase. His anxiety is apparent in his subsequent cross-examination of his butler, Mr. Stevens:

> I mean to say, Stevens, this *is* a genuine grand old English house, isn't it? That's what I paid for. And you're a genuine old-fashioned English butler, not just some waiter pretending to be one. You're the real thing, aren't you? That's what I wanted, isn't that what I have?[32]

The destabilization of Englishness apparent here and throughout *The Remains of the Day* suggests that the rise of cultural hybridity in the 1980s should be attributed in no small part to its compatibility with enterprise culture. Mr. Farraday's probing questions come not because he rejects or desires to deconstruct Englishness; to the contrary, he is enamored by the possibility of acquiring "authentic" Englishness by purchasing icons of national heritage. Prior to the era of enterprise culture in the 1980s,

Farraday's aspiration was infeasible. Englishness was perceived as an essence separate from, though often manifested through, heritage objects. Selvon's West Indians might dress like Englishmen, but they were neither taken to be English nor perceived as likely to hybridize English culture. By the late 1980s, however, Farraday's aspiration becomes much more reasonable: an entire "heritage industry" was premised on the idea that tourists from home and abroad could experience and "buy" Englishness. Indeed, according to Robert Hewison, the Thatcher administration promoted the consumer as a model for citizenship in ways that belied her rhetoric of restoring Victorian values.[33]

The rhetoric and metaphors used to describe hybridity by cultural theorists are similarly consistent with the goals of Thatcherism and enterprise. Bhabha's stated aim of establishing "new structures of authority" by dismantling existing authorities and breaking away from established traditions could easily be misappropriated to rationalize Thatcher's efforts to dismantle trade unions, privatize industries, and foster an individualist entrepreneurial spirit. E. San Juan Jr. suggests that similarities are not confined to rhetoric but also include basic assumptions about identity. According to San Juan, hybridity theories assume that identity is a commodity that may be understood through paradigms "based on the dynamics of market exchange-value whereby assorted goods can be made equivalent."[34] The consumer becomes the model hybrid subject, mixing and matching identities without committing himself or herself to a static set of traditions or community.

The point here is not to minimize philosophical and political differences between advocates of enterprise culture and cultural hybridity but to suggest that their similarities enabled the latter to gain broad purchase in a political climate in which multiculturalism was a fashionable term and not often a serious goal. Nor should we conclude from criticisms such as San Juan's that hybridity can only reproduce existing structures of power. As Steven Connor notes, the mimicry of Englishness in *The Remains of the Day* provoked considerable anxiety among its first reviewers, who almost uniformly insisted on emphasizing the purportedly Japanese characteristics of the author and his novel, even though Ishiguro himself was raised in Great Britain since the age of five and his novel focuses almost exclusively on English characters.[35] Indeed, Ishiguro's novel suggests that one of the more significant criticisms of Bhabha's theory needs qualification. Parry faults Bhabha for envisioning an agonistic rather than antagonistic relationship between the colonizer and colonized, suggesting that he is "positing colonialism as a competition of peers rather than a struggle between the subjugated and the oppressor."[36] While this criticism is valid for conceptions of hybridity in postcolonial nations struggling for independence from Britain, it is less so in the British context where the social tensions between white Britons and minority populations are shaped by the widespread desire among the latter to be accepted as British.

RUSHDIE'S RETURN TO ROOTS

The novels of Salman Rushdie are cited more than the works of any other novelist in debates concerning hybridity, though the tendency to view *The Satanic Verses* as a kind of "proof text" for Bhabha's theory has obscured the distinctive evolution of his thinking. Rushdie initially formulates his vision in a novel devoted to the history of post-independence India, *Midnight's Children* (1980). In this novel, the 1,001 magically gifted children born within the first hour of independence form a group called the Midnight Children's Conference in order to discuss how they might contribute to the development of their nation. The organizer of the conference and protagonist of the novel, Saleem Sinai, calls upon his fellow children to reject partisanship and ideology:

> Do not permit the endless duality of masses-and-classes, capital-and-labour, them-and-us to come between us! We … must be a third principle, we must be the force which drives between the horns of the dilemma; for only by being other, by being new, can we fulfil the promise of our birth.[37]

Saleem's vision of a "third principle" is immediately rejected by his fellow children, particularly his rival Shiva. Yet the failure to enact this ideal is not an indication of its worthlessness. Every successful political movement in *Midnight's Children* achieves its ends through sectarian violence; independence itself represents a disappointment as much as a triumph, as the former colony becomes the separate nations of India and Pakistan. The ideal of a "third principle" is valuable precisely because it has never been enacted, and is thus not tainted with a history of partisanship or violence. And the novel articulates the need for a "third principle" by exploring how historical choices guided by sectarianism and self-interest have led to present social ills.

The similarities between Rushdie's "third principle" and Bhabha's "third space" are caused, in no small part, by a shared frustration with "multicultural" initiatives in Great Britain. During the 1980s, Rushdie increasingly concluded that neither Labour nor Conservative parties were willing to confront the racial tensions plaguing the country, and efforts to promote multiculturalism were insufficiently idealistic, mired in political compromise and low expectations. In one of his most inflammatory essays, "The New Empire within Britain," Rushdie condemns multiculturalism as a means of perpetuating imperialism. He declares: "Multiculturalism is the latest token gesture towards Britain's blacks, and it ought to be exposed, like 'integration' and 'racial harmony', for the sham it is."[38] According to Rushdie, multiculturalism in Britain is introduced as a means of limiting violent political protests against systemic racism, not as a means of addressing its root causes or transforming British society. And because multiculturalism is motivated by expediency rather than the desire for justice, its implementation frequently discourages genuine intercultural dialogue. Cultural differences are portrayed as either trivial issues of taste or incommensurable beliefs, rendering mutual understanding either unnecessary or impossible.

Rushdie has become one of the most influential postwar British writers, and *The Satanic Verses* represents the culmination of more than a decade of reflection about the possibility of cultural hybridity. In his essays, Rushdie trumpets the novel's focus on hybridity: "*The Satanic Verses* celebrates hybridity, impurity, intermingling, the transformation that comes of new and unexpected combinations of human beings, cultures, ideas, politics, movies, songs ... It is a love-song to our mongrel selves."[39] Yet the opposition between hybridity and purity in *The Satanic Verses* is much more complex than the opposition between the "third principle" and sectarianism in *Midnight's Children*. As Simon Gikandi recognizes, the originality of *The Satanic Verses* in Rushdie's oeuvre and British fiction as a whole lies in its critique of both the terminologies of authenticity and purity used by nationalists and the terminologies of migrancy and hybridity used by postcolonial writers and theorists. Gikandi writes: "neither term [home or exile] is endorsed or negated entirely. The novel insists on being read as a set of irresolvable oxymorons or as a series of what Fredric Jameson has defined as antinomies. There is, in fact, a crossing over from home to exile, exile to home."[40]

Gikandi's insight is important to keep in mind because the plot of the novel implies a rejection of hybridity. The novel opens with a magical realist account of Bombay film star Gibreel Farishta and actor Saladin Chamcha hybridizing into "Gibreelsaladin and Farishtachamcha" as they fall toward the English Channel from their exploding plane.[41] Yet the novel closes with a sentimental account of Chamcha leaving England to return to his childhood home in India, where he reconciles with his father; reclaims his real name, Salahuddin Chamchawala; and finds romantic bliss with Zeenat Vakil that he never found with his ultra-English wife, Pamela Lovelace. Any endorsement of hybridity is presumably further undercut by the fact that Saladin's newfound happiness is possible only after Gibreel commits suicide.

The novel's conclusion implies not an outright rejection of cultural hybridity but rather significant concerns about its potential consequences. Earlier in the novel, Saladin is mistaken for an illegal immigrant and incarcerated. He is subjected to verbal and physical abuse by the police, who deny him his rights and, after they discover he is a British citizen, conceal their actions by locking him up in a sanatorium. In another magical realist move, Rushdie portrays Saladin's interactions with the police as literally hybridizing him. Their inhumane treatment transforms him into an animal, a "demi-goat" complete with horns and hooves (163). Saladin is informed by another prisoner that their transformation is the result of how they are represented by the English: "They have the power of description, and we succumb to the pictures they construct" (168). Hybridity is portrayed here not as a liberatory strategy but the dehumanizing result of living in a racist society. Dialogue is disrupted by the police insistence that Saladin is no longer even speaking, just bleating like a goat (159).

Saladin's transformation reveals how theories of cultural hybridity often rely on questionable metaphors. In contrast to nineteenth-century ideas of biological hybridity, cultural hybridity in postcolonial accounts presupposes a constructivist notion of identity. Particularly in accounts influenced by poststructuralist theory, such as Bhabha's, constructivism is characterized in radical terms, suggesting not only that identities are inculcated rather than biologically given but also that individuals have a great deal of control over the kinds of affiliations they make. Identities are characterized as performed, and Rushdie portrays this mentality in the character of Saladin. As the initial description of him makes apparent, Saladin believes that he can construct and then perform his identity as if it were only another acting role:

Mr. Saladin Chamcha had constructed this face with care – it had taken him several years to get it just right – and for many more years now he had thought of it simply as *his own* – indeed, he had forgotten what he had looked like before it. (33)

Yet the paragraph ends with a description of how Chamcha's equally constructed English accent slips when he undertakes a return trip to India after a fifteen-year absence. Such slips only increase after he arrives in India, undercutting more optimistic characterizations of performance that imply that identities may be chosen or modified at will. To take the meta-phor of performance seriously means to recognize that identities represent enactments for others, and are profoundly influenced by the contexts of a performance as well as the reactions of those witnessing it. Saladin's identity for the police who incarcerated him was as much a performance as his English persona, but the scene reveals what the earlier one only implies: performance often is not determined by the actor's desires.[42]

Both Rushdie and Bhabha have been criticized for celebrating a notion of identity based on performance. Yet, as early as his essay "The Commitment to Theory" (1989), Bhabha has been careful to distinguish himself from other poststructuralist and postmodern theorists who celebrated the idea that identities might be appropriated and discarded, mixed and matched without respect to cultural and historical contexts. For Bhabha, the idea of cultural hybridity opens up the possibility of moving beyond identity polit-ics altogether. "The fragmentation of identity is often celebrated as a kind of pure anarchic liberalism or voluntarism," Bhabha writes, "but I prefer to see it as a recognition of the importance of the alienation of the self in the con-struction of forms of solidarity ... The crucial feature of this new awareness is that it doesn't need to totalize in order to legitimate political action or cul-tural practice."[43] Bhabha's complex and evocative language makes it easy to overlook the distinction he is drawing, and his reliance on Rushdie's work as a central example to demonstrate his theory has not helped to resolve the issue because Rushdie himself has been subject to similar accusations.[44] But the sources for Bhabha's theory were not only cosmopolitan migrants or comprador intellectuals, as sometimes alleged; Bhabha himself suggests that he was inspired by the working-class men and women involved in the miners' strike of 1984–85.[45] Bhabha observed that people involved in the strike were motivated by different values and commitments, and that these values were to some degree in conflict; yet the strikers were nonetheless able to negotiate a common political cause among themselves. Thus, Bhabha's fantasy of "elud[ing] the politics of polarity and emerg[ing] as the others of our selves" should not be taken as a vision of appropriating the cultural practices and traditions of other groups; rather, it represents a vision of pol-itical activism that honors the various values and motivations of individuals working toward a common cause.[46]

Rushdie's most significant contribution to debates surrounding hybrid-ity and multiculturalism in Great Britain comes from his insistent ques-tioning of the assumption that cultural hybridity promotes progressive politics. Despite Bhabha's rhetoric of moving beyond polarities of left and right, his examples consistently demonstrate a preference for progressive causes. Indeed, debates surrounding hybridity have been waged largely among left-leaning scholars. A reading of Rushdie's nonfictional writings during the 1980s would suggest that he, too, shares this assumption. *The Satanic Verses*, however, can be read to suggest otherwise, that conceiving of identity in terms of metaphors of performance serves the interests of enterprise culture more than progressive political movements.[47] This more pessimistic view is apparent in Saladin's ardent support of Margaret Thatcher for the majority of the novel; it is even more apparent in the portrayal of Saladin's boss, the advertising and media executive Hal Valence. Valence's fortune depends on selling the idea that identity can be constructed and reconstructed; the man himself is described as "pure, self-created image, a set of attributes plastered thickly over a body that was, in Hal's own words, 'in training to be Orson Welles'" (266). The model of late capitalism that he embodies thrives in a postmodern environment in which subjectivity can be characterized, following Iain Chambers, as "provisional, contingent, composed in a speech of becoming, where the performative event takes precedence over any structural grammar" (118). While Chambers's notion of subjectivity might be politically progressive to the extent that it subverts static social hierarchies, Thatcher's economic and social policies were never focused toward preserving them. Despite her rhetoric of Victorian values, the Prime Minister was committed to a broad social transformation whose goal, according to Valence, is "literally to invent a whole goddamn new middle class in this country" (270). Thus, Chambers's claim that exile represents a defining symbol for this global age becomes a sad reality in the figures of the new middle class, who demonstrate no loyalties to anything other than profit. Such people, in Valence's words, are: "People without background, without history. Hungry people. People who really *want*, and who know that with [Thatcher], they can bloody well *get*" (270). Even Thatcher loyalists such as Saladin are dispensable once they no longer offer a marketable commodity; when customer surveys indicate diminished interest in ethnic stars, Valence fires Saladin despite his plea that they have a contract.

The shift toward a sentimental narrative of "return to roots" that occurs in the final sections of the novel, however, should not be read as a rejection of hybridity in the face of its appropriation by advocates of enterprise culture. Rather, it represents a means of preserving the egalitarian ideals that both Bhabha and Rushdie associate with the concept by introducing an essentialistic component to identity. The problem with hybridity in the marketplace is that minorities or those with limited access to capital have minimal say in how people are perceived, what social codes govern public

essentialism

interactions, and what identities are available. Yet, instead of focusing on the possibility of creating a utopian third space, Rushdie asserts that identity is not in fact entirely malleable. Even when Saladin takes on the form of a demi-goat in response to the inhumane treatment to which he is submitted, his values and perceptions remain largely consistent. Earlier in the novel, Saladin's conversation with Zeeny suggests that the metaphor of performance does not necessarily require that identity is defined in radically constructivist terms. Zeeny insists that Saladin's Englishness is nothing more than a "shell" that can be cracked to reveal an Indian self beneath (57). This idea of an essentialistic core of identity is emphasized toward the end of the novel. In a particularly striking passage, Saladin is portrayed as recovering parts of himself long abandoned:

> Saladin felt hourly closer to many old, rejected selves, many alternative Saladins – or rather Salahuddins – which had split off from himself as he made various life choices, but which had apparently continued to exist, perhaps in the parallel universes of quantum theory. (523)

The recovery of an essential self signified by the text's reversion to the name Salahuddin provides the necessary check to an enterprise culture in which all identities are defined as commodities. Saladin discovers that his rejected selves cannot be bought, sold, or even permanently renounced. The preservation of particular features of an individual's self ensures the possibility that hybridity could at least theoretically be the result of a genuine cultural interchange rather than rampant consumerism or postmodern eclecticism.

The irony that promoting the ideal of cultural hybridity ultimately requires defending a quasi-essentialistic conception of identity is not lost on Rushdie, whose works throughout the 1980s vigorously rejected terminologies of authenticity, roots, and purity. In Rushdie's previous novel, *Shame* (1983), for example, the narrator declares: "Roots, I sometimes think, are a conservative myth, designed to keep us in our places."[48] Nor does this sensibility disappear in *The Satanic Verses*, as the quotation in the last paragraph indicates. Rushdie insists that Saladin recovers multiple selves rather than a single identity, lending credence to Martin Corner's argument that the ending of the novel rejects the "nostalgia for authenticity."[49] But here, in his most controversial novel, Rushdie portrays a return to roots and at least some nominal idea of authenticity out of an awareness that cultural hybridity remains viable as a politically progressive ideal only as long as some elements of identity are not readily reducible to commodities.

PERFORMING IDENTITY IN KUREISHI

Rushdie's conception of an essentialistic hybridity has rarely been endorsed or imitated by subsequent authors, nor is it apparent even within his own later writings. The violent protests against *The Satanic Verses* and the often contemptuous rhetoric employed by Rushdie's supporters polarized public debates over multiculturalism in ways that discouraged the more nuanced claims made in the novel. The press in Britain and the United States, in particular, cast the so-called "Rushdie affair" in hyperbolic terms, portraying the "civilized world" under siege.[50] The *fatwa* declared in 1989 by Iran's Ayatollah Khomeini against Rushdie for writing *The Satanic Verses* only reinforced such a perception in the minds of many Britons, and encouraged xenophobic portrayals of Islam and Muslim immigrants. Authors and public intellectuals who might otherwise have been critical of such simplifications felt personally touched by Rushdie's plight, and denunciations of Iran and Rushdie's critics by luminaries including Norman Mailer and Wole Soyinka reinforced the equation of fundamentalism and essentialism. Rushdie himself followed this practice in defending his novel, derisively characterizing his critics as "apostles of purity."[51] Thus, even after Rushdie sought a rapprochement with Muslims in the 1990s, few seemed interested in more essentialistic conceptions of hybridity.

It should not be entirely surprising, then, that reflections on hybridity in the post-Thatcher era were inspired less by the emergence of New Labour or a more radical left movement than by the rise of Islamic fundamentalism in Great Britain. Hanif Kureishi's *The Black Album* (1995), for example, portrays fundamentalism as a potentially compelling alternative to multiculturalism. The repudiation of a corrupt, soulless, and decaying West preached by Riaz Al-Hussain strikes a chord with the novel's protagonist, Shahid Hasan, who finds himself with little prospect for the future. Studying at a college in London known for gang rivalries more than academics, Shahid finds companionship and a sense of purpose when he joins Al-Hussain's Islamist group, even though he is increasingly repelled by their intolerance, ignorance, and violent acts. The rejection of both assimilation and hybridity by Al-Hussain appears all the more compelling when contrasted with the inarticulate and pessimistic rhetoric of the intellectual left in the novel, embodied by Dr. Brownlow, one of the instructors at Shahid's college. Brownlow laments his loss of faith in socialism and the working class, and is unable either to diagnose the source of the left's failure or to propose a vision for a better future. After initially dismissing the working class as "a bunch of fucking greedy, myopic c-cunts," Brownlow becomes increasingly incoherent, a point that Kureishi emphasizes by making Brownlow a stutterer: "No, no, it's more complicated. Very complicated ... I can't say they've betrayed us – though I think it, I do! It's not true, not true! They've b-b-betrayed themselves!"[52]

Kureishi preserved the ideal of hybridity in his more famous, pre-*fatwa* novel, *The Buddha of Suburbia* (1990), by redefining it in terms of personal reinvention or self-fashioning rather than more utopian visions of political or social transformation. The novel opens with the bold, though qualified, assertion by its biracial protagonist that he embodies Englishness: "My name is Karim Amir, and I am an Englishman born and bred, almost."[53] His claim is belied by the racism he endures, but Karim is successful at transforming himself to conform with the latest fashion trends in ways that first-generation immigrants such as his father and Nasser of *My Beautiful Laundrette* could scarcely imagine. He even learns to exploit his ethnic identity as a kind of cultural capital that enables him to get acting jobs despite his lack of experience or training. Indeed, Karim's successes have led Sukhdev Sandhu to argue that Kureishi is attempting to move beyond hybridity altogether toward a notion of aggregation. According to this idea, Karim can learn to "wear as many masks, create as many personae, explore as many new avenues as he wishes."[54] But the novel's focus on acting and performance as the defining metaphors for identity means that social change occurs almost exclusively on the level of the individual. Karim may find success as an actor and lover, but it requires abandoning strong commitments to any group or political vision. His brief flirtation with the Communist Party is as shallow and fleeting as his attraction to flared pants. Even when he regrets his ignorance of Indian culture, he can conceive of such knowledge only as another commodity that might bring him advantage. At the funeral of his father's best friend, Karim notes: "So if I wanted the additional personality bonus of an Indian past, I would have to create it."[55] Karim's claim of affinity with other Indians at the funeral does not imply any sense of political solidarity or duty. And the possibility of broader social transformation is entirely abandoned in the novel's final scene: Karim and his family celebrate his new role on a soap opera even as the television in the background announces Thatcher's electoral victory.

The fairy tale quality of the conclusion to *The Black Album* indicates the more significant difficulties Kureishi faces in articulating a viable vision of hybridity in the 1990s. Karim's adventures in self-fashioning were certainly hindered by the racial prejudices of those around him, but Karim is relatively free to pursue his aspirations because they corresponded with the anti-establishment ethos of the 1970s. Shahid, in contrast, comes of age a decade later, in an environment that places significant pressure on British Muslims to demonstrate their affiliations publicly. Disillusioned with mainstream political parties, Shahid finds himself forced to choose between the fundamentalism of Al-Hussain and the postmodernism of Deedee Osgood, a tutor from the college and Dr. Brownlow's wife. His affair with Deedee can hardly be seen to provide a model for British multiculturalism, however. The two lovers agree to form their own private community "[u]ntil it stops being fun" (287), but neither has made any provision for their future. Even their escape from London is possible only due to the timely and violent intervention of Shahid's older brother, Chili, who arrives as Al-Hussain and his followers are assaulting the two lovers for Shahid's perceived treachery.[56] The fantasy resolution to the novel is subsequently reaffirmed by the discovery that Al-Hussain's followers have scattered after a botched attempt to firebomb a bookstore. Islamic fundamentalism is presented as a self-destructive phenomenon, and the most violent member of the group is burned to death by his own firebomb. But the unnamed casualty of the conflict is Shahid's Muslim identity, which appears to be shed at the end of the novel without remorse.

Although *The Black Album* ultimately condemns both Brownlow's socialism and Al-Hussain's fundamentalism, it is difficult to discern a political vision that it endorses. As Bart Moore-Gilbert notes, Kureishi's problem is more complex than that faced by earlier critics of Thatcher, such as Malcolm Bradbury and David Lodge.[57] Their satires of the Prime Minister depended on highlighting discrepancies between her rhetoric and actual political policies. By the late 1980s, however, Thatcher had abandoned the idea of consensus or "one nation politics" that had defined the British political scene since the end of World War II. The challenge Kureishi faced in writing *The Black Album*, then, was to articulate an alternative vision of national identity, and the postmodern philosophy associated with Deedee appears to provide the basis for Kureishi's alternative. Under Deedee's influence, Shahid discovers the apparent fluidity of identity; near the close of the novel, he declares: "There was no fixed self, surely our several selves melted and mutated daily?" (285). But in the absence of any idea of a common social good, Shahid's discovery becomes tied to the pursuit of pleasure. Deedee encourages Shahid to perceive identity as a performance, and in a central scene of the novel she dresses Shahid up in drag (127–28). Here, too, the fluidity of identity lacks any significant political implications; it serves simply as enticing foreplay for the lovers. In this context, Shahid and Deedee's inability to articulate a more significant commitment to each other at the end of the novel is unsettling. The pursuit of pleasure has replaced the desire to effect political change apparent earlier in the novel, with the result that the vision of cultural hybridity, already diminished in *The Buddha of Suburbia* to an idea of personal reinvention, has almost disappeared.

Kureishi's focus on pleasure can be dismissed as escapist, but it highlights an often unstated assumption about human nature underlying theories of cultural hybridity. For theorists of hybridity including Chambers and Bhabha, hybridity is characterized as a fundamentally desirable state of being. People who opt for a "pure" fixed identity are consistently portrayed as ignorant, repressed, or repressive – the clear implication is that hybridizing is a "natural" phenomenon, and something in human nature gravitates toward mixing. Critics of hybridity have often tacitly accepted this assumption. Dirlik, Parry, San Juan, and others have rejected hybridity as the privilege of elite migrants, but such a criticism implies its desirability. Kureishi, in contrast, recognizes that fundamentalist Islam has come to thrive in Great Britain because it provides disaffected minorities with coherent identities in ways that notions of multiculturalism and hybridity have not. To the extent that Kureishi's protagonists occupy a state of "in-betweenness,"[58] it is a terrifying and unstable position. Shahid cannot be both Muslim and postmodern; he cannot maintain his relationships with both Al-Hussain and Deedee.[59] In a post-*fatwa* world, identities appear to be both exclusive and inescapable, a declaration of political and moral values as much as a description of who one is. In such an environment, Bhabha's vision of moving "beyond" identity is simply not sustainable.

THE ENDS OF HYBRIDITY

The *fatwa* against Rushdie has proved to be a significant event for a number of younger writers in Britain, and images of Britons burning copies of *The Satanic Verses* have been replayed not only in *The Black Album* but also in Zadie Smith's *White Teeth* (2000) and Monica Ali's *Brick Lane* (2003). The riots provoked by Rushdie's novel in many ways confirmed reservations about hybridity that have been apparent in Afro-Caribbean and South Asian fiction since the 1950s, and novels published since the mid-1990s have largely abandoned Rushdie's celebratory vision of a hybrid nation. *Brick Lane* is indicative of a much more modest and practical vision, one that is sensitive to abiding obstacles. In particular, Ali highlights the economic and biological assumptions underlying the idea that identity is a performance. The protagonist of *Brick Lane*, Nazneen Ahmed, is a young immigrant from Bangladesh married to a much older husband, Chanu, who resists his wife's efforts to learn English or to travel outside of the home. The explorations of Rushdie's and Kureishi's protagonists are rarely limited by education, linguistic barriers, responsibilities for others, or their own biology. Nazneen, in contrast, has only rudimentary knowledge of English, and she is forced to spend long hours at home sewing in order to earn enough money to provide for her two daughters. Perhaps most significantly, her own body limits what kinds of identities she can perform. While she is pregnant, Nazneen feels that it has become only one of a series of restrictions placed on her: "She looked and she saw that she was trapped inside this body, inside this room, inside this flat, inside this concrete slab of entombed humanity."[60]

Brick Lane nonetheless remains committed to an attenuated form of cultural hybridity because, like *The Black Album*, it portrays political activism as inevitably degenerating into self-consuming violence. The most striking example of the negative effects of activism is presented through Nazneen's lover, Karim. Karim begins the novel as a kind of admirable cultural hybrid, a devout Muslim and child of immigrants who nonetheless proudly claims that Britain is his country.[61] His initial efforts to organize Bengalis living on the estates are motivated by the desire for all individuals to participate in the British political system, not to promote isolationism or revolt. Yet Karim becomes increasingly intolerant of cultural differences and his own hybridity as he becomes more engaged in organizing his community. He abandons Western dress in favor of panjabi pajamas and a skullcap; shortly thereafter, he begins spouting Islamist conspiracy theories about the attacks on September 11, 2001. The novel emphasizes the tragedy of his transformation by portraying the march he organizes to protest British racism degenerating into a riot in which rival Bengali gangs fight each other and loot Muslim shops and homes. Witnessing the chaos around him, Karim can only lament, "Man, what it is, it's a mess! It's not even *about* anything anymore. It's just about what it is. Put anything in front of them now and they'll fight it. A police car, a shop window, anything."[62]

Ali's skepticism about both political activism and utopian scenarios of intercultural dialogue leaves her novel strangely inflected by a kind of "post-ideological" celebration of entrepreneurial individualism. Long after Thatcher has fallen from grace, *Brick Lane* presents characters who learn to exploit enterprise culture; who shrink away from affirming specific political or religious ideologies or even broadly based identity politics; and who shift their focus away from claiming political equality to acquiring fiscal independence. Nazneen ultimately learns to reject both her husband's disillusionment with Great Britain's false promises of egalitarianism and her lover's radicalism. Her solution is to work hard in order to provide a better life for her children. And this focus on fiscal independence provides unexpected dividends. In the final scene, Nazneen is taken by her daughters and her friend Razia to an ice rink, giving her the opportunity to live out a fantasy she has had since her earliest days in her adopted country. When she protests that one cannot skate in a sari, Razia replies: "This is England … You can do whatever you like."[63] The image of cultural hybridity here – ice skates and saris – does not connote a broader political or social transformation for the country or even a kind of personal freedom that Shahid and Deedee aspire toward at the end of *The Black Album*. Nazneen and Razia are taking an afternoon off from work as a special occasion. Nor is Razia's insistence on wearing a sweatshirt with a Union Jack printed on the front accompanied by anything resembling the bold rhetoric that Karim employs in *The Buddha of Suburbia*. Razia's clothing stands as a symbol of personal pride about her citizenship, not a political statement about the future of Great Britain.[64]

A similar reluctance to make political demands for broader social transformation is found even in novels that purportedly celebrate hybridity. The almost instant canonization of Zadie Smith's *White Teeth* is intimately linked to its promotion of what Laura Moss calls "everyday hybridity."[65] According to this idea, Smith represents a third generation of black British writers who can finally take for granted that the United Kingdom is their home, and this confidence enables them to present hybridity in less controversial and confrontational terms than previous generations could. In one of the most cited passages of the novel, the narrator declares that the results of "the century of the great immigrant experiment" can now finally be seen on a playground:

> It is only this late in the day that you can walk into a playground and find Isaac Leung by the fish pond, Danny Rahman in the football cage, Quang O'Rourke bouncing a basketball, and Irie Jones humming a tune. Children with first and last names on a direct collision course … It is only this late in the day, and possibly only in Willesden, that you can find best friends Sita and Sharon, constantly mistaken for each other because Sita is white (her mother liked the name) and Sharon is Pakistani (her mother thought it best – less trouble).[66]

Passages such as this exemplify, for Dominic Head, Smith's capacity to dismiss the relevance of cultural "roots" in ways that earlier authors, including Rushdie, never could.[67] What is particularly intriguing here are the assumptions underlying such an argument. The everydayness of hybridity in this account suggests that social change is an organic process rather than the result of sustained political activism, and the novel confirms this attitude. The children in the scene above are hybrids by virtue of birth, not the result of any actions on their part. A similar sense that hybridity is an inevitable and universal condition appears throughout the novel. As a result, the novel can promote the idea of a hybrid, multicultural Britain simply by uncovering the "impure," multifaceted histories of its characters. No intercultural dialogue is necessary because, as Alsana Iqbal notes, no one is purely English. Even the apparently ultra-English Chalfen family turn out to be third-generation immigrants who have changed their names to conceal signs of foreignness. The insistence upon syncretism, as Peter Childs astutely recognizes, ensures that hybridity cannot be escaped.[68]

In many respects, however, *White Teeth* follows *The Satanic Verses* in presenting a plot that undercuts its own more celebratory rhetoric about multiculturalism. In the paragraphs that follow the description of the multicultural playground, Smith portrays a fear of hybridity among not only the English but also immigrants like Alsana. The portrayal of her fear is satirical, but the narrator concedes that "[i]t is both the most irrational and natural feeling in the world" (272). The satirical tone is also directed at the idea that England represents a "Happy Multicultural Land" (384). Irie Jones, daughter of an English father and a Jamaican mother, is consumed with self-loathing, belying any hope that the multicultural vision of the playground can be generalized to British society as a whole. Indeed, like Saladin Chamcha of *The Satanic Verses*, Irie ultimately rejects her early efforts to mimic Englishness in order to "return" to a fantasy postcolonial homeland. In Irie's case, however, the fantasy has no grounding in personal experience because she was born and raised in Great Britain.

White Teeth ultimately attempts to link its "return to roots" narrative to neither an idea of identity politics nor essentialism but rather to a "rootless" cosmopolitanism. Irie's growing interest in the life of her Jamaican grandmother is not primarily guided by the desire to create an alternative history for herself or to establish some privileged cultural knowledge; instead, she sees in it the possibility of escaping her existing ties to family and England. She seeks "the perfect blankness of the past" (332). She collects a hodgepodge of newspaper articles, birth certificates, maps, but does not bother even to read them; she marks each piece with an X and places it under the sofa on which she sleeps. In this way, the novel sees her escaping the cultural traditions in which she was raised. Cultural traditions are repeatedly characterized in negative terms throughout the novel, narrowing characters' scope of vision and constraining their desires. At one point, the narrator declares that tradition is "even more sinister" than religion (161). According to this idea, a preoccupation with the past and tradition leads individuals to organize themselves according to race, gender, religion, or other exclusive identity groups in ways that conceal the purportedly syncretic nature of all identities. Irie's commitment to syncretism gives her the insight to articulate what appears to be the utopian fantasy promoted by the novel as a whole: "In a vision, Irie has seen a time, a time not far from now, when roots won't matter anymore because they can't because they mustn't because they're too long and they're too torturous and they're just buried too damn deep. She looks forward to it" (437).

White Teeth captures the utopianism guiding Bhabha's conception of hybridity in ways that even Rushdie's work never does. As noted earlier, Bhabha is committed to the recovery of cultural traditions or effaced histories only insofar as it represents a necessary precondition to creating an environment in which a more genuinely multicultural Britain might emerge. Rushdie's cosmopolitan migrants largely share Bhabha's sense that traditions inhibit the exploration of new identities. What Rushdie appears unwilling to accept, however, is the extent to which the idea of authenticity must be abandoned in the process. The "blankness" that Irie seeks would be abhorrent to Rushdie. Indeed, the unexplored anxiety in *The Satanic Verses* is the possibility that hybridity involves the elimination of the idea of authenticity altogether. Saladin's mimicry of Englishness is understood as a kind of cultural masquerade in which he performs identities; the novel never entertains the possibility that his Indian identity is simply one more mask. Saladin's lover Veeny is frustrated and saddened when she sees that he looks "just like a blank" when he is not performing (61), and she commits herself to help him recover his authentic Indian identity.

The fantasy of finally dispensing with roots and authenticity in *White Teeth* raises the possibility that the notion of hybridity may soon be eclipsed by terms less associated with identity politics. Hybridity proved to be such a powerful notion in British fiction published during the past three decades largely because it provided the means for authors to broaden conceptions of Britishness. As the novels explored in this chapter indicate, however, while the idea of hybridity helped to challenge notions of a stable and fixed national identity, it rarely provided a viable model for social change. And the renewed interest in humanism among artists and scholars alike may be guided, in part, by a sense that it might capture more fully the utopianism that initially fueled postcolonial theories of hybridity. Smith herself abandons discussions of hybridity and roots in her third novel, *On Beauty* (2005), focusing instead on the legacies of humanism in art and philosophy. Dominic Head has identified similar concerns in *White Teeth*, arguing that the novel's vision of a world without roots demonstrates affinities with Paul Gilroy's notion of "planetary humanism."[69] For Gilroy, ideas of "race" are ethically indefensible because they represent latent legacies of fascism, and hybridity is inescapably tied to its historical place within discourses of race. Only by moving beyond the idea of race itself toward a notion of a planetary humanity can there be hope of resuscitating "democratic and cosmopolitan traditions that have been all but expunged from today's black political imaginary."[70] Gilroy readily recognizes that such a project is utopian in the current political climate, and that the function of his argument is not to effect the radical transformation he envisions but rather to establish the preconditions for it. But skeptics might note similarities to the rhetoric Bhabha employed in describing his vision of a third space. That scholars such as Dominic Head can read *White Teeth* in terms of both hybridity and humanism suggests that they are at least not incompatible, and it remains to be seen whether the shift away from hybridity might lead to significantly different ideas of what constitutes multicultural Britain.

CHAPTER 5

Ghosts of essentialism: racial memory as epistemological claim

Whereas hybridity has been the source of heated debate, essentialism has not: the theoretical strawman for more than thirty years, it has been repudiated by scholars of every theoretical position. The oddity here is that essentialism, as it is typically defined, presents such an absurdly untenable position that is hard to imagine who its advocates currently are and why it would even merit serious scholarly rebuttals. Nor are the critiques of essentialism helpful in this regard: rarely do they identify contemporary proponents of the idea that individuals within a particular ethnic, gender, or religious group possess from birth a common "essence" that is homogeneous and unchanging.[1] Yet the enduring hold essentialism maintains in the humanities is apparent in the fact that scholars continue to rehabilitate qualified versions of the idea: "nominal essences," "nonessentialist essentialism," "fluid essences," and, perhaps most famously, "strategic essentialism."[2] Calling for academics to take "the risk of essence," Stephen Heath and Gayatri Spivak asserted in the late 1970s and 1980s that self-conscious forms of essentialism could create political solidarities among otherwise diverse groups of individuals that must not be neglected despite the risk of lending credence to regressive beliefs about essence.[3] Proponents of strategic essentialism have been motivated not only by a pragmatic sense that progressive minority political movements need to employ all the tools at their disposal but also by a nagging perception that essence is unavoidable. Spivak speaks of the "unavoidable usefulness" of essence despite the fact that it is "very dangerous."[4] Even explicitly constructivist theories like Spivak's deconstruction depend on essentialistic assumptions, according to Diana Fuss. "In my mind," Fuss argues, "it is difficult to see how constructionism can *be* constructionism without a fundamental dependency upon essentialism."[5]

Rethinking the resilience of essentialism within academic discourses becomes increasingly urgent in the face of the resurging interest in identity and identity politics. Since the mid-1990s, poststructuralist dismissals of identity as "pernicious and metaphysically inaccurate"[6] have increasingly been challenged by feminist philosophers and cultural critics including Linda Martín Alcoff, Naomi Schor, Sandra Harding, Christine Battersby, and Sonia Kruks; race theorists including Kwame Anthony Appiah and Henry Louis Gates Jr.; and, most recently, "postpositivist realists" including Satya Mohanty, Paula Moya, and Michael Hames-García. The third group, in particular, has made a compelling argument for viewing identities as powerful sources of knowledge and experience. If there has been a move to renew interest in identity by redefining it in explicitly anti-essentialist terms, however, many scholars and the public at large continue to associate identity with essence. Walter Benn Michaels represents one of the more eloquent if outspoken advocates of this position, arguing that assertions of cultural identity depend on prior assumptions of "racial ontology."[7] Michaels's argument can be read as part of a larger political trend in the United States that characterizes race consciousness as a form of racism and an obstacle to social progress.[8] Responding to this argument requires not only following Mohanty's lead in rejecting the assumed connection between identity and essence but also reconsidering how essentialism is understood. Fuss's concern that "a certain paranoia around the perceived threat of essentialism" has foreclosed more ambitious investigations into specificity and difference is as valid today as it was when she voiced it back in 1989.[9]

While it is impossible to address all forms of essentialism within the space of a chapter, one form in particular has represented an embarrassment to scholars of ethnic American literatures: racial memory. The idea of racial or blood memory implies that individuals can "remember" events that were not personally experienced because they share an often mystical or genetic connection with firsthand witnesses. Racial memory is nearly ubiquitous to ethnic American novels in the latter part of the twentieth century. Frank Chin's *Donald Duk*, Paule Marshall's *Praisesong for the Widow*, N. Scott Momaday's *House Made of Dawn*, and Toni Morrison's *Beloved* represent only a small sample of novels that implicitly or explicitly invoke the idea of racial memory. Yet the paucity of scholarly attention devoted to racial memory in literary texts that are otherwise the subject of so many books and articles points to the embarrassment and even anxiety that the concept provokes. Racial memory flies in the face of the defining metaphors of ethnic and cultural studies, which Stuart Hall identifies as "unsettling, recombination, hybridization and 'cut-and-mix.'"[10] In contrast, Momaday eschews the highly qualified and theoretically nuanced versions of essentialism mentioned above – asserting, for example, that it is "an obvious and foregone conclusion [that] the Indian and the white man perceive the world in different ways."[11] In perhaps his most provocative statement to date, Momaday claims the "existence of intrinsic variables in man's perception of his universe, variables that are determined to some real extent on the basis of his genetic constitution."[12] Read at face value, this claim challenges what has become a basic, almost foundational truth in the humanities: the idea that identity is a social construction and not a biological fact.

Momaday's assertions provoke an intriguing question that traditional analyses of essentialism have difficulty answering: what would lead ethnic minority writers to invoke forms of essentialism that previously justified a history of racist and imperialist policies? The tendency in academic scholarship to read essentialism in ontological terms, as Michaels does, fails to provide answers that can account for the complexity of racial memory in ethnic American fiction. Ontological readings focus attention on the ways in which essentialism involves positing a presocial "being" who is defined by an "essence" that predetermines an individual's identity in racial terms. But literary texts such as *Beloved*, *Donald Duk*, and *House Made of Dawn* do not use racial memory to construct identity in terms of exclusion, homogeneity, and stability, as the ontological reading of essentialism would predict. As a large body of scholarship has shown, these texts challenge such notions of identity, insisting instead that identity arises out of a long and difficult process of social interactions. Thus, unqualified dismissals of racial memory as "absurdly racist," to use Arnold Krupat's phrase,[13] may be less useful than shifting the way essentialism is analyzed, to consider it in more epistemological rather than ontological terms. This would involve focusing on the extent to which racial memory in these texts enables, prohibits, or otherwise transforms cultural knowledge. Put in Mohanty's terms, the key question is what is the epistemic significance of essentialism.

My analysis builds on the work of Mohanty and others who have argued for the epistemic significance of identity. "Identities are theoretical constructions that enable us to read the world in specific ways," Mohanty argues, rejecting the tendency to read identity in terms of being and ontology.[14] I will argue that certain forms of essentialism have a similar epistemic significance, enabling individuals to redefine how they perceive themselves and the social ascriptions attributed to them. The epistemological focus proposed here could begin to address oversimplified dismissals of essentialism and, in the process, respond to the call by E. San Juan Jr. (2002) to reassess the fundamental guiding principles of ethnic studies.

A critical re-examination of essentialism could represent a crucial part of such a reassessment, for the dominant conception of essentialism within ethnic studies does not provide a compelling explanation for its enduring attraction among academics and artists. Ultimately, essentialism remains alluring not because it implies the existence of static identities or common experiences that define a people; rather, it implies the possibility for certain personal experiences to yield reliable knowledge about broader social patterns of exploitation.

RACIAL MEMORY AS KNOWLEDGE CLAIM

The work of N. Scott Momaday serves as the focal point for my exploration because no other contemporary ethnic American author has achieved such long-standing literary prominence while still consistently portraying identity in terms that are highly susceptible to charges of essentialism.[15] The idea of racial memory is present even in his first, Pulitzer Prize-winning novel, *House Made of Dawn* (1968). It becomes central to his thinking several years later in his essay "The Man Made of Words," which was initially presented at the First Convocation of American Indian Scholars in 1970. In this address, Momaday describes a meteor shower that occurred on November 13, 1833. The story of its occurrence, according to Momaday, has been so significant to Kiowa cultural identity that it continues to be told to this day. He insists that it is retained not simply as a historical event, however, but as a memory passed down from generation to generation: "So deeply impressed upon the imagination of the Kiowas is that old phenomenon that it is remembered still; it has become a part of the *racial memory*."[16] This claim is justified by noting that it was previously asserted by a now-deceased elder, Ko-sahn, who also "remembered" the event:

And in the racial memory, Ko-sahn had seen the falling stars. For her there was no distinction between the individual and the racial experience, even as there was none between the mythical and the historical. ("Man," 102)

That Momaday's early formulations of racial memory never received the criticism his later characterizations did speaks to the preoccupations and anxieties that have guided ethnic studies. While "racial experience" certainly suggests an essentialistic characterization of Native Americans, Momaday does not claim that it has a biological or genetic basis in "The Man Made of Words" or other early works. Only after he starts making explicit references to the "genetic constitution" of Native Americans in some later pieces such as "Personal Reflections" does his theory elicit significant critical responses from scholars of ethnic American literatures. But particularly within the academic environment of the 1980s and early 1990s, in which postmodern and poststructuralist theories held a significant, if not dominant, position, Momaday's earlier invocations of racial memory could be read in metaphorical terms. The first major book on Momaday's writing, Matthias Schubnell's *N. Scott Momaday: The Cultural and Literary Background* (1985), never entertains the possibility that racial memory should be read literally; subsequent works on Momaday produced by Susan Scarberry-García, Louis Owens, and Chadwick Allen have tended toward the same conclusion.[17] Momaday himself seems to encourage this kind of reading. The description of racial memory in "The Man Made of Words" comes in the context of a broader argument for a constructivist account of Native American identity. "[A]n Indian is an idea which a given man has of himself," he asserts ("Man," 97). Anticipating Joan Scott's famous claim that "experience is a linguistic event,"[18] Momaday states: "It seems to me that in a certain sense we are all made of words; that our most essential being consists in language ... We are what we imagine. Our very existence consists in our imagination of ourselves" ("Man," 96, 103). The conflation of personal and vicarious experience apparent in his characterization of racial memory can thus be read simply as a recognition that the events of his own life are mediated through the same linguistic forms that have been used to describe the meteor shower and other Kiowa traditions.

The tendency by scholars of ethnic studies to read portrayals of racial memory in purely metaphorical terms reflects a desire to reconcile the multiple and sometimes conflicting goals within the discipline. The goal of challenging negative stereotypes of ethnic minorities might incline scholars to condemn Momaday's conception of racial memory as essentialistic. Krupat's dismissal of racial memory as racist would, for example, appear to be guided by this line of thinking. Krupat has received significant criticism, however, in large part because another central goal among ethnic studies scholars has been the reconstruction of experiences of oppressed populations left out of imperial histories.[19] Indeed, the second goal has often been perceived to be the necessary precondition for accomplishing the first. Rey Chow characterizes the situation eloquently when she writes that the inescapable reality facing many exploited populations is that "[t]he native's victimization consists in the fact that the actual evidence – the original witness – of her victimization may no longer exist in any intelligible, coherent shape."[20] To move beyond the status of victim

requires, according to Chow, access to accurate histories of victimization – histories that have been systematically suppressed. In this context,
portrayals of racial memory by Momaday and other ethnic American
authors become politically palatable, if theoretically problematic, because
they potentially offer sources of knowledge that are not determined by
the post-Enlightenment epistemologies that have guided the production
of Western historical narratives. For scholars struggling to compensate
for the fact that there are often few if any remaining firsthand sources to
provide memories left out of historical records, Momaday's conflation of
personal knowledge, historical research, and imaginative speculation is
alluring despite its potential to be deemed essentialistic.

The problem is that existing theories of strategic essentialism provide
neither an answer to critics such as Walter Benn Michaels nor an interpretation of racial memory that lends any credence to the claims made by
the authors who invoke the term. Spivak's advocacy of "a *strategic* use of
positivist essentialism in a scrupulously visible political interest" is motivated by a sense that success within political arenas requires temporarily
compromising theoretical insights into the constructed nature of collective identities.[21] For Spivak as much as for Michaels, then, racial memory has no epistemological significance. It could be useful in establishing
political coalitions among diverse populations, but it cannot help individuals to interpret their personal experiences or to clarify their moral
responsibilities. To the contrary, the cultivation of an ethnic, gender, or
class consciousness among members of a population involves implicitly
endorsing the economic and social forces that created stratification in the
first place. Thus, from Spivak's perspective, Momaday should employ the
terms *Native American* or *Indian* only temporarily as a means to accomplishing a political end, and his ultimate goal should be moving "beyond"
identity.

A response to Michaels that is more compatible with Momaday's ideas
could involve developing Mohanty's argument that identities are best
understood not as strategic positions but as theoretical constructions
that enable individuals to interpret their social location and personal
experience.[22] According to this account, racial memory need not be read
as either a simple metaphor or a strategy but rather as part of an epistemological inquiry into the conditions that have led ethnic minorities to
perceive themselves as alienated both from a mainstream white culture
and from a marginalized culture associated with their ancestors. In other
words, Mohanty suggests that the examination of certain experiences historically associated with an identity group could help other individuals

identified with that group to understand their current social circumstances whether or not they consciously affiliate themselves. This idea is apparent in Momaday's later novel, *The Ancient Child* (1989). Set, as the protagonist is called, is a middle-aged artist of international renown who has compromised his art in the name of satisfying a white bourgeois clientele. Yet nothing in his personal experience or immediate life provides him with the means to analyze and diagnose the sources of his unhappiness; seduced by his own success, he has internalized the values of the art world he resents. Set recognizes that he needs to look beyond his personal experiences in order to interpret his situation, and his "longing for something beyond memory" guides him to learn more about the Kiowa culture of his paternal ancestors.[23] As was the case in Momaday's earlier major works including *House Made of Dawn*, *The Way to Rainy Mountain*, and *The Names*, *The Ancient Child* portrays Kiowa mythic narratives as providing a crucial source of knowledge for characters to use in interpreting their life experiences. By recasting his personal experiences in relation to the "Kiowa story of Tsoai," as it is referred to in the opening pages of the novel, Set is able to redefine his priorities and to establish more healthy relationships. Momaday marks his psychological growth by portraying him transforming into a bear at the end of the novel, just as the boy in the Kiowa story did before him. His final words in the novel, "Yes. I am *set*,"[24] recognize that his new self-perception is intimately linked to a new affiliation with Kiowa cultural identity; "Set" is not only his nickname but also the Kiowa word for bear.

Momaday's insistence on retaining the terminology of racial memory even in later works such as *The Ancient Child* suggests that he differs somewhat from Mohanty in his belief that a certain kind of essentialistic thinking is a necessary precondition to gaining more accurate knowledge about an individual's social circumstances. As demonstrated earlier, Momaday does not invoke racial memory to claim that all Native Americans have precisely the same experiences, but he does appear to believe that some kind of racial memory is necessary for establishing an individual's Native American identity. Intriguingly, racial memory is necessary not only for acculturated individuals like Set; even characters in the mythic narrative plot line of *The Ancient Child* rely on racial memory for their knowledge. The epilogue, for example, describes the life of the great-great-grandson of the woman who witnessed the boy's transformation into a bear, and the narrator declares that this descendent knew Tsoai "in the current of his blood."[25] In this final scene, Momaday makes no reference to genetics or biology as the source of racial memory. Yet if *The Ancient Child* suggests that Momaday's most extreme genetic claims might not be representative of a conception of racial memory developed and refined over thirty years, the novel nonetheless portrays identity using metaphors and language that historically have been associated with essentialism. Momaday does not provide readers with less inflammatory terminologies of tribal memory or narrative identity but continues to invoke the language of blood. Such invocations would be unnecessary and counterproductive according to Mohanty's theory of identity in large part because it assumes that all human beings, given the right circumstances, have the capacity to distinguish between reliable knowledge and mystification. Set's inability to make such distinctions without access to racial memory suggests that Momaday does not share such optimism.

ESSENTIAL KNOWLEDGE

Chadwick Allen's work provides a useful lead for understanding why Momaday retains the idea of racial memory throughout his career. Allen argues that Momaday's conception of racial memory should be read against a historical context in which an individual's genetic composition was used by the United States government to regulate the activities of Native Americans and to disqualify individuals who did not appear Indian enough from receiving federal Indian status and the benefits associated with it. In Allen's reading, racial memory represents a trope for the "appropriation and redeployment of the U.S. government's attempt to regulate American Indian personal and political identities through tabulations of 'blood quantum' or 'degree of Indian blood.'"[26] The epistemic significance of racial memory, according to this idea, comes from its transformation of ethnic identity. By redefining ethnicity in terms of racial memory rather than blood quantum, Momaday rejects governmental efforts to impose an external definition of Native American identity. Racial memory represents a conflation of imagination, storytelling, and genetics that cannot be objectively measured or verified. Insofar as race is defined by possessing "racial memory," it becomes a social construction determined by the tribal community rather than a biological fact certified by outsiders.

As Allen's argument indicates, racial memory is not invoked by Momaday to resolve ontological questions about what constitutes race; if anything, it complicates such questions by challenging widespread assumptions that race is a readily identifiable category. But its usage is motivated by a recognition that racial categories have significant effects on how individuals perceive themselves whether or not such categories have any biological basis. "Once labels are applied to people," Kwame Anthony Appiah writes, "ideas about people who fit the label come to have social and psychological effects. In particular, these ideas shape the ways people conceive of themselves and their projects."[27] Thus, if race or other identity categories are social constructions, this does not necessarily imply that individuals can change the ascriptions attributed to them. Individuals do not choose their identities in isolation; identities arise out of ongoing interactions with others, and represent a response to facts that are outside of a person's control. From birth, individuals are located within particular places, social networks, and religious institutions. As people mature, they may respond differently to the social circumstances of their birth and upbringing, but no one can entirely ignore them.[28]

The power of social ascriptions to direct an individual's explorations of identity are painfully if humorously apparent in Frank Chin's *Donald Duk*. In sharp contrast to Momaday's characters, the young eponymous protagonist of Chin's novel desires nothing more than to assimilate into mainstream white American society, declaring, "Hey, everybody's gotta give up the old and become American. If all these Chinese were more American, I wouldn't have all my problems."[29] This fantasy cannot be realized, however, because those around Donald continually ascribe to him a Chinese identity. In his school, for example, his teachers bring him in front of the class to pronounce Chinese phrases and his fellow students question him about Chinese history as if he possessed some inherited expertise, despite the fact that he was born and raised in the United States. Donald himself internalizes these ascriptions and fails to recognize the extent to which his knowledge of Chinese culture and history is based on American stereotypes.

The critique of demeaning and essentialistic portrayals of Chinese in *Donald Duk* does not involve a broader rejection of essentialism, however. Characterizations of "the timid, introverted Chinese" immigrants and their helplessness against the "violently individualistic and Democratic Americans" presented in Donald's history class are not refuted by the presentation of factual historical data countering such perceptions (2), although Donald and his white friend Arnold Azalea do present such data near the end of the novel (151–52). Instead, Chin invokes racial memory as the necessary antidote to negative social ascriptions. Through a series of dreams, Donald relives the experiences of Chinese immigrants working to build the Central Pacific leg of the transcontinental railroad, with particular focus on the day the workers set the world record for the most miles of track laid in a single day. The legitimacy of Donald's racial memory of the experience is ratified at the end of the novel when he and Arnold present to their class a history book that contains a photo of the Chinese workers, and Donald's face is clearly depicted among them.

That Chin felt it necessary and appropriate to invoke racial memory in order to counter racist portrayals of Chinese is striking because it suggests that he, like Momaday, finds critiques based on empirical historical evidence insufficient to transform the perceptions of mainstream white society or ethnic American populations. The stability of prevailing identity stereotypes in the face of contradictory evidence can be attributed, according to Christine Battersby, to the fact that they appeal to the founding metaphysical categories that have informed Western notions of individuality and subjectivity since Aristotle.[30] The Aristotelian notion of essence identifies a single conception of what constitutes humanity regardless of culture, race, or gender. The practical result of this conception is that a fairly narrow and culturally contingent idea of humanity is cast as the universal norm against which all others are judged. In other words, there are not "separate but equal" masculine and feminine essences; women are botched men who failed to develop their full potential to be "human" while forming in their mother's womb. Battersby's argument could be extended to the racial identities under consideration in this chapter. This logic suggests that negative portrayals of racial minorities employ essentialistic reasoning, yet such reasoning does not identify multiple racial essences, simply a single "ideal" essence against which other races are measured and found wanting. The portrayals of Chinese and white Americans in Donald's history book confirm this. Timidity and introversion are not alternatives to individualism but indicators of the failure of Chinese immigrants to develop this characteristic. Efforts by disempowered groups to conceive of essentialistic identities for themselves thus represent not a capitulation to but a critique of Western metaphysics.

The combative rhetoric Chin employs in his nonfictional essays, however, has made it difficult for scholars to appreciate the complexity of racial memory in his fictional works. In "Come All Ye Asian American Writers of the Real and the Fake" (1991), for example, Chin accuses fellow Asian American authors Maxine Hong Kingston, David Henry Hwang, and Amy Tan of producing revisionist histories of Chinese immigrants that reinforce racist stereotypes.[31] The binary of "real/fake" histories that Chin employs in his argument is simplistic, and has been rightly criticized as "essentialist dogma."[32] Yet Chin is not ignorant of the extent to which Asian American identity represents what Lisa Lowe calls a "racial

formation" that is produced from an ongoing and often contentious negotiation between the state and its citizens.[33] In his first play, *The Chickencoop
Chinaman* (1972), Chin insists that Chinese American identity is a social
construction; his protagonist, Tam Lum, declares: "Chinamen are
made, not born."[34] Chin and the other editors of the literary manifesto
AIIIEEEEE! An Anthology of Asian-American Writers (1974) emphasize
this conception of identity in their reading of the play, asserting that Lum
is "forced to invent a past, mythology, and traditions from the antiques
and curios of his immediate experience."[35] Even his critique of Kingston's
revision of the Fa Mu Lan legend in *The Woman Warrior* seems motivated
less by a belief that cultural traditions should never be changed than by a
sense that Kingston seems uninterested in distinguishing between more
and less accurate knowledge. Chin asserts: "We expect Asian American
writers, portraying Asia and Asians, to have a knowledge of the difference
between the real and the fake. This is a knowledge they have admitted they
not only do not possess but also have no interest in ever possessing."[36]

This last point is crucial to understanding Chin's literary works.
While his portrayals of racial memory in *Donald Duk* are motivated in
no small part by a desire to provide a corrective to the work of other
Asian American authors, Chin seems more interested in the possibility
that essentialistic identifications with ancestral figures can help individuals to make sense of their experiences in light of their social location
and the ways in which it shapes self-perceptions.[37] As *Donald Duk* makes
apparent, mainstream portrayals of ethnic populations have served to
perpetuate social inequalities by obfuscating the experiences and epistemologies of individuals identified with such populations. The history books
in Donald's class conceal the contributions made by Chinese immigrants
to the growth and development of the United States in order to limit the
aspirations of Chinese Americans. The success of this strategy is apparent
in the fact that Donald never seeks out knowledge that might contradict what he learns in the classroom until after he perceives a personal
connection to the past in his dreams. Only after he perceives himself
as personally experiencing the lives of Chinese immigrants working on
the railroad is he able to reevaluate his internalized racism. Chin is careful not to suggest that Donald's racial memories are the sole cause of his
transformation; rather, they inspire him to engage in an exploration of
the history of Chinese immigrants that, in turn, leads him to reinterpret
his own experience. After he experiences his dreams he begins to look at
his surroundings in a new way, recognizing things he had never noticed
previously, such as the images of the Chinese folk hero Kwan Kung all

over Chinatown (82). As long as Donald passively accepts the conception of Asian Americans presented to him, he is incapable of perceiving
Chinese culture as possessing viable and fundamentally different values
from those he learns in class and through the media.

The specific experiences or events described as racial memories thus
do not represent a genetic inheritance; to the contrary, racial memories refer to knowledge that individuals do not possess, at least initially,
but must acquire in order to counter negative social ascriptions of themselves. As Avery Gordon argues in her book *Ghostly Matters: Haunting
and the Sociological Imagination*, there is a whole range of experiences
about individuals' everyday lives that they are prevented from fully
understanding by exploitative institutions of power. "In a culture seemingly ruled by technologies of hypervisibility," Gordon argues, "we are
led to believe that neither repression nor the return of the repressed, in
the form of either improperly buried bodies or countervailing systems of
value or difference, occurs with any meaningful result."[38] To the extent
that these technologies are successful, individuals do not remember their
own exploitation or recognize cultural practices that might endorse values
that challenge established systems of power. The implication of Gordon's
argument is that if individuals are "haunted" by residual traces of these
experiences and subsequently desire to acquaint themselves more fully
with them, they would not be appealing to a timeless racial or sexual
essence. Rather, they would be drawing upon whatever limited knowledge they currently possess, and the recognition of a set of experiences
only partially felt or understood could lead individuals to sense a broader
field of cultural knowledge with which they would have been more fully
and personally acquainted if not for the intervention of outside forces.
In the case of *Donald Duk*, Donald has had his dreams for some time;
however, until Uncle Donald confronts him about his self-loathing, the
dreams are incomprehensible nightmares: "they are all bad because they
are all about Chinese he does not understand" (25). Donald's increasing
capacity to understand the dreams over the course of the novel does not
imply that his identification with his great-great-grandfather and other
Chinese immigrants working on the railroad leads him to recover their
experiences in some unmediated fashion, although Donald does envision
himself interacting with them in his dreams. Rather, the dreams represent
a significant form of knowledge because they enable Donald to combine
his imaginative fantasies, his repressed frustration with racist descriptions
of Chinese Americans, and his historical research into the experiences of
Chinese immigrants. To use Gordon's terms, both Chin's and Momaday's

characters are "haunted" by Chinese and Kiowa traditions, respectively, with which they have gained only limited familiarity while growing up. And by asserting the existence of racial memory, they can insist on the possibility of redefining their ethnic identities in light of their own historical research and reconstructions rather than being condemned to draw upon existing stereotypes.

The idea of racial memory proposed here, however, does not endorse what Sonia Kruks calls an epistemology of provenance – the idea that certain experiences inherently "belong" to a certain group and that other people cannot understand them. Like Michaels, Kruks demonstrates significant misgivings about identity politics and the essentialistic identity claims typically associated with them. Recognizing that identity politics can be enabling for marginalized groups, Kruks nonetheless considers the risks of endorsing epistemological and ethical relativism to be too significant. In her account, identity politics "threatens to undercut notions of shared (or even communicable) experience to such an extent that possibilities for a broadly based emancipatory politics are de facto subverted."[39] Yet the history that Chin creates in his novel supports rather than subverts the idea of shared and communicable experience. The history of Chinese Americans is not cast as separate from that of mainstream white America; to the contrary, it represents an integral though effaced part of American history. Chin takes pains to show that Arnold learns as much as Donald about the history of Chinese immigrants and that their joint efforts to acquire such knowledge provide the basis for solidarity not difference. Even though Donald, not Arnold, is characterized as experiencing racial memory, the two boys learn to confront their teacher and his racial stereotypes together. Donald and Arnold have different relationships to the knowledge of the experiences of Chinese immigrants, a difference that arises from their different social locations and personal identifications. But racial memory is not invoked by Chin or Momaday to alienate mainstream white American readers. Rather, the term provides the means to acknowledge the inescapable reality that each individual is, in Alcoff's terms, "always already in the world, committed to a large array of beliefs, engaged in ongoing projects and practices."[40] Arnold and Donald can share similar goals even though the knowledge they acquire has different implications for how they perceive themselves and their relationships to others.

Chin emphasizes the communicability even of experiences that are characterized as racial memories. Initially, Donald's dreams are no more comprehensible to the novel's readers than to its protagonist; Chin ensures this situation by refusing to provide any description of them whatsoever. Once Donald overcomes his internalized racism, however, he and readers witness them simultaneously. This is significant because if Chin were claiming that only Chinese Americans could possess such experiences, then he could have limited the description of the dreams to what Donald chooses to retell. Instead, Chin emphasizes that Donald himself receives these experiences in mediated form, just as readers do: "The dream comes on like a movie all over his eyes" (25). The cinematic simile invoked here indicates the potential for anyone to witness the events portrayed in Donald's dream. Chin studiously avoids the language of blood or genetics in his portrayal of the dreams, suggesting that other characters and readers do not necessarily need to make the essentialistic identification with Chinese American ancestors that Donald does. Similar identifications are unnecessary because Donald's identification enables him to interpret the previously incoherent and fragmentary accounts of Chinese American railroad workers into a coherent narrative form – the "movie" of his dreams – which subsequently can be apprehended by anyone willing to question mainstream portrayals of Chinese Americans. Perhaps the most significant indication of Chin's optimism in this regard is that Donald himself comes to rely less and less on his dreams as a source of knowledge as the novel progresses; increasingly, his knowledge is the result of his own research, conversations with older Chinese Americans, and his interactions with Arnold.

Momaday also portrays the knowledge designated as racial memory to be communicable; however, he more explicitly cautions against the conclusion that such knowledge can be divorced from the social circumstances in which it was produced. In "The Man Made of Words," for example, Momaday asserts that Ko-sahn's racial memories give her an attitude toward the environment that all Americans need to emulate: "We had better learn from it. Surely that ethic is merely latent in ourselves … We must live according to the principle of a land ethic. The alternative is that we shall not live at all" (102). By referring to Ko-sahn's racial memory as "latent" in all Americans, Momaday reaffirms the idea that anyone theoretically could possess her knowledge. Simply learning the story of the meteor shower, however, is insufficient. The knowledge Momaday attributes to Ko-sahn results from her effort to interpret her personal experiences with respect to the values and beliefs of those who have transmitted the story over the generations. And this identification would be possible only by learning about the cultural and historical contexts of the story.

The different attitudes toward the communicability of experience held by Chin and Momaday point to the very different cultural and political contexts in which they are writing. Chin has worked over his career to document the contributions made by Chinese immigrants and their descendents to the growth of the United States; both his fictional and nonfictional writings insist that American history cannot be understood without telling the history of Chinese Americans. That Arnold and Donald can find the material evidence for such claims in a public library emphasizes the communicability of the experiences of Chinese Americans. Momaday, in contrast, has worked to preserve a tribal, national consciousness that is separate from the one developed by European colonists and their descendents. Racial memories describe experiences before the arrival of Europeans and establish the enduring connection of tribal populations to lands that have been seized. As a result, the question of access to cultural knowledge is intertwined with questions of political claims to territory. Chadwick Allen even speaks of a "blood/land/memory complex" in the writings of Momaday and other Native American authors.[41] Momaday's resistance to the idea that cultural knowledge can be equally available to all, then, is motivated by the recognition that similar rhetoric has been used historically to modify, violate, and ignore treaty obligations.

In his more recent characterizations of Native American identity, Momaday continues to struggle with the challenge of conceiving of identity without having either to rely on invocations of genetics or to admit that anyone could legitimately claim to be Native American. According to this revised understanding, individuals who refuse to identify with at least certain events or experiences that historically have shaped the existence of Native American tribes cannot claim to be Native American. Reflecting on the 500th anniversary of Columbus's "discovery" of America, Momaday writes:

I have been asked, how do you define an Indian, is it a matter of blood content? I say no, an Indian is someone who thinks of themselves as an Indian. But that's not so easy to do and one has to earn the entitlement somehow. You have to have a certain experience of the world in order to formulate this idea. I know how my father saw the world, and his father before him. That's how I see the world.[42]

An act of identification requires more than rudimentary knowledge of the history and culture of a particular group. It also requires individuals to be willing to view their personal experiences in light of those who have been previously associated with the identity label. Momaday's assertion that he shares the worldview of his father and grandfather, in this context, is not meant to justify his claim to Native American identity on genetic grounds. His claim that he knows how his paternal ancestors perceived the world emphasizes that his own identification is based on his lifelong efforts to learn about their lives as a means of providing guidance for his own. Thus, Momaday's portrayals of identity even at this late stage of his career continue to be open to accusations of essentialism, but not a notion of essentialism based on the idea of genetics or timeless essences. Rather, Momaday's portrayal is essentialistic in that he portrays the lives of his paternal ancestors as having sufficient coherence and stability that he can reconstruct them in a form that could subsequently be used as a pattern for his own life.

THE BURDEN OF THE BLOOD

Over the course of this chapter, I have argued against the idea that racial memory necessarily signifies an effort to claim cultural identity through an appeal to a stable and unchanging racial "essence." The central place Momaday and Chin give to the imagination in their historical reconstructions rejects the idea of a fixed, stable past that could be claimed as a genetic inheritance. Momaday's and Chin's works suggest instead that racial memory can signify vicarious experiences that individuals define as central to how they conceive of themselves and their relationships to larger collectives. While this line of reasoning still constitutes essentialism for critics such as Michaels, its difference from the narrowly defined Aristotelian notion of essence means that criticisms tied to that definition do not necessarily apply to racial memory. It is not always the perception of genetic privilege that guides individuals to recover or to acquire greater familiarity with the cultural traditions identified as racial memories; rather, it is often a sense of regret over lacking knowledge that would allow them to share in activities important to their parents and grandparents and to understand many of their own experiences while growing up.

The epistemic significance of racial memory, then, resides in its potential to change how an individual can relate to specific events or experiences. Racial memory recasts knowledge in very personal terms. The ideas, feelings, and perceptions related by these "memories" shape an individual's worldview in ways that other more abstractly felt knowledge does not. It would become increasingly difficult, for example, for Momaday to ignore the effects of acculturation on himself or other Native Americans as he increasingly identifies Kiowa stories as racial memories.

This becomes apparent during a 1970 discussion about Native American oral traditions. Momaday confesses early in the discussion that his own fluency in Kiowa is rather limited: "I had to rely to a great extent on people who are much more conversant with the language than I am. My father speaks it very well. He did some of the interpreting for me."[43] But the initial issue of Momaday's fluency rapidly shifts to a general conversation on the condition of other Kiowas: "I know for a fact that very few young Kiowas, to name but one tribe," Momaday states, "are learning to speak Kiowa. It is a language that is dying very quickly."[44] Racial memory, in this context, leads Momaday to perceive similarities in experience between himself and other Kiowa whom he has never met. And this recognition of shared experience shapes how he can perceive his own project of reconstructing Kiowa traditions and stories. Even his more autobiographical works convey a sense that he writes on behalf of others who have experienced cultural alienation. The prologue to *The Way to Rainy Mountain*, for example, speaks of the oral tradition as having "suffered a deterioration in time," and that what remains is "fragmentary."[45] At the same time, he insists that the idea of Rainy Mountain is nonetheless "as crucial and complete as it ever was" because it can be accessed vicariously through narratives such as his own.

Perhaps the most crucial implication of this conception of racial memory is that knowledge is inseparable from moral responsibility. This responsibility extends not only to other Kiowa and to readers interested in Kiowa culture and history; Momaday suggests that it also extends to the material and people he depicts. As Ko-sahn herself states, her continued existence is contingent upon Momaday's representation. Her apparently relativistic assertion, "You have imagined me well, and so I am," underlines this fact ("Man," 99). Because Momaday recognizes that her existence to the majority of his readers is confined to his writings, he feels a responsibility to render her justly. This is not to suggest that racial memory provides a specific set of ethical guidelines for behavior. Nor does this suggest that morality is based simply on kinship loyalty. In claiming that an Indian is a "moral idea" (97), Momaday asserts that the cultural knowledge required to identify oneself as an Indian involves a broader awareness of, among other things, every human's responsibility to care for the environment. Hence, the idea of an "American land ethic" is a logical result of an exploration into Native American history and culture (101). All knowledge entails greater awareness of the circumstances of others and the ways in which the knower can affect such circumstances, and it is this awareness that Momaday elsewhere terms the "burden of the blood."[46]

I have argued throughout this chapter that certain forms of essentialistic thinking can be vital to undoing what San Juan calls the conditioning
of individuals' "epistemological apparatus" by exploitative institutions.[47]
As my analysis has shown, racial memory concerns what knowledge an
individual considers relevant to his or her identity, how knowledge is
interpreted, and what he or she feels the need to learn on the basis of
what he or she already knows. And narratives exploring this process of
redefining the individual's relationship to knowledge can have implications for a much broader range of readers than those who identify with
the ethnic category to which a racial memory is linked. If San Juan is
correct that economic and social structures exist to exploit all populations, then understanding how such exploitation is enacted with respect
to a particular population can provide insight into its enactment for other
populations. Such a claim would not imply the existence of some grand
metanarrative of victimization or deny genuine differences among the historical experiences of ethnic minority populations. Rather, it would lend
credence to Mohanty's argument that the experiences of oppressed populations merit a kind of "epistemic privilege" precisely because they can
reveal social mechanisms of exploitation to American society as a whole:

That would help explain why granting the possibility of epistemic privilege to
the oppressed might be more than a sentimental gesture; in many cases in fact
it is the only way to push us toward greater social objectivity. For granting that
the oppressed have this privilege opens up the possibility that our own epistemic
perspective is partial, shaped by our social location, and needs to be understood
and revised hermeneutically.[48]

The hope for achieving greater social objectivity ironically guarantees
that essence will continue to be a haunting presence in academic scholarship as well as in ethnic American fictions. Greater objectivity requires,
in part, a continual re-examination of existing historical narratives of
the United States and their portrayals of minority populations. And this
re-examination often involves positing alternative narratives of the past
that may not, initially at least, have compelling material evidence to support them. As Chow and Gordon indicate, the exploitation of certain
ethnic populations has succeeded in no small part because the lives and
experiences of their members have been effaced in existing records. In such
instances, historical reconstructions tend to have an essentialistic quality
to them, but this does not necessarily inhibit critical and self-conscious
inquiry. The fact that essentialistic portrayals posit a nondiscursive reality means that they can be subjected to analysis and refuted as contrary
material evidence becomes available. The idea of race that was used by the

Western powers to justify colonialism and slavery, for example, depended on a set of essentialistic assumptions about biological differences among races that was not sustainable upon interrogation. According to the account of essentialism presented here, only those assumptions that are capable of being refined in light of new knowledge represent potentially reliable ones. That Momaday abandons his claim for a genetic basis of racial memory in "Confronting Columbus Again" indicates his own willingness to modify, if only tacitly, his assumptions, and this is a promising sign for scholars interested in his work. Momaday's refined characterization of racial memory encourages readers to perceive essence not as the goal or conclusion of inquiry but as its starting point. Racial memory is invoked not to provide a fixed or static characterization of individuals but to encourage imaginative explorations of existing portrayals of minority populations from alternative points of view. And the possibility that such explorations might provide more accurate descriptions of human experiences than currently exist will remain tantalizing enough to ensure that essence remains a part of academic discourses in the humanities for the foreseeable future.

CHAPTER 6

Amitav Ghosh and the aesthetic turn in postcolonial studies

While a renewed interest in aesthetics is apparent throughout the humanities, it is particularly striking in postcolonial studies. As recently as 2003, Deepika Bahri lamented what she saw as a "remarkable lack of a sufficiently developed critical framework for addressing 'the aesthetic dimension' (in Herbert Marcuse's words) of postcolonial literature."[1] For decades, the term *aesthetics* – when it appeared in scholarly discussions at all – signaled little more than opprobrium.[2] Since the publication of Bahri's *Native Intelligence: Aesthetics, Politics, and Postcolonial Literature*, however, aesthetics has become a central preoccupation among postcolonial scholars, and books including Nicholas Brown's *Utopian Generations* (2005) and Ato Quayson's *Aesthetic Nervousness* (2007) signal a potentially significant shift in the field. Postcolonial studies first acquired disciplinary legitimacy, according to Robert Young, by devaluing the "aesthetic qualities" of a work and focusing instead on its depiction of "representative minority experience."[3] So, a reversal is not without significant risk. Modern notions of aesthetics, as they emerged in eighteenth-century European thought, were intimately linked to the intellectual and ideological justifications for worldwide colonial expansion. Focusing on the aesthetics of postcolonial literary texts thus risks denying cultural differences under a universalizing, Enlightenment discourse, drawing attention away from political concerns in favor of a rarefied formalism, and realigning the field with its most conservative forebears including Matthew Arnold, Edmund Burke, and T. S. Eliot, for whom aesthetics involved an elitist notion of "high culture" that devalued artistic works produced from Britain's colonies.

Bahri's intervention in *Native Intelligence* has been so timely because it proposes a compromise between the two dominant strands of postcolonial scholarship, which Laura Chrisman and others have characterized as materialist/historicist and culturalist/textualist.[4] The Frankfurt School Critical Theory that provides the framework for *Native Intelligence* enables Bahri to address concerns by materialist critics that postcolonial theories are inattentive to connections between artistic production and global flows of capital; it also enables her to rationalize the study of elite, metropolitan texts that have been widely consumed by Western audiences and crowned with Western literary prizes. The negative utopianism for which she argues provides a compelling alternative to the cosmopolitan migrant utopianism endorsed previously by Homi Bhabha and Iain Chambers, and her readings of Salman Rushdie, Rohinton Mistry, and Arundhati Roy usefully situate their works in a critical though inseparable relation to the material histories surrounding their production.

The risk in promoting aesthetic theories identified with Frankfurt School thinkers is that they might come to dominate how aesthetic questions are read across the board. The very powerful readings produced by Bahri and Brown, for example, presuppose an unnecessarily extreme opposition between so-called positive and negative utopias inherited from Frankfurt School thinking. According to this idea, utopian thinking is either positive in the sense of attempting to represent the concrete features of an alternative world directly or negative in the sense of gesturing toward an alternative world that can be intimated but neither represented nor known at the present moment. The preoccupation with negative utopias by Theodor Adorno, Walter Benjamin, and, to a lesser degree, Herbert Marcuse is founded on assumptions about the worldwide dominance and stability of capitalism, and its apparently unlimited capacity to appropriate utopian representations within a system that commodifies all features of existence. Bahri herself recognizes that Frankfurt School theorists failed to account for the importance of the unique histories of anticolonial resistance. Yet she follows Adorno in characterizing positive utopian thinking as mere "pseudo-reflection,"[5] arguing that what is required is an insistent interrogation of the very idea that we can know what utopia might look like. Brown simply dismisses positive utopias as politically useless and reactionary in that they simply rearticulate current social life in futuristic forms.[6] But even among the most famous authors emerging during the era of decolonization, the novel provides the opportunity to articulate utopian aspirations in positive terms. Readers of Wole Soyinka's *Season of Anomy* (1973), Ngũgĩ wa Thiong'o's *Devil on the Cross* (1980), and Chinua Achebe's *Anthills of the Savannah* (1987) can find very specific descriptions of idealized communities – their ethnic makeup, their economic system, their governance, their attitude toward religion and the supernatural. In the latter two novels, these communities are rapidly eliminated by forces bent on preserving a neoimperialist form of capitalism. But their brief presence suggests that the distinction between positive and negative utopian thinking is not rigid, and the *promesse du bonheur* to which Adornean negative utopias gesture may in fact be more fully realized when combined with efforts to articulate more precisely the needs that must be addressed, and perhaps even the constitutive features of a more utopian world.

My project complements the recent aesthetic turn in postcolonial studies by exploring how aesthetic categories central to Enlightenment reason are reclaimed and redeployed within postcolonial contexts. Particularly within Southeast Asia, Dipesh Chakrabarty argues, European thought has been indispensable, though inadequate, to think through the experiences of political modernity in non-Western nations.[7] Given the centrality of the aesthetic to the formation of modern nation-states in Western Europe and the dominant ideological forms of class society appropriate to them, the importance of sentiments, affections, and bodily habits – the so-called aesthetic realm – to forms of postcolonial reasoning needs to be explored.

Taking my lead from Simon Gikandi's claim that European conceptions of the aesthetic were often valued most by individuals from populations who were deemed incapable of aesthetic experience, I would like to pay particular attention to constructions of beauty in postcolonial literary texts.[8] My focus is guided in part by the desire to bring Frankfurt School nonidentitarian aesthetics into conversation with Kantian and hermeneutic schools of thought. The insistent reappearance of beauty in the political philosophy of both Marcuse and Adorno suggests its enduring capacity to motivate anti-imperialist sentiment. Highlighting this point is particularly important because contemporary discussions of their aesthetics often demonstrate a curious aversion to beauty. This absence is ironic given that Marcuse criticizes Marxist aesthetics for rejecting the idea of the beautiful,[9] and Adorno devotes three chapters of his *Aesthetic Theory* to the topic. My focus on beauty is also guided by the sense that the aesthetic has played a crucial role in the constitution of both colonial and anticolonial thought in ways that have not been fully recognized. The aesthetic has had a mixed career within Western thinking, but it has been crucial to utopian thinking not only among theorists identified with the Frankfurt School. As Terry Eagleton and Geoffrey Galt Harpham suggest, the centrality of the aesthetic to modernity and Enlightenment thinking has to do precisely with its capacity to provide at least a theoretical basis for a utopian society.[10] Kant argued that every judgment of taste presupposes a *sensus communis* – a sense that judgments can and must have universal validity.[11] By making beauty an object of consensus, Kant models in aesthetic judgment a process of intersubjective communication that, in the words of Tobin Siebers, makes "aesthetics indispensable to a democratic conception of political judgment" and the conception of utopia itself.[12]

This chapter explores the engagement with aesthetics undertaken by the Indo-Burmese author Amitav Ghosh. Since his first novel, *The Circle of Reason* (1986), Ghosh has explored the dehumanizing effects of capitalism and imperialism, and his work has been contrasted favorably with Rushdie's by materialist scholars.[13] Yet his repeated declarations of his aesthetic debt to V. S. Naipaul – who perhaps more than any other postcolonial author has been vilified for his putative sympathies with Empire – highlight his complex and evolving attitude toward the aesthetic.[14] For Ghosh, questions of aesthetics are intimately related to questions of utopia, and he has consistently portrayed in positive terms his notion of a more egalitarian society. As was the case with Achebe, Soyinka, and Ngũgĩ, utopias in Ghosh's works tend to be destroyed by the forces against which they respond. Yet his novels refuse to characterize them as failed projects, and they play a crucial role in his efforts to identify in the notion of beauty the possibility of communicating experience while respecting cultural differences.

AESTHETICS SPACES AND IDENTIFICATION

While Ghosh has portrayed utopian communities since *The Circle of Reason*, the connection between aesthetics and utopian thinking is most fully developed in his fifth major work, *The Glass Palace* (2001). Ghosh himself has described this sprawling, multigenerational narrative as both a "family memoir" and a "history of the Indian diaspora in Southeast Asia."[15] The novel traces the tumultuous history of modern Burma (also known as Myanmar since 1989) primarily through the families of Rajkumar (an amoral Bengali entrepreneur who emigrates to Burma at an early age) and Uma Dey (an Indian independence activist). Their lives are shaped by violence: the 1885 deposing of the Burmese royal family by the British, two World Wars, and the 1962 military coup. Yet *The Glass Palace* provocatively portrays its characters seeking out spaces associated with beauty and art, particularly in moments of political crisis. In the first pages of the novel, eleven-year-old Rajkumar dreams of witnessing the marvels reputed to be in the Glass Palace, the residence of the royal family. His opportunity arrives after the British military sack the palace, and crowds of Burmese are looting its contents. Rajkumar's second son, Dinu, becomes enraptured decades later by the natural beauty of the Malayan countryside beyond his family's rubber plantation. He becomes increasingly absorbed with photographing his surroundings as the Japanese military machine moves across Southeast Asia. Late in the novel, an elderly Dinu holds weekly discussions about aesthetics among students, artists, and dissidents in his photographic studio, which he names the Glass Palace. These discussions provide a space in which to speak freely for people who have been educated by the military regime of Myanmar to accept what Dinu calls "the habit of obedience."[16] Answering young revolutionaries who consider aesthetic matters irrelevant to politics, Dinu declares, "I quoted Weston … Weston reflecting on Trotsky … that new and revolutionary art forms may awaken the people or disturb their complacency or challenge old ideals with constructive processes of change" (439; ellipses in original).

The unambiguously positive portrait of Dinu's circle runs counter to Adorno's nonidentitarian aesthetics, which suggests that artworks cannot represent a more egalitarian world disentangled from capitalist exploitation.[17] Works of art participate in the reification of human relations to the extent that they impose an aesthetic form onto the formless diversity of life. Thus, Adorno proposes a kind of existential corollary to the familiar point that capitalism depends on mystifying the means of production: language necessarily involves an act of violence whereby the object of representation is defined exclusively in terms of the subject's categories of understanding. Positive utopian thinking, then, is not simply wrongheaded but dangerous in that it promotes such violence; art "achieves an unreal reconciliation at the price of real reconciliation."[18] Any consolation that art might provide renders everyday life that much less intolerable, and, in so doing, reduces the possibility that people will risk actions necessary to change their economic and social conditions. According to this line of thinking, then, the portrayal of Dinu's circle fails to recognize how efforts to envision alternatives from the present vantage point only contribute to the increasingly totalizing grip of capital by providing a melancholic consolation: utopia exists in art, if not in life.[19]

The utopian portrait of Dinu's Glass Palace is intriguing given that Ghosh shares with Frankfurt School thinkers some fairly basic assumptions about the political and economic conditions governing the globe. In a 1995 essay entitled "The Fundamentalist Challenge," he declares:

Today, for the first time in history, a single ideal commands something close to absolute hegemony in the world: the notion that human existence must be permanently and irredeemably subordinated to the functioning of the impersonal mechanisms of a global marketplace.[20]

The worldwide hegemony of capitalism is perhaps the most fundamental axiom of Adorno's thought, and his entire aesthetic theory can be read as a response to this first principle. Nonidentitarian thinking emerges from the sense that artistic representations are incorporated within a capitalist system committed to perpetuating itself through commodifying all elements of human existence. Ghosh is also clearly sympathetic to Adorno's more existential critique of language's inadequacy to represent its objects. In the preface to his book of essays *Incendiary Circumstances* (2005), for example, Ghosh echoes the challenge issued by nonidentitarian thinking when he asks: "is it possible to write about situations of violence without allowing your work to become complicit with the subject?" (x). In other words, can the artist represent his or her subject matter without appropriating or commodifying it?

Ghosh's decision to portray the dissident leader Daw Aung San Suu Kyi as the political inspiration for Dinu's Glass Palace, then, seems puzzling, as does his description of Aung San Suu Kyi herself near the end of the novel. Indeed, the novel explicitly portrays her as an aesthetic figure in at least two prominent senses of the term. First, she is identified as a figure of beauty. "She was beautiful almost beyond belief," notes Dinu's visiting niece, Jaya (466). Second, she is identified with the notion that people must safeguard spheres of existence outside of politics. She is the only leader Dinu has ever believed in, not because of her tactical skills, integrity, or success:

she's the only one who seems to understand what the place of politics is ... what it ought to be ... that while misrule and tyranny must be resisted, so too must politics itself ... that it cannot be allowed to cannibalize all of life, all of existence. To me this is the most terrible indignity of our condition – not just in Burma but in many other places too ... that politics has invaded everything, spared nothing ... religion, art, family ... (467; ellipses in original)

This portrait invites readers to engage in precisely the kinds of identification with literary characters of which Adorno is contemptuous. From Adorno's perspective, the portrayals of Dinu's Glass Palace and Aung San Suu Kyi would confirm the inevitability of current conditions, limiting the capacity of readers to sense the possibility of fundamentally different alternatives. The novel provides, in other words, consolation for the world as it is rather than an intimation of the world as it could be.

Both Ghosh and Adorno locate in beauty a kind of utopian promise that an alternative to the present repressive system must exist; however, their different conceptions of beauty highlight their different understandings of utopian thinking. Adorno reverses the tendency of

Western aesthetics since Hegel to prioritize artistic over natural beauty, suggesting instead that art has value only insofar as it is an imitation of natural beauty. Adorno's reversal is motivated neither by a Romantic sensibility that infuses nature with some spiritual dimension nor by an ecological consciousness that bases human development in terms of sustainable economic practices. Rather, natural beauty is characterized by an "essential indeterminateness" because nature itself represents a "plenipotentiary of immediacy."[21] The term *natural beauty* functions as a placeholder to describe those things in the world that have yet to be appropriated by capitalism, and the category is important because it provides the basis for an allegory of the limits of bourgeois society's capacity to extinguish alternatives to itself. "Natural beauty is the trace of the nonidentical in things under the spell of universal identity," Adorno declares.[22] Put another way, nature functions as the repository of the "nonexistent" that Adorno identifies as the basis of all genuine utopian thinking. The existence of natural beauty is utopian not because it provides a sign of the more humane natural world or an image of a reconciled Nature and humanity, as it did for Kant, but because it indicates that capitalism can never entirely appropriate all features of existence.

Ghosh's notion of beauty, at least as it is associated with Aung San Suu Kyi, resonates more with Kantian than Adornean aesthetics. Kant famously defined beauty as that which defies an observer's rules, laws, and other pregiven concepts and categories of understanding.[23] Jaya finds herself absorbed by Aung San Suu Kyi's beauty precisely because the latter defies everything she expected to see in Myanmar. Aung San Suu Kyi's speech was "completely unlike anything she'd ever heard" (466), and her laughter infects the large crowd that has risked the wrath of military intelligence to see her. She is "beautiful," in other words, because she physically embodies the hopes of the Burmese people to produce an alternative political regime in their lifetimes. When Jaya finds herself thinking that "it was impossible to behold this woman and not be half in love" (467), she models something distinctly similar to Kantian judgment in positing a *sensus communis*, a universal validity to her judgment of taste. She makes no attempt to force her judgment on others, but she does feel the need to engage with those around her to validate it. The novel reinforces Jaya's aesthetic judgment by having Dinu declare that Aung San Suu Kyi defies efforts even by the military regime to categorize her. Noting that the government has labeled her an imperialist, Dinu declares that such efforts only highlight their illegitimacy.

A similar ideal of beauty functions as the basis for the group that meets at his Glass Palace. The gatherings at Dinu's photographic studio are entirely voluntary, unplanned, and Dinu himself resists enforcing his standard of taste as the model. The novel emphasizes aesthetic and cultural differences among participants, differences that are never entirely dissolved, although the participants typically choose to keep returning. Here again, something like Kant's *sensus communis* emerges, where participants are allowed to defer temporarily their commitments to the outside world in pursuit of a disinterested discussion of aesthetic values. The model of debate and exchange that the gatherings embody provides a symbolic representation of a community learning to balance the contradictory impulses of freedom and social responsibility.[24]

In terms of the formal dimensions of the novel, the narrative exemplifies the notion of beauty its characters describe by deliberately eliding generic expectations, blending fiction and nonfiction.[25] The "Author's Notes" that end *The Glass Palace* declare that Ghosh is creating a "parallel, wholly fictional world" (471), yet the novel repeatedly emphasizes its basis in historical fact. The narrative is prefaced with a map of Southeast Asia, locating the work in time (the map notes that it presents "Territorial Boundaries ca. 1945") and place (the map presents an image of where the original Glass Palace was located). The "Author's Notes" identify an exhaustive list of sources, and Ghosh declares that he read "hundreds of books, memoirs, travelogues, gazetteers, articles and notebooks, published and unpublished" in preparation for writing (471); additionally, he provides an extensive list of people interviewed, and locations visited. Even his concession that he presents a fictional world is qualified by his declaration that he has deliberately fictionalized certain events and omitted certain sources out of "fear of reprisals against those concerned" by agents of Myanmar's military regime (473). The apparent fictionality of the text thus appears to be a rhetorical necessity rather than an indication of creative autonomy. The formal features of the novel encourage readers to downplay the artifice inherent in having characters articulate and dispute conceptions of beauty. Whereas Adorno advocated an art whose formal features stand in tension with its content, Ghosh uses the formal features of *The Glass Palace* to encourage readers to view its content as a gloss on current political events. Or, put another way, for Adorno, aesthetic form emphasizes that utopian alternatives can never be entirely eradicated, and the experience of beauty emerges from a kind of contentless form; for Ghosh, in contrast, aesthetic form emphasizes the permeability between lived and imagined worlds, and the experience of beauty emerges from a sense that alternatives are always apparent in everyday life.

Ghosh's insistence on the permeability between lived and imagined worlds is motivated by a concern that memories of life under repressive regimes are often lost. In the "Author's Notes," Ghosh emphasizes that he was "forced" to create a fictional world because so many of the original memories were fading or censored (471). Fiction becomes a necessary means of preserving and communicating fragmentary experiences, and the representation of fictional characters such as Dinu underscores the continuing inability of the military regime to direct or restrict the lives of its citizens. Ghosh never denies that his fictionalization of life in contemporary Myanmar risks simplifying or sentimentalizing political dissent, repackaging it for consumption by first world audiences. But his more basic concern that such experiences might be lost altogether to the outside world and other dissidents outweighs concerns about the violence perpetuated by literary representations. The quasi-existential character of Adorno's wholesale critique of representation emerges from a particular historical vantage point from which capitalism appeared to have an almost uniform world dominance. The relative isolation of Myanmar from the market system and the continued capacity of dissidents including Aung San Suu Kyi to challenge the regime, in contrast, provide the grounds for Ghosh to perceive a far more uneven world landscape, in which artists could "reimagine the space[s] for articulate, humane, and creative dissent" (*Incendiary Circumstances*, 137) that are at least partially beyond the control of state power.[26] Such a possibility animates not only Ghosh's descriptions of Dinu's Glass Palace but also the generic form of the novel. Ghosh's declaration that *The Glass Palace* is a "family memoir" rather than a more explicitly politically engaged literary form such as social realism or protest literature recalls Dinu's concern that politics in Myanmar threatens to "cannibalize all of life." While the chapters leading up to the final scene of the novel focus on Dinu's Glass Palace and the visit to Aung San Suu Kyi, the very last scene shifts its emphasis away from the political to the familial. Jaya relates to Dinu her most enduring memory of his father, Rajkumar. The memory concerns not political dissidents or speeches or protests but a moment of quiet domestic happiness, a wryly sweet version of the consummation scene between the novel's two primary families: Jaya describes to Dinu how her son discovered an elderly Uma and Rajkumar naked in bed together, and witnessed his first kiss.

My point is not to dismiss the relevance of Adorno's aesthetic theories but rather to suggest that we might benefit from extending Dipesh

Chakrabarty's argument for provincializing Europe – that while modernity may indeed represent a dominant world-system, it has been experienced historically in such radically different ways that the ontological assumptions underlying modern European political and aesthetic thought may limit how postcolonial literatures can be understood.[27] Ghosh's aesthetics are shaped by a much more heterogeneous, fractured, and fluid conception of modernity that Adorno's, and this is reflected in Ghosh's willingness to risk representing utopian communities.[28] Ghosh is not insensitive to the limited capacity of language to represent experience. As will become apparent later in this chapter, Ghosh's insistence on representing beauty and utopian communities comes not despite but because of his sense that Enlightenment thinking has been guided by a desire to appropriate non-European others within a single dominant historical narrative that gives primacy to colonial empires and, more recently, to neocolonial forms of economic exploitation.

UTOPIAS POSITIVE AND NEGATIVE

The engagement with Kantian aesthetic thinking in Ghosh's work can be traced back to his first novel, *The Circle of Reason*, in which he highlights the historical connection between aesthetics and instrumental reasoning. Indeed, for Yumna Siddiqi, the central question of the novel is whether its "succession of utopian projects" can utilize an "alternative, nonrepressive rule of reason" that divorces the emancipatory elements of Enlightenment reason from its coercive elements.[29] Early in the novel, the rural Indian schoolteacher, Rationalist, and Pasteur fanatic Balaram declares that empirical reasoning does not belong to the West but is universal. "Science doesn't belong to countries. Reason doesn't belong to any nation," he declares. "They belong to history – to the world."[30] In the small village of Lalpukur, he undertakes schemes to decontaminate residents and refugees alike with carbolic acid, and founds The Pasteur School of Reason with its Kantian departments: the Department of Pure Reason and the Department of Practical Reason. The text clearly satirizes his ambitions, but he does provide a model for local villagers to combine education with vocational training that enables them to remain self-sufficient while continuing their studies. Balaram himself understands his utopian project as having an aesthetic quality, describing his plan as "[s]imple and beautiful: knowledge coupled with labour" (109). Similar visions of beauty as the embodiment of a highly organized community underline the utopian thinking of characters for the majority of the novel. When Balaram's nephew and ward, Alu, later envisions his own utopian community, he too sees it as the realization of Pasteur's vision (280). Alu's socialist community bans money because he equates it with impurity. "No money, no dirt will ever again flow freely in the Ras," he declares (281).

The success of both Balaram's Pasteur School of Reason and Alu's Ras signals a simultaneous fascination and discomfort with utopian schemes based on aesthetic ideals. *The Circle of Reason* does not characterize the aesthetic as inherently coercive: Balaram's and Alu's projects neither fail nor become repressive, but are eradicated by agents of the states in which they reside. Yet the novel demonstrates significant anxieties about the historical outcomes that emerge when aesthetics becomes central to political discourse. The final utopian figure in the novel, Dr. Uma Verma, rejects the notion of utopia built on an aesthetic ideal in favor of a kind of syncretism best exemplified by the cremation ceremony she organizes for Alu's companion Kulfi. Dr. Verma's presence in the novel provides a counterpoint not only to the Enlightenment rationalism endorsed earlier by Balaram but also to the socialism of her colleague Dr. Mishra. In the span of twenty pages, she is portrayed as rejecting her father's obsession with books as a longing for order lacking in the world (395); criticizing the socialism of Dr. Mishra as one more orthodoxy (409); and, in the midst of her cobbled-together cremation ceremony, declaring that action cannot wait for a more organized or pure world. "Nothing's whole anymore," she says. "If we wait for everything to be right again, we'll wait for ever while the world falls apart. The only hope is to make do with what we've got" (416–17).[31]

Rereading *The Glass Palace* through the lens of *The Circle of Reason*, it becomes apparent that Ghosh takes pains to portray the dystopian potential of communities based on an aestheticized notion of order. Put another way, Ghosh tempers the portrait of the second Glass Palace with the cautionary tale of the first. The Burmese Queen is so insistent on making everyone around her conform to her principles of order and decorum that she punishes anyone who would defy them, killing the King's closest relations and disowning her own children when they fail to live up to her expectations. Indeed, the novel is filled with examples of what Marc Redfield has called the "potentially dehumanizing thrust of aesthetic formalization."[32] Uma Dey's husband – the District Collector in charge of monitoring the Burmese royal family after they have been exiled to a small coastal village in India – provides the clearest allegory of the dark side of aesthetic education. As one of the few Indians to rise to prominence in the Civil Service, Beni Prasad Dey is obsessed with demonstrating his legitimacy, which he sees measured in terms of his mastery of British culture and social mores. His sense that British military and political superiority is couched in an aesthetic superiority becomes apparent in his attitude toward the Burmese royal family. "But what could they possibly know of love, of any of the finer sentiments," he thinks to himself, "these bloodthirsty aristocrats, these semi-illiterates who had never read a book in all their lives, never looked with pleasure upon a painting?" (131). An Arnoldian sensibility is apparent in how he measures their capacity to experience love by their familiarity with Western art forms. In the mind of the Collector, the Queen's lack of a proper aesthetic education leads to her monstrous cruelty. Yet his own life, which he deliberately models on an aesthetic ideal, is portrayed as lacking genuine passion or sympathy. On learning that Uma is planning to leave him, he laments: "I used to dream about the kind of marriage I wanted ... To discover together the world of literature, art: what could be richer, more fulfilling?" (149). In practice, however, life becomes an intolerable obsession with fulfilling proper form and etiquette, and the Collector ridicules his wife on a daily basis for improperly arranging the silver and a myriad of other such failings. Even his suicide by paddling out to sea in an old racing scull left behind by an Englishman seems strikingly formal and cold, without any reflection on the costs to Uma.

The dark side of aesthetic appreciation identified in Ghosh's fiction has historically nagged efforts to extract a political philosophy out of Kant's *Critique of Judgment*: to balance the need to respect and preserve difference with the longing to retain the possibility of universality. Kant's aesthetic theory has intrigued interlocutors from Schiller to Hannah Arendt and Jean-François Lyotard because of its assertion that universally compelling norms can emerge from the interactions between free and independent subjects. Or, as Tobin Siebers puts it, "Beauty is a vision of a plural universe in which self and other necessarily meet – a universe in which one must contend with others and other logics ... with purposes beyond our meddling and understanding."[33] The aesthetic involves intimately personal affections, sentiments, and feelings that are not subsumed by rational cognition or the categories of understanding on which it depends, yet aesthetic judgments draw individuals into dialogue with others. Precisely because an individual feels that his or her judgments should have universal validity he or she is led to share experiences with others. That aesthetic judgments presuppose universal validity or a *sensus communis* does not necessarily mean that they impose a single, monolithic and universal notion, although this has often been the historical reality. As the debates in Dinu's Glass Palace attest, sharing experiences may not lead to consensus nor does every effort to communicate experience succeed in overcoming barriers of language and philosophical bias. The potential for dialogue that the aesthetic permits always risks collapsing into the demand for assent (as demonstrated by the District Collector toward Uma), and the notion of consensus on which beauty is based always risks becoming a tool for silencing dissenting voices and projecting a homogeneity and transparency that do not in fact exist.

On the formal level, *The Glass Palace* emphasizes the conflicting tendencies of the aesthetic by establishing a series of dialectical oppositions through its characters. Uma Dey's political activism, for example, emerges in explicit contrast to her husband's tendency to impose an aesthetic order on the world around him. Perhaps the most significant opposition in the novel, however, emerges between Uma's nephew Arjun and Dinu. In the latter half of *The Glass Palace*, Ghosh employs both a positive and a negative utopianism, traced in Dinu's and Arjun's narratives respectively. In contrast to the affirmative portrait of Dinu's Glass Palace discussed earlier, the portrayal of Arjun's experiences in the British military demands that readers extrapolate from his errors and intuitions. As one of the first generation of Indian officers serving in the British army, Arjun takes great pride in the traditions and protocols of his unit. Although his nonmilitary friends and family perceive him to be a mercenary or a tool of British imperialism, he sees himself as part of a special fellowship, the "First True Indians" (242). Renouncing the dietary codes and restrictions with which they were raised, the Indian officers proudly consume the ham, beef, alcohol, and cigarettes that make up the diet of their English counterparts, pronouncing themselves "the first Indians to be truly free" (242–43). In many respects, Arjun's error repeats the District Collector's: the belief that an aesthetic education could enable the formation of a shared community of taste or a *sensus communis*, which would in turn provide the basis for political and even national solidarity. Although such a belief animated many of Kant's interpreters, Kant himself was careful to avoid addressing the question of whether a *sensus communis* could be built, or even whether it actually exists.[34] For Arjun, however, a shared community of taste is produced simply by adopting English values rather than by encouraging an ongoing dialogue among individuals. Despite Arjun's rhetoric, the basis of taste was determined for the Indian officers by the English; the cultural heterogeneity of the Indian officers was subsumed in the name of an aesthetic ideal to which they all assented but did not arrive at by themselves.[35] As a result, they lose their capacity to communicate with the

Indian soldiers under their command. Only after the British forces are routed by the Japanese invaders does Arjun even recognize his inability to communicate with his batman about personal issues.

Arjun's ultimate inability to find a basis for solidarity leads him to despair, and the novel identifies the problem in terms of the imagination. Struggling to understand his discomfort around Indian soldiers, Arjun recognizes that he and his fellow officers "had always known the country to be poor, yet they had never imagined themselves to be part of that poverty: they were the privileged, the elite. The discovery that they were poor too came as a revelation. It was as though a grimy curtain of snobbery had prevented them from seeing what was plainly before their eyes" (302). While he eventually becomes capable of imagining himself in a new way – of lifting the "grimy curtain" of ideology – through conversations with his batman and others, he cannot learn to describe his situation without the language and terms of the British. Whereas Dinu retains the hope that Western conceptions of the aesthetic are not simply ideological props, Arjun laments that the British have "colored everything in the world as we know it. It is a huge, indelible stain which has tainted all of us. We cannot destroy it without destroying ourselves" (446).

The opposition between Arjun and Dinu never devolves into a simplistic binary between error and truth; indeed, the formal pattern of the narrative exemplifies the notion of beauty presented in the novel, much as the generic disruptions discussed in the last section did. The oppositions between characters and their worldviews diminish through dialogue. Ghosh portrays Dinu questioning his own epistemological bases of judgment after his final conversation with Arjun, who by this time stands committed to violently resisting the British despite lacking weapons, supplies, and increasingly even men under his command. Dinu subsequently finds his artistic beliefs challenged by his wife, Daw Thin Thin Aye. Struck by her innovative writing, which blends classicism with folk usage, Dinu questions her decision to make all her characters speak Burmese despite their diverse cultural backgrounds. She responds:

Where I live … every house on the street speaks a different language. I have no choice but to trust my readers to imagine the sound of each house. Or else I would not be able to write at all about my street – and to trust your reader is not a bad thing. (459)

No less than in Arjun's narrative, the imagination is invoked to resolve the apparent impossibility of communicating experience. Indeed, the ideological mystification that prevents Arjun from identifying with the Indian soldiers under his command is presented as an extreme form of a more general existential condition, one that is particularly acute in culturally and linguistically diverse societies like Myanmar and India.[36] Thus, Thin Thin Aye's decision to make all of her characters speak a single language is not entirely different from Arjun's effort to insist on a single standard of taste among Indian officers, but the assumptions guiding the former are very different. The act of trusting the reader to imagine differences that cannot be conveyed through aesthetic form acknowledges that efforts to communicate experience depend on active engagement and interpretation rather than passive reception.

There is, then, a broad allegory to be drawn from Ghosh's writing about the interdependence of Kantian and Adornean aesthetics. If Kantian aesthetics and its potential political implications are to be divorced from the historical violence perpetuated by Enlightenment thinking – as Jonathan Loesberg and others have sought to do – then a rigorous nonidentitarian critique along the lines proposed by Adorno is necessary.[37] Put another way, the argument that negative utopian thinking is insufficient for the needs of many writers outside of Europe and the United States is counterpointed by the argument in this section that positive utopian thinking is unable to divorce itself from its most pernicious tendencies. In *The Glass Palace*, Ghosh attempts to render both positive and negative utopian thinking within the aesthetic form of the novel, in such a way that the two modes of thinking mutually correct each other. The portrayals of the Burmese Queen, the Collector, and Arjun emphasize the inescapable dangers of utopian thinking, and emphasize that Dinu's vision of people engaged in disinterested debate is a heuristic rather than a reality. Dinu's Glass Palace proposes the conditions under which individuals are invited to engage with each other in ways that respect potentially intractable differences, and Arjun's inability ever to escape from his own biases reminds readers that such conditions are rarely, if ever, met.

THE HORIZON OF COLLECTIVE IMAGINATION

The role ascribed to the imagination in interpreting reality and creating solidarity is one of the most significant developments in Ghosh's thinking. The imagination is not even a significant topic of discussion in *The Circle of Reason*. The primary impediments to utopian projects have nothing to do with internalized ideology that must be overcome through an act of imagination. While the community living in the Ras may initially doubt Alu's proposal for waging "war on money" (241), these doubts are rapidly overcome when the proposal is accompanied by a concrete outline for implementation. There is, in other words, no ideological work necessary to create the conditions for a more utopian society, simply a practical logistical task of figuring out how to compensate everyone fairly for their labor. Even in defeat, Alu's supporters do not understand their failure in terms of an incapacity to see their own exploitation, as Arjun does in *The Glass Palace*. As he is being led away by the secret police, Professor Samuel, key architect of Alu's vision, smiles and shouts: "How many people will you send away? The queue of hopes stretches long past infinity" (409). As indicated earlier, resistance is cast as an inevitable byproduct of an imperialist capitalist system. Hope thus replaces the need for imagination in Ghosh's first novel. Or, hope might be understood to represent a proto-imagination that turns the recognition of unsatisfied needs into a passionate desire to see the world transformed.

The crucial shift in Ghosh's thinking occurs after the 1984 assassination of Indian Prime Minister Indira Gandhi by her Sikh bodyguards. In his essay "The Greatest Sorrow," Ghosh writes that the targeted violence against Sikhs in the wake of the assassination and the government's collusion caused a profound "epistemic upheaval" for the entire country (*Incendiary Circumstances*, 54). Elaborating on a lecture by Ranajit Guha on Hegel and South Asian history, Ghosh argues that the nation-state has for the past 200 years provided the epistemological foundation for collective experience across the globe, making possible the writing of history as a narrative that organizes time into a coherent narrative linking past, present, and future. According to this idea, the nation-state becomes the central protagonist in the narrative of history, and its development represents the movement toward ever higher forms of ethical civilization. The civil violence that emerges in the 1980s in India, Sri Lanka, and elsewhere, according to Ghosh, effects a worldwide rethinking of the assumption that the nation-state should serve as "the grid on which history is mapped" (48). If the state can serve the efforts of one group to eradicate another, then it ceases to embody a disinterested ideal for producing solidarity.

The imagination, then, has the crucial task of enabling individuals to reinterpret the past outside of the narrative frame of nation. Consciously rejecting Fredric Jameson's assertion that Third World literature is preoccupied with composing national allegories, Ghosh portrays national boundaries as "shadow lines" that have no physical basis or long cultural history.[38] The Bengali families Ghosh follows in *The Shadow Lines* have ties that cross borders, and the crucial event that drives the plot of the novel – the murder of the narrator's relative and role model Tridib by a crowd involved in the 1964 riots – is literally incomprehensible to the narrator for the majority of the novel because he understands the personal experiences of his family members in terms of the national news. Indeed, the centrality of the nation to the meaning of personal life stories leads to traumatic consequences for those whose experiences do not fit. Without an historical narrative in which to place the events of 1964, they become literally meaningless for the narrator. The narrator admits that it took him fifteen years to recognize that the riots he witnessed as a child in Calcutta were linked to the riots in Dhaka, in which Tridib was murdered while trying to rescue a distant relative from a mob. The narrator conveys the traumatic quality of these events by establishing a comparison with the perceived historical significance of the 1962 war with China. Noting that he and his friends could all recollect a surprising number of details about their lives during that period, the narrator discovers that his friends cannot even recall that riots occurred in 1964. His friends dismiss his recollections as mere fantasies, pointing out that the university library has shelves of books on the 1962 war and nothing on the events of 1964. The few newspaper accounts that the narrator eventually manages to discover categorize the attacks as launched by vaguely defined "anti-national elements," and merit less attention than an important cricket Test match against England.[39] Here, again, the novel emphasizes that nationalism provides the dominant lens through which journalists and historians alike understand events, and events that fail to fit within this narrative tend to be given less attention than others, like the cricket match or the war against China, that do.

To the extent that nationalism establishes a set of biases that prejudice all readings of the past, the imagination assumes a hermeneutic task that resembles its function during an aesthetic experience: to apprehend without recourse to pregiven categories of understanding. In the first paragraphs of the novel, the narrator notes that the name he uses to describe his father's aunt in writing, Mayadebi, is different from the word he used in actual conversations with her, Mayathakuma. Ghosh thereby highlights the levels that readers are removed from the experiences of characters by establishing barriers between the narrator and readers, who will never be able to view the experiences the narrator describes in the way that he did. Yet the narrator immediately thereafter points to his own failure of identification; he concedes that he imagines Tridib, Mayadebi's second son, looking just like himself when he was a boy. The narrator thus faces the same epistemological problem as his readers – that any effort to acquire historical knowledge of events removed from his personal experience involves distortion. Even the most highly precise description of an event or place or person cannot re-create the hermeneutic biases that guided the initial viewer or eliminate the biases of readers attempting to reconstruct the initial experience. Distortion becomes the defining, if not constitutive, feature of imagining in *The Shadow Lines*.

Ghosh nonetheless takes pains to show that such distortions do not limit the imagination's capacity to provide accurate historical knowledge. Put another way, the novel takes a surprisingly optimistic attitude toward the capacity of imagining to reconstruct the experiences of others even while acknowledging the impossibility of identifying with the people who had those initial experiences. When the narrator visits London while on research for his Ph.D. dissertation, he visits the locales described to him as a child by Tridib, who lived there during World War II. He demonstrates a remarkable ability to navigate London, based solely on his imaginative reconstructions of Tridib's stories. To the amazement of Tridib's sister Ila and her English friends, the narrator can describe the layout of the house in which Tridib lived forty years earlier. The narrator recalls that Tridib himself insisted on the paramount importance of using the imagination to acquire knowledge of a place: "the one thing he wanted to teach me, he used to say, was to use my imagination with precision" (24).

While the notion of imagination articulated in *The Shadow Lines* anticipates the role it is assigned in *The Glass Palace*, Ghosh demonstrates significant reservations about the epistemological significance of the imagination in works published during the intervening years. He significantly downplays the role of imagination in the historical reconstruction of a pre-Western cosmopolitanism in *In an Antique Land: History in the Guise of the Traveler's Tale* (1992). Ostensibly, the work follows Ghosh's travels to a small village in Egypt for fieldwork research on his Ph.D. dissertation in anthropology, and his subsequent research into the story of an eleventh-century slave of a Jewish trader named Ben Yiju. Bomma, as the slave is known from documents recovered from the Geniza of the synagogue of Ben Ezra in Cairo, is part of a flourishing transcontinental trade economy that connects Africa, the Middle East, and Southeast Asia. Indeed, Ghosh repeatedly contrasts this "shared enterprise" with the imperialist capitalism introduced in the eighteenth century by Europeans. According to Ghosh's narrative, the ruthless and militaristic approach of the Europeans decimated the highly developed cultures based on "accommodation and compromise" (288), and sought to eliminate every trace of the past that might imply legitimate alternatives to itself.[40] Ghosh's project can thus be seen in terms of Marcuse's notion of "critical remembrance," where the representation of broken promises of the past can provide a sense of inspiration for future utopian projects. And some version of this spirit was caught by the Anglo-American academy, with Ghosh's book receiving glowing praise from anthropologists Clifford Geertz and James Clifford among others for providing a model of a "multicultural bazaar" and "traveling cultures" in an era of globalization.[41]

The shift in focus away from explicit meditations on imagination toward a selective, perhaps tendentious, historical reconstruction of an alternative tradition of cosmopolitanism points to a problem with the notion of imagination articulated in *The Shadow Lines.*[42] Acts of imagining in the earlier work were almost exclusively described in terms of an individual's mental activities. The imagination enables the narrator to reconstruct Tridib's personal experiences, but it fails to accomplish its modern ideological function – healing social rifts between individuals and groups by providing the basis for a common sense. The novel does not focus on how particular images could capture an entire community, and provide a basis for self-definition. To the contrary, *The Shadow Lines* demonstrates significant suspicion of such activities: the closest thing in the novel to a collective imagination would be the histories of nationalism that cast the nation-state as the essential basis for self-definition and meaning. Such collective reconstructions actually introduce ideological distortions rather than provide an accurate description of reality, as the omission of the 1964 riots from the historical record indicates. Accurate interpretations of reality require the narrator or other individuals to divorce themselves from the images and histories presented to them. In much the same way that Schiller understood aesthetic education as a process that would temporarily withdraw individuals from the world in order to encourage a free play that would provide the basis for freedom, the free play of the imagination in Ghosh's *The Shadow Lines* provides the necessary basis for a more genuine freedom than what the state offers because it is a freedom based on the individual having the ability to assess accurately what his or her options are, and to make a choice based on knowledge of those options. But, as we have repeatedly observed throughout this study, the problem of how to communicate experience remains a problem.

The more considerable attention to problems of representation in *In an Antique Land* indicates the difficulty, if not impossibility, of translating the notion of an individual imagination into a positive notion of a collective imagination. Throughout *In an Antique Land*, Ghosh portrays intractable misunderstandings in his conversations with the Egyptians at his field research site. The Muslims around him cannot understand Ghosh's unwillingness to convert to their religion. Nor can Ghosh convey the logic of his worldview to them, despite his education, knowledge, and worldliness – i.e., his cosmopolitanism. This impasse becomes acutely apparent when the topic of circumcision is raised. Villagers convey their shock and disbelief that Ghosh is not circumcised:

> In Arabic the word "circumcise" derives from a root that means "to purify": to say of someone that they are "uncircumcised" is more or less to call them impure. "Yes," I answered, "yes, many people in my country are 'impure'." I had no alternative; I was trapped by language.
> "But not you …" He could not bring himself to finish the sentence. (62)

The primary impediment to realizing or restoring the eleventh-century model of cosmopolitanism is not intolerance, and Ghosh repeatedly portrays the villagers trying to converse with him, trying to understand. Rather, language is characterized as weighted with histories of religious and philosophical biases that cannot be overcome. The problem, in other words, is not a lack of sympathy but rather the sedimentation of repeated language use, and the habits of thought created by it. The preoccupation with aesthetics in later works such as *The Glass Palace* is anticipated here: the fantasy of experiencing the world without pregiven categories of understanding represents the only possibility of moving beyond the impasse that separates Ghosh from his interlocutors. Hence, the reversal from *The Shadow Lines* is significant. The earlier work concludes with a "redemptive mystery" shared between the narrator and May Price (an English woman romantically involved with Tridib and indirectly responsible for his death) – an aesthetic or even quasi-spiritual experience that is largely independent of language (246); *In an Antique Land*, in contrast, founders on apparently insuperable obstacles presented by language.

The problem is thus not best understood through the lenses of Adorno, Marcuse, and Benjamin. For all of their differences, these thinkers shared a fundamental sense that the ideological implications of aesthetics mean that artists face a stark choice: to reject positive portrayals of utopia for their ideological complicity or to reproduce the ideology of capitalism, imperialism, and/or fascism. Adorno is quite clear that the utopian potential of remembrance is drawn from broken promises made in the past, not from any successful community that existed in the past. "Ever since Plato's doctrine of anamnesis the not-yet-existing has been dreamed of in remembrance," he writes, "which alone concretizes utopia without betraying it to existence. Remembrance remains bound up with semblance: for

even in the past the dream was not reality."[43] Ghosh demonstrates a fascination with the possibility that conversations might nonetheless reach
a point beyond where conversants were initially capable or comfortable,
based on their ideological biases. This suggests something much closer to
the thinking of Hans-Georg Gadamer, who insisted that meaning was
not linked to a specific person or work of art but rather arose out of critical engagements as individuals struggled to arrive at a "fusion of horizons." In the context of Ghosh, this helps to understand the nature of the
problem of utopia for him. As he makes apparent even from *The Circle
of Reason*, the challenge is not identifying characteristics of an ideal society. Ghosh is very specific in his portraits. Nor is the challenge divorcing
the characteristics of an ideal society from potential complicity with or
appropriation by imperialist powers. Ghosh is quite clear in *In an Antique
Land* that an alternative strand of cosmopolitanism can be reconstructed,
which has its own legitimate genealogy for individuals to draw upon
in the effort to remake the current globalized system dominated by the
West. Rather, the problem facing a utopian writer is how the work of
art or any conversation, for that matter, can create a basis of common
sense: taste is not in fact uniform and individuals will always have irresolvable differences that are not based on abstract rational grounds that
can be adjudicated.

Put in more concrete terms, *In an Antique Land* can identify in inter-
continental trade a basis or logic for people of different cultures to come
together, but Ghosh's work fails to explain convincingly why this basis of
cosmopolitanism does not necessarily devolve into exploitation. Indeed,
Ghosh's historical narrative establishes a sense of determinism that
counters the very point of his reconstruction. This becomes particularly
apparent when Ghosh describes the 1509 battle between the Portuguese
navy and a transcontinental fleet put together by representatives of
Gujarat, Calicut, and Egypt. Ghosh finds a curious moral to this battle
which sealed the fate of cosmopolitanism and paved the way for centuries
of European imperialism:

By the time the trading nations of the Indian Ocean began to realize that their
old understandings had been rendered defunct by the Europeans it was already
too late … As always, the determination of a small, united band of soldiers tri-
umphed easily over the rich confusions that accompany a culture of accommodation and compromise. (288)

According to this narrative, the only long-standing basis for solidarity
appears to be the determination to extract profit from others, which is

precisely the argument against which Ghosh directs his work. If Ghosh is correct that the Western imperial powers attempted to eliminate militarily and philosophically all alternatives to themselves, his narrative of their triumph does not point to the contingency of Western imperialism but, if anything, its inevitability. Cosmopolitanism fails to prepare people for war, but it also fails on epistemological grounds: the "old understandings" underestimate the greed that is apparently a defining feature of human nature.

Ghosh is clear about the stakes in finding an alternative basis for coming together: the reproduction of Western historical narratives of development. In a crucial scene – an earlier version of which was published in 1986 as "The Imam and the Indian" – Ghosh finds himself in a heated debate with an old village Imam. The debate quickly devolves into an argument over who has superior military technology, Egypt or India. In contrast to the scenes described earlier, however, the argument does not hinge on cultural or linguistic misunderstandings. "At that moment, despite the vast gap that lay between us, we understood each other perfectly," Ghosh states (236). To invoke the terminology though not the argument of Gadamer, the two debaters have achieved a "fusion of horizons" that guarantees an intractable disagreement. Recalling that a fusion of horizons, for Gadamer, meant that conversants share not the same values but a sense of what futures are conceivable or possible, the language of development promoted by Western Europe provides the limit or horizon beyond which neither the Imam nor Ghosh can conceive. In other words, the Imam and Ghosh share a basis for judgment, though it is one that guarantees that they can never arrive at a common community. Ghosh notes:

it seemed to me that the Imam and I had participated in our own final defeat, in the dissolution of the centuries of dialogue that had linked us: we had demonstrated the irreversible triumph of the language that had usurped all the others in which people once discussed their differences. We had acknowledged that it was no longer possible to speak, as Ben Yiju and his Slave, or any one of the thousands of travelers who had crossed the Indian Ocean in the Middle Ages might have done: of things that were right, or good, or willed by God; it would have been merely absurd for either of us to use those words, for they belonged to a dismantled rung on the ascending ladder of Development. (236–37)

The scene provides perhaps the clearest indication that an internalized sense of historical determinism is a hermeneutic problem as much as a political or economic one. As long as the Imam and Ghosh fail to rethink the basis of their judgments, they remain unable to work together or to retrieve an alternative history of cosmopolitanism, which is the central project of *In an Antique Land*.

It is not altogether surprising that his next work of fiction, *The Calcutta Chromosome* (1995), approaches epistemological problems very differently. The novel represents Ghosh's first work of science fiction, and re-creates a hypothetical history of the discovery of the mechanism for the transmission of malaria. The protagonist of the novel, a computer programmer named Antar, begins to unravel this history when he comes across the identity card of a former acquaintance and coworker, L. Murugan, while doing a routine scan for his job. What Antar comes to discover is that British scientist Ronald Ross, the man credited with the discovery of the manner in which malaria is conveyed by mosquitoes, was fed his research by a shadowy group seeking to discover a secret for transmitting consciousness from body to body. This group practices what Murugan calls "counter-science,"[44] which is built on assumptions that contradict Western empiricism. They believe that knowledge is inherently self-contradictory because "to know something is to change it, therefore in knowing something, you've already changed what you think you know so you don't really know it at all: you only know its history."[45] Here, then, Ghosh provides a system of knowledge that stands outside of the narrative of development and the epistemology associated with it, precisely what was lacking in *In an Antique Land*.

Yet the resolution to *The Calcutta Chromosome* emphasizes the cost of positing a radically alternative epistemology. In the near-future New York in which Antar lives, international capitalism has succeeded in penetrating every aspect of human life. Antar works at home alone, and his every moment is monitored by computers to ensure his maximum productivity. There is, in other words, no privacy or separation between work and leisure space. Set against this backdrop, it makes sense that the only alternative the novel can provide is a shadowy cult devoted to "counter-science," whose rituals can never be directly represented. The novel ends with Antar apparently being inducted into the group, who reassure him in the final page: "We're with you; you're not alone; we'll help you across."[46] But readers are given no access to the world on the other side – it is left very much in terms of the negative utopias proposed by Adorno, Bahri, and Brown. To acknowledge the novel's central claim – that to know the world is to change it – limits the possibility of ever describing utopia, for in doing so it too would change. It appears as if Ghosh concedes Adorno's claim: that aesthetic redemption always comes at the expense of actual redemption. But this represents a very difficult bargain for Ghosh, who has emphasized that his utopian cosmopolitan society would be based on conversation. Such a basis requires a minimal communicability of experience, and this is precisely what the novel cannot provide in its final moments. The novel can provide intimations of it, presenting the familiar Ghosh scene of a doughnut shop in Penn Station in which Antar and other cosmopolitans enjoy coffee and conversation. But this can only be a very rough approximation, given that the coffee drinkers are all part of an international migrant economy that moves bodies across nations in order to conform with the flows of capital. It is not an enduring space, and survives only in the brief moments that its patrons can spare from their work.

THE ENDS OF THE AESTHETIC

Ghosh's renewed interest in aesthetics and the imagination in *The Glass Palace*, then, represents an effort to overcome the impasses reached by *In an Antique Land* and *The Calcutta Chromosome*. Crucial to this effort is the portrayal of the uses to which the aesthetic was put by entrepreneurs intent on exploiting the resources of Britain's colonies. The centrality of Enlightenment aesthetic thinking is apparent in the most significant capitalist enterprise in the novel, the Morningside Rubber Estate. This project – born of the partnership between Rajkumar and his mentor Saya John and implemented by Saya's son Matthew and daughter-in-law Elsa – creates vast wealth for the families during World War I, as competing empires desperately need natural resources such as rubber to sustain their war machines. The estate provides profit by exploiting natural resources and human labor, and the novel makes it clear that the discourse of aesthetics is crucial to rationalizing its existence. "It's beautiful, isn't it?" Elsa declares to Rajkumar's wife Dolly as they pass thousands of rubber trees, all aligned geometrically for efficient extraction (172). Dolly herself admires the labor it must have taken to clear the jungle, but is uncomfortable with what she sees: "there was something eerie about its uniformity; about the fact that such sameness could be imposed upon a landscape of such natural exuberance" (172). Elsa's narrative is striking for its implicit invocation of the categories of the beautiful and sublime that emerged in Enlightenment thinkers such as Kant and Edmund Burke. Elsa relates how "horrified" she felt when she first came to the area: "The place was beautiful beyond imagining, but it was jungle – dense, towering, tangled, impassable jungle" (172). The jungle becomes an embodiment of the sublime, something whose grandeur exceeds the capacity of the imagination to understand it, thereby filling the witness with feelings of horror and pleasure. What capitalism requires, then, according to this narrative, is the domestication of the sublime into the beautiful. The literal imposition of order by destroying and then replanting the trees becomes a metaphorical imposition of a political, social, and moral order.

Elsa's husband Matthew similarly understands capitalism to involve the introduction of the aesthetic into non-Western spaces. When the District Collector's widow Uma describes the workers as slaves, Matthew is quick to reinvoke the language of aesthetics. He says: "It's no easy thing to run a plantation, you know. To look at, it's all very green and beautiful – sort of like a forest. But actually it's a vast machine, made of wood and flesh. And at every turn, every little piece of this machine is resisting you, fighting you, waiting for you to give in" (201). The logic here is that the apparent beauty is not natural but rather the product of human (that is, Western) labor. The language of beauty also enables an interesting slippage, whereby the humanity of the laborers is denied: they are simply a part of the totality of the scene – part of nature – as indicated by his description of the "machine" as "wood and flesh." And the description of this system as a machine further enables him to suggest that everything is a product of his labor, denying any pre-existing social order or ecosystem.

The direction the argument takes between Uma and Matthew indicates Ghosh's sense that the discourse of aesthetics inevitably produces a counter-discourse of resistance. By folding his laborers into an undifferentiated natural world that is rendered beautiful, Matthew inadvertently posits an opposing tendency toward a "sublime" existence that resists the order he brings. His aesthetic discourse enables him to assert that rationality and justice guide his system of administration, but the consequence is that he cannot attribute acts of resistance, insubordination, or even laziness on the part of his employees to either his rule or their own agency, because they have no agency as parts of an undifferentiated nature. Thus, resistance becomes a feature of nature itself, and nature in turn becomes a potential metaphor for the inevitability of resistance to capitalism. Uma recognizes this when she asks the question, "What on earth are you going to do if your tappers decide to take a lesson from your trees?" (202).

Ghosh does not evince the predilection for the sublime over the beautiful that has characterized literary theories and continental philosophy over the past several decades. From Hayden White to F. R. Ankersmit to Jean-François Lyotard to Nicholas Brown and Amy J. Elias, the sublime has been characterized as implicitly emancipatory in contrast to a fascist beauty.[47] Ghosh, however, never undercuts Dinu's or Uma's assertions about beauty. Rather, aesthetic discourses are inescapably heterogeneous in the sense that Chakrabarty describes the political – a notion that defies any single effort to conceptualize it.[48] Whatever the hopes of Schiller and later Romantics, the historical emergence of aesthetics as a legitimatory discourse of capitalism presents real limits to its usefulness.[49] It nonetheless has a certain unruliness, and always has the potential to be unhinged from its initial ideological function. As the scene indicates, the discourse of beauty ends up highlighting the inevitability of resistance, despite every measure taken to ensure order. Despite the fact that Matthew has every single rubber tree imported from a reliable clonal seed, the limits of engineering the social and natural world are mapped in the very representations of the natural world provided by Western discourses. In other words, aesthetics is heterogeneous in the sense that it legitimizes and critiques simultaneously. It should be no surprise then that Adorno himself never entirely rejected beauty, despite his over-quoted assertion that poetry after Auschwitz is barbaric. With both Adorno and Ghosh, there is nothing inherent to nature that provides a kind of map for utopia or resistance. Rather, its position within systems of understanding makes it a sign of ineradicable utopian aspirations.

Thus, Ghosh provides a response to concerns that the resurging interest in aesthetics in the humanities might signal a return to a formalism isolated from history or another universalizing discourse that takes culturally contingent values as transparent and "natural." The aesthetic itself, as Ghosh makes clear, emerges historically as a crucial feature of modernity and Western efforts to reorganize everything on the planet within a single controllable economic system. The appeal to aesthetics by capitalists like Matthew and later by the dissidents like Dinu may involve an appeal to a notion of beauty that appears ahistorical, but this is the ideological work to which the aesthetic is put rather than anything to do with the aesthetic itself. The focus on a specifically aesthetic community at the end of the novel, in contrast to utopias in Ghosh's earlier works, needs to be read in this context. Dinu's declaration that aesthetic spaces exist outside the realm of politics is analogous to the claim of a nature that continually defies the efforts of estate owners to mold the jungle to their needs. The aesthetic promises to provide a space for a collective imagination, reconciling the notion of individual imagination identified by *The Shadow Lines* with the critique of it presented by *In an Antique Land*.

Whether the unruly discourses of aesthetics have the capacity to serve the specific disciplinary needs of postcolonial scholars is another question. Postcolonial theory emerged out of a specific crisis of legitimacy in the

Anglo-American academy in the 1980s. Scholars like Robert Young who insist that it has more revolutionary roots in 1960s independence movements are not incorrect, but the fact that postcolonial theory experiences such a particular boom when it does and where it does has more to do with the needs of English departments to defend their own existence at a time of budget cuts and an anti-intellectual environment promulgated by conservative governments in the United States and Great Britain. Thus, postcolonial theory has always had at least a triple labor: to understand the successes and failures of revolutionary anticolonial movements to establish viable states after gaining independence; to provide a theoretical lens for understanding the emergence and function of literature produced since the late 1950s; to provide a political ground for scholars to justify their own existence. The third task, which has provided much fodder for critics of the field from Aijaz Ahmad to E. San Juan Jr., does not necessarily invalidate the former tasks. As Simon Gikandi notes, people "burdened with the stigma of difference turned to art (and other modern categories) to affirm their universal identity as human beings."[50] The aesthetic, in other words, remains invaluable despite the repeated and by now pro forma deconstruction of universal identity. Chakrabarty's notion of heterogeneity provides only one obvious way of moving beyond the impasse of unqualified affirmation or absolute negation that has haunted so many discussions. Postcolonial studies has been at the forefront of efforts to challenge the universalizing tendencies of modern European thought, and it in turn could benefit from a more thorough investigation of the deliberate refusal to reduce thought to a single set of categories that has been at the heart of modern aesthetic discourses.

Conclusion: imagining together?

This study has argued that a renewed interest in the imagination among contemporary Anglophone writers comes as a response to the perceived consolidation of an imperialist form of capitalism as a world-system. The texts in this study characterized the epistemological task assigned the imagination as one that requires identifying individual experiences in terms of broader economic, political, and social conditions. The imagination, in other words, is consistently conceptualized in intersubjective terms, and the novels in this study struggle to portray what it might mean to imagine together: characterizing imagining not as an individual pursuit that withdraws people from the world around them but as a social practice that engages people with the experiences and worldviews of others.

We also observed, however, that to the extent that novels portray anything resembling a "politics of imagining," such portrayals tend to cast human relations in highly abstracted terms, divorced from the class systems, racial ascriptions, and cultural differences that limit the range of possible interactions among people. If philosophers of the imagination including Ricoeur, Brann, and Kearney argue for a utopian dimension to imagining, this should not be surprising. As all of the authors in this study recognize, to posit the existence of the imagination in the contemporary context is to concede both that the senses are bombarded by various forms of propaganda and that the mental activities associated with human rationality are often insufficient to overcome the distortions they cause. To posit the existence of the imagination, in other words, presupposes a melancholic recognition of a world-system and the limited ability of individuals to stand outside of it. Indeed, theories of the imagination have historically played a role in limiting the kinds of interactions individuals can have and the range of social formations that are conceivable. As Ian Baucom and Rita Barnard have both recently noted, modern notions of the imagination did not simply open up possible realms of existence but also foreclosed them. Hobbesian political theory invokes the imagination, according to Baucom, in order "to outlaw [the era prior to the state] as epistemologically ungraspable and historically catastrophic"; Barnard similarly concludes: "The origins of the state are therefore *sensu stricto* unimaginable."[1]

The ambivalent and often inconsistent attitudes toward the imagination demonstrated by the authors in this study indicate their acute awareness of the ideological ends to which it has so often been put. Indeed, from Coleridge to Appadurai, modern theories of the imagination have struggled to separate its productive and its pernicious tendencies, in part by drawing distinctions between imagination and fancy or fantasy. The distinction emerges in Hobbes's 1651 *Leviathan*, which breaks from the tendency prior to the seventeenth century to use the Greek *phantasia* and the Latin *imaginatio* interchangeably.[2] Coleridge's 1817 *Biographia Literaria* established definitively the modern distinction between a positive, autonomous, creative imagination and a negative, heteronomous, mimetic fancy.[3] More interesting than the distinction itself, which concludes volume 1 of the *Biographia Literaria*, is Coleridge's insistence earlier in chapter 4 that all societies are progressively moving toward such a distinction.[4] Coleridge writes:

It is not, I own, easy to conceive a more opposite translation of the Greek *Phantasia* than the Latin *Imaginatio*; but it is equally true that in all societies there exists an instinct of growth, a certain collective, unconscious good sense working progressively to desynonymize those words originally of the same meaning.[5]

Not only does the definition of imagination require an explicit distinction from fantasy, according to Coleridge; modernity itself as a historical phenomenon can, to no small degree, be measured by the extent to which the imagination acquires its uniqueness. While Appadurai would not state this so baldly, his insistence that the imagination is the key component of a new global order comes at the end of a paragraph that began with his assertion that the imagination is "[n]o longer mere fantasy" – that is, we have arrived at an historical moment in which imagination and fantasy are no longer synonymous.[6]

The distinction between imagination and fantasy has been crucial to efforts to define the conditions necessary for individuals to imagine together. The distinction enables Appadurai, for example, to concede that much of our image-making capacities reproduce the mass media images with which we are bombarded on a daily basis. At the same time, the distinction insists upon an ineradicable capacity of humans not only to create images; more importantly, the goal of imagining is ultimately the construction of collectivities, connecting the individual to broader networks. Appadurai emphasizes the collective dimension of imagining – what he calls imagining as a social practice – in terms that distinctly echo Coleridge's definition of the imagination as something that "struggles to idealize and to unify":[7] "It is the imagination, in its collective forms, that creates ideas of neighborhood and nationhood, of moral economies and unjust rule, of higher wages and foreign labor prospects. The imagination is today a staging ground for action, and not only for escape."[8]

The notion that the imagination is crucial to defining the necessary preconditions to communicating experience runs against the dominant understanding of literary value that now circulates within literary studies as a discipline. As Dorothy J. Hale compellingly argues in a recent *PMLA* essay on the changing profession, literary studies has trumpeted the heterogeneous collection of political theorists which it takes as sources, yet it has largely failed to acknowledge that "the heterogeneity of these political influences has coalesced in a surprisingly unified account of literary value."[9] Martha Nussbaum no less than Judith Butler identifies the value of literature in terms of the "felt encounter with alterity" that it appears to produce. Hale argues: "Incomprehension of the other yields knowledge of the self: we are made to recognize our operative interpretive categories as our own 'regime of the norm.'"[10]

The preoccupation with the imagination among contemporary Anglophone authors qualifies this assessment. Alterity is indeed a crucial feature of the experience of reading, yet alterity is presented in such a manner as to appear potentially intelligible. The distinction from the quasi-Levinasean notions of alterity that dominate academic discussions is important because simple incomprehension need not lead to questioning of our own regimes but often to a sense of alienation or perceived threat. Yet, whether we are talking about beauty in Amitav Ghosh or blood memory in N. Scott Momaday, contemporary Anglophone novels consistently explore various modes of communicating experiences in ways that preserve differences. Momaday's insistence on blood memory, for example, certainly confronts many readers with a sense of alterity, yet his repeated invocations of the imagination and his assertions that identity is the product of imagination provide the necessary means for readers to feel that they can and potentially should engage with experiences that are radically different from their own.

Put more polemically, if the imagination has a small place in literary studies outside of Romanticism, this is in part because it challenges the discipline's "regime of the norm." If the imagination historically has served the ideological function of supporting the universality of bourgeois subjectivity and the aesthetic function of certifying the cultural capital of literary works, it has also served a utopian function of expanding the boundaries of community beyond the obvious markers of affiliation such as nation, race, religion, and class. The renewed interest in the imagination among contemporary novelists, then, suggests a far riskier and more ambitious project than Hale describes; beyond "knowledge of the self" that the experience of alterity affords, the novels in this study press readers to undertake the task of understanding the often obscured interdependence between the self and others – to interpret personal experiences in relation to unfamiliar sets of social, economic, and political conditions, which are represented in mediated form through the novel. The task itself can sound improbable, naïve, and informed by misguided assumptions about what constitutes "human nature." But the epistemological significance the novels in this study attribute to the imagination – and their proposal that imagining can function as a social practice that enables individuals and groups to engage critically with the environments in which they live – invites readers to question "incomprehension of the other" as a foundational assumption guiding literary studies.

Notes

PREFACE AND ACKNOWLEDGMENTS

1 For some useful surveys on the history of imagination, see Richard Kearney, *The Wake of Imagination: Toward a Postmodern Culture* (Minneapolis: University of Minnesota Press, 1988); Edward S. Casey, *Imagining: A Phenomenological Study*, revised edn. (Bloomington: Indiana University Press, 2000); Eva T. H. Brann, *The World of the Imagination: Sum and Substance* (Savage, MD: Rowman & Littlefield, 1991); and James Engell, *The Creative Imagination: Enlightenment to Romanticism* (Cambridge, MA: Harvard University Press, 1981).

2 Even if we restrict ourselves to post-World War II efforts by Eva T. H. Brann, Edward S. Casey, Cornelius Castoriadis, James Engell, Richard Kearney, Paul Ricoeur, and Gilbert Ryle, it is hard to disagree with Ricoeur's suggestion that contradiction might be a structural trait of the imagination. The terms to which it historically has been linked in Western European and North American thinking – ideology, utopia, aesthetics, Romanticism, among them – are themselves resistant to definition. As a result, characterizations of the imagination often seem circular, contingent upon other terms whose definitions are inseparable from it. Even the very existence of the imagination is debatable, whether it represents a single, identifiable faculty or a collection of mental processes.

3 Arjun Appadurai, *Modernity at Large: Cultural Dimensions of Globalization* (Minneapolis: University of Minnesota Press, 1996), 31.

4 Richard Kearney, *The Wake of Imagination*, 3.

5 Saree Makdisi's analysis of the "culture of modernity" and its relationship to Romanticism provides a useful starting point for understanding the significance of the imagination. Makdisi argues that modern imperialism and modern capitalism cannot be understood without reference to British Romanticism. The merging of imperialism and capitalism in the nineteenth century, which Makdisi takes to be the defining feature of the modern era, depended on the creation of narratives of universal history through which the chaotic and unruly pasts of peoples across the world were increasingly assimilated within a single, universal conception of historical development. The unified world-system found its earliest expressions, however, in the imaginative prophecies of Romantic literature. By the late eighteenth century, artists

and philosophers were envisioning both the universal history that an imperialist capitalism subsequently made a reality and anti-histories devoted to preserving alternative ways of life and modes of being. Makdisi writes:

> Whereas modernism, in many of its varieties, celebrates the pre- or anti-modern and the archaic as they are on the verge of final eradication or commodification, romanticism celebrates the pre- or anti-modern at the moment at which that eradication is just beginning.

See Makdisi, *Romantic Imperialism: Universal Empire and the Culture of Modernity* (Cambridge University Press, 1998), 10.

1 INTRODUCTION: GLOBALIZATION, IMAGINATION, AND THE NOVEL

1 Makdisi, *Romantic Imperialism*, 13.
2 Nigel Leask provides a compelling account of how the imagination in Coleridge's thought shifted from a "radical critique of the commercial and capitalist order" during 1797–1805 to a "means of legitimizing a traditional cultural élite." See Leask, *The Politics of Imagination in Coleridge's Critical Thought* (Basingstoke: Macmillan, 1988), 1, 5. According to Leask, Coleridge's shift is paradigmatic of the general eclipse of civic definitions of the imagination.
3 T. S. Eliot, "Building up the Christian World," *The Listener* April 6, 1932, 501.
4 In his apocalyptic *The Wake of Imagination*, Kearney declares that the "psychic world is as colonized as the physical world by the whole image industry" (1). Fredric Jameson's *Postmodernism, or, the Cultural Logic of Late Capitalism* (Durham: Duke University Press, 1991) suggests that the era formerly known as postmodernity is defined by questions about the extent to which the imagination has been co-opted:

   > [I]f postmodernism is a substitute for the sixties and the compensation for their political failure, the question of Utopia would seem to be a crucial test of what is left of our capacity to imagine change at all. (xvi)

5 Russell Jacoby, *Picture Imperfect: Utopian Thought for an Anti-Utopian Age* (New York: Columbia University Press, 2005), xiv.
6 Ibid., xvi.
7 André Brink, "Stories of History: Reimagining the Past in Postapartheid Narrative," in Sarah Nuttall and Carli Coetzee (eds.), *Negotiating the Past: The Making of Memory in South Africa* (Cape Town: Oxford University Press, 1998), 31.
8 Throughout this study, I will be following Brann's convention of using the term "imagination" to refer to a faculty of the mind; the term "imagining" refers to the activities engaged in by that faculty.
9 See Richard Rorty, *Philosophy and the Mirror of Nature* (Princeton University Press, 1979); F. R. Ankersmit, *Sublime Historical Experience* (Stanford University Press, 2005); Hans-Georg Gadamer, *Truth and Method*, trans. Joel Weinsheimer and Donald G. Marshall, 2nd revised edn. (New York: Continuum, 1999).

10 Claire Chambers, "'The Absolute Essentialness Conversations': A Discussion with Amitav Ghosh," *Journal of Postcolonial Writing* 41.1 (2005), 30.

11 Gaurav Desai draws the basis for his term "epistemological coloniza-tion" from V. Y. Mudimbe's seminal work, *The Invention of Africa: Gnosis, Philosophy, and the Order of Knowledge* (Bloomington: Indiana University Press, 1988). See Desai, *Subject to Colonialism: African Self-Fashioning and the Colonial Library* (Durham: Duke University Press, 2001), 4.

12 Paul Ricoeur argues that the free play of the imagination anticipated by Kant points to the idea of the imagination as "a general function of what is possible in practice." See Ricoeur, "Imagination in Discourse and in Action," in *Rethinking Imagination: Culture and Creativity*, ed. Gillian Robinson and John Rundell (London: Routledge, 1994), 127.

13 Deborah Elise White, *Romantic Returns: Superstition, Imagination, History* (Stanford University Press, 2000), 2. White herself demonstrates a certain defensiveness about her project, emphasizing that she is not rehabilitating the imagination, but using it to investigate the category of the aesthetic. John Whale's *Imagination under Pressure, 1789–1832: Aesthetics, Politics and Utility* (Cambridge University Press, 2000), provides a very useful account of the shifting attitude toward the imagination among scholars of Romanticism, and he makes a compelling case for the imagination as an "integral and still undervalued component of cultural critique" (1).

14 Forest Pyle, *The Ideology of Imagination: Subject and Society in the Discourse of Romanticism* (Stanford University Press, 1995), 175.

15 Ricoeur argues that utopian thinking is inseparable from the imagin-ation: "May we not say then, that imagination itself – through its utopian function – has a *constitutive* role in helping us *rethink* the nature of our social life?" See Ricoeur, *Lectures on Ideology and Utopia*, ed. George H. Taylor (New York: Columbia University Press, 1986), 16.

16 Pyle, *The Ideology of Imagination*, 175.

17 Quoted in Kearney, *The Wake of Imagination*, 418. See Aristotle, *De Anima*, 427b.

18 Quoted by John Rundell, "Creativity and Judgment: Kant on Reason and Imagination," in *Rethinking Imagination: Culture and Creativity*, ed. Gillian Robinson and John Rundell (London: Routledge, 1994), 91.

19 For further information on Kant's flip-flop on the imagination, see Kearney, *The Wake of Imagination*, 171.

20 Nigel Leask, *The Politics of Imagination in Coleridge's Critical Thought*, 3.

21 Simon Gikandi, *Ngũgĩ wa Thiong'o* (Cambridge University Press, 2000), 42. See also Ngũgĩ, *Decolonising the Mind: the Politics of Language in African Literature* (London: James Currey, 1986), 90.

22 Ngũgĩ wa Thiong'o, *Decolonising the Mind*, 90.

23 Achebe, *Hopes and Impediments: Selected Essays*, 1988 (New York: Doubleday, 1989), 139; italics in original. Subsequent references are given in the text.

24 Leavis, *The Great Tradition: George Eliot, Henry James, Joseph Conrad*, 1948 (New York University Press, 1960), 29. Leavis famously defined Jane Austen as the "inaugurator of the great tradition of the English novel," linking her

greatness to her preoccupation with moral questions: "Without her intense moral preoccupation she wouldn't have been a great novelist" (7).

25 Achebe explicitly defines morality in terms of the capacity to imagine the circumstances of other individuals in his essay "The Truth of Fiction." He writes: "A person who is insensitive to the suffering of his fellows is that way because he lacks the imaginative power to get under the skin of another human being and see the world through eyes other than his own." See Achebe, *Hopes and Impediments*, 149.

26 Abdul JanMohamed, *Manichean Aesthetics: The Politics of Literature in Colonial Africa* (Amherst, University of Massachusetts Press, 1983), 151.

27 Ibid., 283.

28 Ngũgĩ, *Homecoming: Essays on African and Caribbean Literature, Culture and Politics* (London: Heinemann, 1972), xv.

29 Ibid.

30 Ngũgĩ, *Penpoints, Gunpoints, and Dreams: Towards a Critical Theory of the Arts and the State in Africa* (Oxford: Clarendon Press, 1998), 21. Subsequent references are given in the text.

31 Ngũgĩ, *Devil on the Cross*, 188.

32 George Levine's introduction to the edited collection *Aesthetics and Ideology* offers a very useful summary of the rise of ideology as the central question for the humanities in the 1980s and the concurrent dismissal of aesthetics. See Levine, "Introduction: Reclaiming the Aesthetic," in *Aesthetics and Ideology*, ed. George Levine (New Brunswick: Rutgers University Press, 1994), 1–30.

33 For Terry Eagleton, the critical potential of the aesthetic as a category is inseparable from its complicity with the production of modern class society. He writes: "The aesthetic is at once, as I try to show, the very secret prototype of human subjectivity and early capitalist society, and a vision of human energies as radical ends in themselves which is the implacable enemy of all dominative or instrumentalist thought." See Eagleton, *The Ideology of the Aesthetic* (Oxford: Blackwell, 1990), 9.

34 Isobel Armstrong, *The Radical Aesthetic* (Oxford: Blackwell, 2000), 41.

35 Shierry Weber Nicholsen argues for a notion of "exact imagination" in Adorno's late work, although Nicholsen's term is a translation of *exacte Phantasie* rather than the terminology of *Einbildungskraft*, which Kant used more often. See Nicholsen, *Exact Imagination, Late Work: On Adorno's Aesthetics* (Cambridge, MA: MIT Press, 1997), 4. Nicholsen rationalizes her translation by arguing that Adorno was evoking Kant's work rather than Freud's (229 n.9).

36 Adorno, *Aesthetic Theory*, 1970, trans. Robert Hullot-Kentor, ed. Gretal Adorno and Rolf Tiedemann (Minneapolis: University of Minnesota Press, 1997), 109.

37 Ibid., 60.

38 See Deepika Bahri, *Native Intelligence: Aesthetics, Politics, and Postcolonial Literature* (Minneapolis: University of Minnesota Press, 2003), 6; Nicholas

Brown, *Utopian Generations: The Political Horizon of Twentieth Century Literature* (Princeton University Press, 2005), 22–23.

39 Hans Robert Jauss challenged Adorno's *Aesthetic Theory* on similar grounds. For Jauss, Adorno's aesthetics of negativity denies the basic communicative character of art, insisting on an abstract "either–or" of negativity or affirmation. See Jauss, *Aesthetic Experience and Literary Hermeneutics*, trans. Michael Shaw, intro. Wlad Godzich (Minneapolis: University of Minnesota Press, 1982), xxxvii. Jauss, a student of Gadamerean hermeneutics, insisted that aesthetic experience involves an active process of assent and rejection.

Kearney makes a suggestive point in this regard: the utopian theories of the Frankfurt School might benefit from a linkage to what he calls a critical hermeneutics of imagination. See Kearney, *Poetics of Imagining: Modern to Post-Modern* (New York: Fordham University Press, 1998), 223. While the point is never fully developed, the difference in position between Kearney and Adorno becomes apparent in their attitude toward Samuel Beckett. For the latter, Beckett is heroic in his rejection of representation and imagination, and Adorno intended to dedicate *Aesthetic Theory* to him. Kearney, in contrast, sees Beckett as symptomatic of a pessimistic postmodernism that considers the endorsement of a "postmodern aesthetic of failure" the only viable option left (*The Wake of Imagination*, 309). The deconstruction of imagination in Beckett's *Imagination Dead Imagine* and other late works resists despair to the extent that it refuses the binary of hope/despair altogether in favor of a notion of undecidability. But this option sacrifices the possibility of the utopian horizon of history that Kearney considers essential for any collective political action. Recognizing that the political implications of hermeneutics have often remained only implicit (Gadamer frustrated critics and advocates alike with his unwillingness to address political concerns more directly), Kearney's implicit thesis seems to be that the critical potential of Frankfurt School thinking provides a corrective to hermeneutics even as hermeneutics returns the favor.

40 Samuel Beckett's own suspicions of the imagination can be found, for example, in his early study *Proust* (1931), where he declares: "Imagination, applied – a priori – to what is absent, is exercised in vacuo and cannot tolerate the limits of the real." See Beckett, *Proust* (New York: Grove Press, 1931), 56.

41 Brown, *Utopian Generations*, 12.

42 My thinking here is indebted to Daniel Little's theory of "microfoundations" for social explanations. See Little, *Microfoundations, Method, and Causation* (New Brunswick: Transaction Publishers, 1998). For Little, the focus of Marxist social science on so-called macro-explanations of social phenomena needs to be complemented by detailed accounts of "the circumstances of individual choice and action that give rise to aggregate patterns" (4). This microfoundational approach helps to explain why social groups so often do not act in their own best interests.

43 Rob Nixon, *Homelands, Harlem and Hollywood: South African Culture and the World Beyond* (New York: Routledge, 1994), 1.

44 André Brink, *Writing in a State of Siege: Essays on Politics and Literature* (New York: Summit Books, 1983), 221.

45 Dipesh Chakrabarty, *Provincializing Europe: Postcolonial Thought and Historical Difference* (Minneapolis: University of Minnesota Press, 1986), 149.

2 AESTHETIC REVOLUTIONS: WHITE SOUTH AFRICAN WRITING AND THE STATE OF EMERGENCY

1 The State of Emergency declared in July 1985 initially covered thirty-six magisterial districts. It was expanded across the country on June 12, 1986, in anticipation of the tenth anniversary of the student uprising in Soweto.

2 Paton continued to write after helping to found the Liberal Party in 1953; however, he published only two more novels, *Too Late the Phalarope* (1953) and *Ah, But Your Land Is Beautiful* (1981), both of which were considered weak efforts in comparison to *Cry, the Beloved Country*.

3 See Rachel Donadio, "Post-Apartheid Fiction," *The New York Times* December 3, 2006, online.

4 Linda Hutcheon, *The Politics of Postmodernism*, 2nd edn. (London: Routledge, 2002), 3.

5 See Elleke Boehmer, "Endings and New Beginning: South African Fiction in Transition," in *Writing South Africa: Literature, Apartheid, and Democracy, 1970–1995*, ed. Derek Attridge and Rosemary Jolly (Cambridge University Press, 1998), 51; Fredric Jameson, *Postmodernism, or, the Cultural Logic of Late Capitalism* (Durham: Duke University Press, 1991), xvi. Among white South African writers, Coetzee was submitted to the harshest criticism. See Sue Kossew, "Introduction," in *Critical Essays on J. M. Coetzee*, ed. Sue Kossew (New York: G. K. Hall & Co., 1998), 1–17, for a succinct review of the history of Coetzee reception. See also Benita Parry's thoughtful critique in "Speech and Silence in the Fictions of J. M. Coetzee," in *Critical Perspectives on J. M. Coetzee*, ed. Graham Huggan and Stephen Watson (Houndmills: Macmillan, 1996), 37–65.

6 André Brink, *Reinventing a Continent: Writing and Politics in South Africa 1982–1995* (London: Secker and Warburg, 1996), 55. Mark Sanders provides a very useful analysis of the inescapable complicity of South African intellectuals and artists who opposed apartheid. See Sanders, *Complicities: The Intellectual and Apartheid* (Durham: Duke University Press, 2002).

7 The argument presented here is consistent with Abiola Irele's notion of a distinct African imagination. For Irele, white writers including Brink, Coetzee, and Gordimer may legitimately be considered African writers but do not display "the sense of a connection to an informing spirit of imaginative expression rooted in an African tradition." See Irele, "The African Imagination," *Research in African Literatures* 21.1 (1990), 60.

8 Albie Sachs, "Preparing Ourselves for Freedom," in *Writing South Africa: Literature, Apartheid, and Democracy, 1970–1995*, ed. Derek Attridge and Rosemary Jolly (Cambridge University Press, 1998), 239.

9 Njabulo S. Ndebele, *South African Literature and Culture: Rediscovery of the Ordinary* (Manchester University Press, 1994), 67.

10 See Michael Chapman, *South African Literatures* (London: Longman, 1996), 402.

11 Felicity Wood, "Interview with André Brink," *English Academy Review* 18 (2001), 112. Wood's characterization of Brink is useful, but can be misunderstood. The explicit embrace of postmodern stylistics in *States of Emergency* represents the culmination of a process occurring over two decades rather than a radical departure. Even when Brink aligned himself with the "Sestigers" in the 1960s, elements associated with postmodernism were apparent in his writings. According to his own genealogy of postmodernism in South African literature, his 1967 *Aspekte van die Nuwe Prosa* (*Aspects of the New Fiction*) was already highlighting "postmodernist practices like self-reflexivity, parody, and the textualization of the world" in the early writings of the European-educated Sestigers, although the term *postmodern* does not appear in this work. See Brink, "South Africa: Postmodernism in Afrikaans and English Literature," in *International Postmodernism: Theory and Literary Practice*, ed. Hans Bertens (Amsterdam: John Benjamins Publishing Company, 1997), 484. Brink's genealogy suggests that the explicit usage of the term coincides with the State of Emergency (484).

12 Brink, *Writing in a State of Siege: Essays on Politics and Literature* (New York: Summit Books, 1983), 206. Subsequent references are given in the text.

13 In perhaps the most thoughtful and damning criticism of Brink's argument, J. M. Coetzee points out that Brink's basic conception of the writer as a witness against state power presupposes that writers can exist outside of the society they critique, uncontaminated by its values. "Is diagnosis carried out from inside or outside of the body?" Coetzee asks. "If from outside, how did the organ find its way out of the body?" See "André Brink and the Censor," *Research in African Literatures* 21.3 (1990), 72. Put another way, Coetzee questions how imagining can be truly transgressive if Brink is correct that an individual's perceptions are shaped by internalized state propaganda. If the imagination is a mental process, it too presumably would be constrained or determined by the biases that enable most white South Africans to tolerate and even support apartheid.

14 Brink, *A Dry White Season* (London: W. H. Allen, 1979), 304.

15 Intriguingly, Brink faults European Romantics for reinforcing a dichotomy between words and acts. "Since the age of the Romantics writers have experienced what one critic termed 'the fatal lure of action,'" Brink writes in a 1976 essay (*Writing in a State of Siege*, 151). According to Brink's argument, it is this false dichotomy that leads to the sense that writers are irrelevant. Brink insists that writing is "effective as a revolutionary act in its own, peculiar, right" (151).

16 Brink, "Stories of History: Reimagining the Past in Post-Apartheid Narrative," in *Negotiating the Past: The Making of Memory in South Africa*,

ed. Sarah Nuttall and Carli Coetzee (Cape Town: Oxford University Press, 1998), 31.

17 Brink makes this point explicitly in his novel *On the Contrary* (1993) when he declares that governments become powerful by fettering the imagination. See Brink, *On the Contrary* (London: Secker and Warburg, 1993), 181.

18 Brink, *States of Emergency* (New York: Summit Books, 1988), 195. Subsequent references are given in the text.

19 To understand Brink's investment in the imagination, it is helpful to draw a contrast between his pre- and post-Emergency characterizations of the political relevance of literature. In one of his most famous pre-Emergency essays, "Mapmakers" (1978), Brink argues that writers in a repressive society have two functions, both of which are associated with the metaphor of mapmaking. According to the first version, writers have a responsibility to "map" the world around them as realistically as possible, defying attempts by governments to conceal their actions. According to the second version, writers have a responsibility to "map" the world around them so that readers can sense the possibility that social conditions could be changed. Brink writes:

> The writer is not concerned only with "reproducing" the real. What he does is to perceive, below the lines of the map he draws, the contours of another world, somehow a more "essential" world. And from the interaction between the land as he *perceives* it to be and the land as he knows it *can* be, someone from outside, the reader of the map, watches – and aids – the emergence of the meaning of the map. (*Writing In a State of Siege*, 169)

This earlier characterization anticipates many of the elements of his later theorizations of imagination. The crucial difference, however, lies in the extent to which realistic representations can be trusted. In the case of "Mapmakers," Brink argues that the second, more utopian "map" emerges from the initial effort to represent the world as accurately and realistically as possible. In his later writings, representations are far less reliable, and the basic activity of imagining involves a "transgression" of sensory perceptions. Reality itself is not available, at least in many instances, through what individuals see or hear, but must instead emerge from a process of critical reflection that defamiliarizes habitual patterns of interpretation and encourages individuals to find correspondences where they otherwise would not have.

20 See, for example, "South Africa: Postmodernism in Afrikaans and English Literature," in *International Postmodernism: Theory and Literary Practice*, ed. Hans Bertens (Amsterdam: John Benjamins Publishing Company, 1997), 483–90. In his encyclopedic study *The Novel: Language and Narrative from Cervantes to Calvino* (New York University Press, 1998), Brink argues that postmodernism is not only an international phenomenon but also a feature of the European novel throughout its history. Brink writes: "My argument is quite simply that what has so persistently been regarded as the prerogative of the Modernist and Postmodernist novel (and of a few rare predecessors), namely an exploitation of the storytelling properties of language, has in fact been a characteristic of the novel since its inception" (6–7).

21 Brink appears to be blending Gadamer with Schiller, or is not adhering precisely to the former. Gadamer specifically distinguishes his conception of play from Schiller's. In contrast to Schiller's *Spieltrieb* or "play drive," Gadamer argues that play "means neither the orientation nor even the state of mind of the creator [of the work of art] or of those enjoying the work of art, nor the freedom of a subjectivity engaged in play, but the mode of being of the work of art itself." See Gadamer, *Truth and Method*, 2nd edn., trans. Joel Weinsheimer and Donald G. Marshall (New York: Continuum, 1999), 101. This distinction is crucial because it enables Gadamer to suggest that art enables individuals to temporarily suspend the "purposive relations that determine active and caring existence" (102), which would not be possible if the individuals were using a work of art deliberately to achieve a state of play.

22 Gadamer, *Truth and Method*, 306.

23 Michael Chapman, for example, finds that images of national crisis are "too easily swallowed into the text of an erotic escapade." See Chapman, *South African Literatures* (London: Longman, 1996), 405. More significantly, Brink's critics have repeatedly pointed to instances where he reproduces the rhetoric of the apartheid regime. Rosemary Jane Jolly's largely sympathetic account of Brink's fiction suggests that he establishes his authority as a writer by engaging in "the substitution of the authority of the narrative voice for that of the bodies of the violated." See Jolly, *Colonization, Violence, and Narration in White South African Writing: André Brink, Breyten Breytenbach, and J. M. Coetzee* (Athens: Ohio University Press, 1996), 28; see also Diala, "Nadine Gordimer, J. M. Coetzee, and André Brink: Guilt, Expiation, and the Reconciliation Process and Post-Apartheid South Africa," *Journal of Modern Literature* 25.2 (2001/2002), 71; Chait, "Mythology, Magic Realism, and White Writing after Apartheid," *Research in African Literatures* 31.2 (2000), 27.

24 Casey, *Imagining*, ix.

25 Ibid., 189.

26 Brann, *The World of the Imagination*, 711.

27 Ibid., 798.

28 White, *Romantic Returns*, 6.

29 See Ibid., 2; Pyle, *The Ideology of Imagination*, 2.

30 Brink, *Imaginings of Sand* (San Diego: Harvest Books, 1996), 4. Subsequent references are given in the text.

31 Quoted by Jolly, *Colonization, Violence, and Narration in White South African Writing*, 21.

32 Gordimer, *Living in Hope and History: Notes from Our Century* (New York: Farrar, Straus and Giroux, 1999), 191.

33 Ibid.

34 Ibid., 193.

35 Gordimer, *The Essential Gesture: Writing, Politics and Places*, ed. Stephen Clingman (London: Jonathan Cape, 1988), 104. Subsequent references are given in the text.

36 "I am a white South African radical … Please don't call me a liberal," Gordimer declares in a 1974 interview with Michael Ratcliffe. Quoted by Clingman, *The Novels of Nadine Gordimer: History from the Inside* (London: Allen & Unwin, 1986), 145; see also Nancy Topping Bazin and Marilyn Dallman Seymour (eds.), *Conversations with Nadine Gordimer* (Jackson: University Press of Mississippi, 1990), 56.

37 There is some disagreement among scholars about the extent of the influence of Lukács on Gordimer. Stephen Clingman notes that Gordimer only began reading Lukács in 1968, and that her interest in realism can be dated earlier. See Clingman, *The Novels of Nadine Gordimer*, 10. Dominic Head provides a more detailed account of a complex appropriation and disavowal of Lukács. See Head, *Nadine Gordimer* (Cambridge University Press, 1994), 12–18.

38 Gordimer, *The Conservationist*, 1974 (Harmondsworth: Penguin, 1978), 22.

39 Ibid., 141. Head provides a complementary reading of *The Conservationist*. Head argues that the novel represents "an enactment of political transition, a decolonization presented as an historical inevitability" (*Nadine Gordimer*, 99), though for Head the inevitability is based less on quasi-Freudian metaphors of psychic repression than on the modernist form of the novel, which progressively dissolves the coherence of Mehring's narrative.

40 Gordimer, *The Conservationist*, 267. For an excellent analysis of the cultural and political significance of place in Gordimer's writing, see chapter 3 of Rita Barnard's *Apartheid and Beyond: South African Writers and the Politics of Place* (Oxford University Press, 2007).

41 Christopher Heywood argues that even some sympathetic reviewers held similar reservations about Gordimer's brand of realism by the early 1960s. For Heywood himself, there are "penalties as well as rewards for Gordimer's fictional method," which demonstrates significant difficulty in achieving an "authentic voice." See Heywood, *A History of South African Literature* (Cambridge University Press, 2004), 201.

42 Gordimer, *July's People*, 1981 (New York: Penguin, 1982), 132.

43 Ibid., 69.

44 Ibid., 29.

45 Ibid., 160.

46 John Cooke comes to a similar conclusion through an analysis of metaphors of "picturing" in the novel. For Cooke, *July's People* represents a departure from Gordimer's earlier novels in how it points to the limitations of observation. "*July's People* develops as Gordimer's most radical renunciation of the knowledge yielded by observation, of which photography is simply the most obvious example." See Cooke, *The Novels of Nadine Gordimer: Private Lives/ Public Landscapes* (Baton Rouge: Louisiana State University Press, 1985), 168; see also Rowland Smith, "Masters and Servants: Nadine Gordimer's *July's People* and the Themes of Her Fiction," in *Critical Essays on Nadine Gordimer*, ed. Rowland Smith (Boston: G. K. Hall & Co., 1990), 150.

47 Gordimer, *Writing and Being* (Cambridge, MA: Harvard University Press, 1995), 130.

48 For Lukács, a successful revolution requires individuals to develop solidarity based on the recognition of their common experiences of exploitation; as he puts it in *The History of Class Consciousness*, "the fate of the revolution (and with it the fate of mankind) will depend on the ideological maturity of the proletariat, i.e. on its class consciousness." See Lukács, *The History of Class Consciousness*, trans. R. Livingstone (London: Merlin Press, 1990), 70.

49 Gordimer's shift away from Lukács can be traced aesthetically. Lukác's insistence that the revolutionary process is carried out on the class rather than the individual level leads him to insist in *The Historical Novel* that genuinely realistic characters are representatives of historical crises rather than significant agents. Using Sir Walter Scott as his paradigmatic example, Lukács argues: "The 'hero' of a Scott novel is always a more or less mediocre, average English gentleman ... Scott thus lets his important figures grow out of the being of the age, he never explains the age from the position of its great representatives, as do the Romantic hero-worshipers. Hence they can never be central figures of the action." See Lukács, *The Historical Novel*, 1937, trans. Hannah and Stanley Mitchell (London: Merlin Press, 1962), 33, 39. The protagonists of at least some of Gordimer's pre-Emergency novels such as *July's People* can be read in these terms, as representatives rather than heroic individuals. Notably, Bam and Maureen are increasingly referred to by generic pronouns such as "the man" or "the white woman" as the novel progresses. In contrast, Hillela of *A Sport of Nature* (1987) is an exceptional character who personally influences the entire course of the history of sub-Saharan Africa.

50 Gordimer, *A Sport of Nature*, 1987 (New York: Penguin, 1988), 161. Subsequent references are given in the text.

51 Adam Smith argues that sympathy is an essential part of a universal human nature. "The greatest ruffian," Smith declares, "the most hardened violator of the laws of society, is not altogether without it." See Smith, *The Theory of Moral Sentiments*, 1759, ed. Knud Haakonssen (Cambridge University Press, 2002), 11.

52 Andrew Vogel Ettin provides a very useful summary of reviews that criticize Gordimer's connection between sexuality and politics. See Ettin, *Betrayals of the Body Politic: The Literary Commitments of Nadine Gordimer* (Charlottesville: University Press of Virginia, 1993), 69–72.

53 Peck, "What's a Poor White to Do? White South African Option in *A Sport of Nature*," in *Critical Essays on Nadine Gordimer*, ed. Rowland Smith (Boston: G. K. Hall & Co., 1990), 163.

54 Head, *Nadine Gordimer*, 136.

55 Gordimer, *My Son's Story* (New York: Farrar, Straus and Giroux, 1990), 117.

56 Ibid., 275, 276.

57 Ibid., 276.

58 Clingman argues for an "implicit dialectic between romanticism and realism" in Gordimer's work, quoting her description of herself as a "romantic struggling with reality." See Clingman, *The Novels of Nadine Gordimer*, 219. According to Clingman, Romanticism represents a utopian yearning for a

world that transcends the boundaries of Gordimer's social and historical limits, and its presence in her writings has progressively declined since *The Conservationist*.

59 Gordimer, *My Son's Story*, 277.

60 Coetzee, *Doubling the Point: Essays and Interviews*, ed. David Attwell (Cambridge, MA: Harvard University Press, 1992), 99.

61 Coetzee, *Age of Iron*, 1990 (New York: Penguin, 1998), 164. Subsequent references are given in the text.

62 Gordimer, "The Idea of Gardening: *The Life and Times of Michael K.* by J. M. Coetzee," in *Critical Essays on J. M. Coetzee*, ed. Sue Kossew (New York: G. K. Hall & Co., 1998), 143.

63 See, for example, Gordimer, "Preface," in *Critical Perspectives on J. M. Coetzee*, ed. Graham Huggan and Stephen Watson (Houndmills: Macmillan, 1996), vii–xii.

64 The argument that politics depends on ethics in Coetzee's work has been made, for example, by Derek Attridge, James Meffan and Kim L. Worthington, Mike Marais, and, to a lesser degree, Jane Poyner. David Attwell makes a similar argument when he suggests that Coetzee's "carefully positioned metafictional constructions" establish an ethical vision that does not also celebrate colonialism's appropriation of the colonized world. See Attwell, *J. M. Coetzee: South Africa and the Politics of Writing* (Berkeley: University of California Press, 1993), 22. Dick Penner's defense of Coetzee does not appeal to the category of ethics, but it does similarly suggest that political crises are symptomatic of a "more fundamental problem: the psychological, philosophical, and linguistic bases of the colonial dilemma." See Penner, *Countries of the Mind: The Fiction of J. M. Coetzee* (New York: Greenwood Press, 1989), xiv.

65 Quoted in Kimberley Wedeven Segall, "Pursuing Ghosts: the Germanic Sublime and J. M. Coetzee's *Disgrace*," *Research in African Literatures* 36.4 (2005), 40.

66 Rushdie, *Shame*, 1983 (New York: Vintage International, 1989), 92.

67 Ibid., 278.

68 Ibid., 90.

69 Coetzee, *Doubling the Point*, 341.

70 Coetzee explicitly notes that the definition of freedom he presents to Attwell is drawn from Kant (ibid.). Although it is unacknowledged in that particular interview, Coetzee's definition also seems reminiscent of Plato's notion of ideal forms. This becomes more explicit during the final interview in *Doubling the Point*, as Coetzee retrospectively discusses the central preoccupations of his writings: "Why should I be interested in the truth about myself when the truth may not be in my interest? To which, I suppose, I continue to give a Platonic answer: because we are born with the idea of truth" (395).

71 Ibid., 98.

72 For a brief history of the connection between imagination and madness in Western philosophy, see the introduction to James Phillips and James

Morley's edited volume *Imagination and Its Pathologies* (Cambridge, MA: MIT Press, 2003), esp. 1–7.

73 Coetzee, *Waiting for the Barbarians*, 1980 (New York: Penguin, 1982), 143.

74 Coetzee himself articulates a similar point, suggesting that Afrikaner Christian nationalism depended on envisioning a "radically discontinuous intervention into time" that sought to suspend any notion of time moving forward (*Doubling the Point*, 209).

75 For Michael Marais, Coetzee shares Adorno's understanding of aesthetic autonomy, a notion which implies that the artwork exists in an unstable relation to the social world in which it was created. Art continually posits the possibility of a world that has not been damaged and deformed, yet the work of art itself can never escape the world in which it was produced. This argument leads Marais to read Mrs. Curren's declaration that apartheid represents a "crime" not as a measure of her growth but rather as an indication of the "dialectical understanding that it is the artwork's estrangement from history *and* inability to take up a position outside it that enables it to criticize society and to do so 'in terms of its own procedures and issues.'" See Marais, "From the Standpoint of Redemption: Aesthetic Autonomy and Social Engagement in J. M. Coetzee's Fiction of the Late Apartheid Period," *Journal of Narrative Theory* 38.2 (2008), 234.

76 Coetzee understands his work to be influenced by philosophical idealism in at least two prominent senses of the term. First, his thinking is idealist in the Platonic sense that he seems to posit freedom as a concept or ideal form that is beyond our capacity to represent or enact, yet which we struggle to approximate. Second, he accepts Attwell's characterization that his work endorses "a linguistic idealism" that views reality and history purely as constructs of language (*Doubling the Point*, 145). Appreciating Coetzee's increasing interest in realism during the State of Emergency is further complicated by his own terminology. In *Doubling the Point*, he makes a point of emphasizing that he prefers to use the word "illusionism" rather than realism, the former term having far more negative connotations (27).

77 Marais, "From the Standpoint of Redemption," 81–82. Sam Durant similarly rejects the notion of a sympathetic imagination, arguing that a properly ethical relationship requires imagination to be placed in abeyance. "In place of the traditional concept of the sympathetic imagination, in which the self attempts to mentally inhabit the position of the other," Durant argues, "Coetzee's fiction works to other the self, to deprive the subject of its privileges until it is reduced to an approximation of the other." See Durant, "J. M. Coetzee, Elizabeth Costello, and the Limits of the Sympathetic Imagination," in *J. M. Coetzee and the Idea of the Public Intellectual*, ed. Jane Poyner (Athens, OH: Ohio University Press, 2006), 130.

78 McClintock and Nixon, "No Names Apart: The Separation of Word and History in Derrida's 'Le Dernier Mot du Racisme'," in *"Race," Writing, and Difference*, ed. Henry Louis Gates Jr. (University of Chicago Press, 1986), 340.

79 Coetzee, *Doubling the Point*, 249, 248.

80 Ibid., 27.

81 Head notes that Coetzee's purportedly highly self-conscious and deliberately artificial writing style has been overstated by scholars who read him in terms of postmodernism. Indeed, for Head, Coetzee attempts to resuscitate aspects of realism even in earlier novels such as *Life and Times of Michael K.*, which rejects many of the conventions associated with nineteenth-century European realism (*J. M. Coetzee*, 9).

82 I discuss Spivak's shifting attitude toward essentialism more fully in chapter 5.

83 Seyla Benhabib, *Situating the Self: Gender, Community, and Postmodernism in Contemporary Ethics* (New York: Routledge, 1992), 15.

84 Geoffrey Galt Harpham argues that scholars of postmodernity, postcolonial studies, gender studies, feminism, and post-Marxist political theory all inherit the "governing presumptions" of modern critical thinking, the most debilitating of which is the idea that virtue and power are natural antagonists. See Harpham, *Shadows of Ethics: Criticism and the Just Society* (Durham: Duke University Press, 1999), 253. Harpham calls for scholars to move beyond their intellectual "fastidiousness," which has led to an obsession with the idea that the margins represent the site of theoretical consistency. Conceding that any move toward the political center and coalition building will involve compromising theoretical values, Harpham nonetheless insists that academics must be "willing to live with that dimension of worldly life irreducible to theory and incommensurate with strict principle, willing to choose among flawed alternatives" (262).

85 Coetzee, *Elizabeth Costello* (New York: Viking, 2003), 196. Subsequent references are given in the text.

86 Kearney, *Poetics of Imagining*, 227.

3 THE PASTORAL AND THE POSTMODERN

1 The characterization of postmodern literature in terms of an explicit reaction against a purportedly naïve realism is apparent, for example, in Linda Hutcheon, *A Poetics of Postmodernism: History, Theory, Fiction* (New York: Routledge, 1988); Alison Lee, *Realism and Power: Postmodern British Fiction* (London: Routledge, 1990), and Peter Middleton and Tim Woods, *Literatures of Memory: History, Time and Space in Postwar Writing* (Manchester University Press, 2000).

2 Several volumes on Victorian realism are conceived of as direct responses to postmodern characterizations, including *Adventures in Realism*, ed. Matthew Beaumont (Malden: Blackwell, 2007); *Knowing the Past: Victorian Literature and Culture*, ed. Suzy Anger (Ithaca: Cornell University Press, 2001). Harry E. Shaw's *Narrating Reality: Austen, Scott, Eliot* (Ithaca: Cornell University Press, 1999) is a very useful single-authored study on realism in light of postmodern critiques.

3 George Levine, "*Daniel Deronda*: A New Epistemology," in *Knowing the Past: Victorian Literature and Culture*, ed. Suzy Anger (Ithaca: Cornell University Press, 2001), 53.

4 Anger, "Introduction: Knowing the Victorians," in *Knowing the Past: Victorian Literature and Culture*, ed. Suzy Anger (Ithaca: Cornell University Press, 2001), 11.

5 Fowles, *Daniel Martin*, 1977 (New York: Signet, 1978), 1. Subsequent references are given in the text.

6 The pastoral has had a very different function within the context of South African literature, for example, where it provided a crucial ideological vehicle for legitimizing territorial claims by white Afrikaners. For excellent analyses of pastoralism in South African literature, see Rita Barnard's *Apartheid and Beyond: South African Writers and the Politics of Place* (Oxford University Press, 2007) and J. M. Coetzee's *White Writing: On the Culture of Letters in South Africa* (New Haven: Yale University Press, 1988).

7 As scholars have noted, *Daniel Martin* clearly demonstrates a preference for the novel over cinema. Katherine Tarbox, for example, declares that Daniel's errors in perception result from his "cinematic writing style." See Tarbox, *The Art of John Fowles* (Athens: University of Georgia Press, 1988), 88. Robert Alter provides a useful qualification, however, suggesting that Fowles is not rejecting visual images altogether. Indeed, in the final scene of the novel, Daniel gains new awareness of *mimesis* as an ongoing, never consummated task while observing a Rembrandt self-portrait. See Alter, "*Daniel Martin* and the Mimetic Task," in *Critical Essays on John Fowles*, ed. Ellen Pifer (Boston: G. K. Hall & Co., 1986), 162.

8 Terry Gifford, *Pastoral* (London: Routledge, 1999), 45. It is illustrative to read how theorists of the pastoral view mid-eighteenth-century poets such as George Crabbe, who were deliberately writing against traditional pastoral forms in the effort to describe the actual conditions of contemporary rural life. Raymond Williams takes Crabbe to be exemplary of a "counterpastoral" tradition; Michael McKeon describes Crabbe as representative of a shift toward "realism" in eighteenth-century pastoral, but McKeon places the word within quotation marks. See Williams, *The Country and the City* (New York: Oxford University Press, 1975), 12, and McKeon, "The Pastoral Revolution," in *Refiguring Revolutions: Aesthetics and Politics from the English Revolution to the Romantic Revolution*, ed. Kevin Sharpe and Stephen N. Zwicker (Berkeley: University of California Press, 1998), 279.

9 Williams, *The Country and the City*, 22, 61.

10 In *The Aristos*, Fowles characterizes socialism as a fundamentally flawed effort to reinterpret Christianity. Its pursuit of social justice depends on "crude theories of equality, of materialism, of history." See Fowles, *The Aristos: A Self-Portrait in Ideas* (Boston: Little, Brown and Company, 1964), 114.

11 Lukács, *The Historical Novel*, 342.

12 Fowles is highly selective in his appropriation of Lukács. According to George H. Gilpin, Fowles goes beyond the model of Lukács's historical

novel by interweaving fiction and autobiography, thereby breaking down the "formal illusion that art and life are separate." See Gilpin, *The Art of Contemporary English Culture* (Houndmills: Macmillan, 1991), 175. Certainly, Daniel Martin cannot be said to fulfill Lukács's notion of typicality, and the novel signals this point in a scene in which Daniel reads the oft-cited passages from *The Historical Novel* on heroes in the novels of Walter Scott (589–90; see Lukács, *The Historical Novel*, 32–33). As noted earlier, it is hard to see Daniel as a "more or less mediocre, average English gentleman," a point which Daniel himself recognizes; at the same time, the novel insists on reading Daniel's crisis as indicative of a more general national crisis.

13 The conception of realism suggested by *Daniel Martin* can be understood in terms of F. R. Ankersmit's defense of what he calls subjective history. Ankersmit challenges the assumption that historians should bracket their political and moral values when writing historical narratives, arguing that such values are not impositions on the past but the result of a historian's understanding of what "really happened." According to this idea, the historian's task is not to attempt to present a value-free narrative but to provide the most compelling *proposal* for understanding the past. Echoing Daniel Martin's characterization of literary language, Ankersmit argues that "the indeterminacy of the relationship between words and things is not a defect but the supreme virtue of all representational use of language." See Ankersmit, "In Praise of Subjectivity," in *The Ethics of History*, ed. David Carr, Thomas R. Flynn, and Rudolph Makkreel (Evanston: Northwestern University Press, 2004), 12. According to this claim, language cannot be precise without some generally accepted epistemological standard for determining how words ought to be related to things. In the absence of such independent standards, historians have the capacity to choose how to view the past. This is crucial because many representable things have no obvious form in the absence of a representation of them; Ankersmit notes, for example, that the labor movement does not exist as an entity separate from representations of it.

14 McKeon, "The Pastoral Revolution," 272.

15 Fowles, *The French Lieutenant's Woman* (1969; New York: Signet, 1970), 81.

16 Fowles, *Wormholes: Essays and Occasional Writings*, ed. Jan Relf (New York: Henry Holt and Company, 1998), 81.

17 Ibid., 84.

18 Ibid., 223, 225.

19 Spargo, *The Ethics of Mourning: Grief and Responsibility in Elegiac Literature* (Baltimore: Johns Hopkins University Press, 2004), 226.

20 In the final paragraph of Jeremy Paxman's *The English: A Portrait of the People*, he invokes Fowles's distinction between Red-White-and-Blue Britain and Green England to argue that amid the decay of nation-states Englishness represents the "nationalism of the future." See Paxman, *The English: A Portrait of a People* (Woodstock: Overlook Press, 2000), 266. As with Fowles, Paxman is very explicit in casting Englishness in pastoral terms as a spirit that can be accessed only through the imagination.

Paxman declares: "In the collective unconscious from which John Major drew his pictures, there exists another England. It is not the country in which the English actually live, but the place they *imagine* they are living in. It touches the reality they see around them at various points, but it is something ideal ... Their relationship with this arcadia is that of some emotional remittance-man" (144).

21 McKeon, "The Pastoral Revolution," 287.

22 Fowles, *Wormholes*, 79.

23 Simon Gikandi argues that "Englishness was itself a product of the colonial culture that it seemed to have created elsewhere." See Gikandi, *Maps of Englishness: Writing Identity in the Culture of Colonialism* (New York: Columbia University Press, 1996), x. Ian Baucom similarly argues that debates over Englishness have been "understood as struggles to control, possess, order, and dis-order the nation's and the Empire's spaces." See Baucom, *Out Of Place: Englishness, Empire, and the Locations of Identity* (Princeton University Press, 1999), 4. The intriguing paradox of Englishness, as Baucom recognizes, is its simultaneous identification with and contrast to Britishness: "that Englishness has been identified with Britishness, which in turn has been identified as coterminous with and proceeding from the sovereign territory of the Empire, and that Englishness has also defined itself *against* the British Empire" (12).

24 My critique differs somewhat from that of Andrzej Gąsiorek, who suggests that Fowles's philosophical commitments undermine his endorsement of socialism. "Fowles's nominal espousal of socialism is overwhelmed by his deep-rooted commitment to existentialism," Gąsiorek writes, "so that he envisions a world of the Few versus the Many, which is simply incompatible with socialism." See Gąsiorek, *Post-War British Fiction: Realism and After* (London: Edward Arnold, 1995), 117. More troubling yet is the sense that the Few are biologically elect, and Daniel Martin's progressive politics are undermined by his tendency to explain socioeconomic inequalities by way of genetic and evolutionary theory. Blame is displaced away from the economic and political organization of society onto its victims.

25 Ackroyd, *Albion: The Origins of the English Imagination* (London: Chatto & Windus, 2002), xix. Subsequent references are given in the text.

26 Fowles, *Wormholes*, 88.

27 Ackroyd, *The Collection*, ed. Thomas Wright (London: Chatto & Windus, 2001), 366, 336. Subsequent references are given in the text.

28 Fowles, *Wormholes*, 79.

29 Paul Gilroy significantly misreads Ackroyd on this point, declaring that *Albion* is "memorable for its casual employment of the language of race." See Gilroy, *Postcolonial Melancholia* (New York: Columbia University Press, 2005), 114.

30 Quoted by Barry Lewis, *My Words Echo Thus: Possessing the Past in Peter Ackroyd* (Columbia: University of South Carolina Press, 2007), 185.

31 In his earlier work, Ackroyd declared that "England is a dispirited nation," one that has insulated itself from modernism by desperately clinging to an

outdated and philosophically untenable liberal humanism (*Notes for a New Culture*, 146). His condemnation of English literature is sweeping:

> Our own literature has revealed no formal sense of itself and continues no substantial language. Our writing has acquiesced in that orthodoxy which has already been described, resting as it does upon a false aesthetic of subjectivity and a false context of realism. And it is this conventional aesthetic which has been reified into the English "tradition." (147)

32 Lewis, *My Words Echo Thus*, 153.
33 Quoted by Gifford, *Pastoral*, 8.
34 Sympathetic readings of Ackroyd's work demonstrate the challenge of reconciling his earlier and later works. Susana Onega, for example, characterizes *Hawksmoor* and *Chatterton* as historiographic metafiction, even though Ackroyd himself rejects the label of postmodernist in an interview with her. See Onega, *Metafiction and Myth In the Novels of Peter Ackroyd* (Columbia, SC: Camden House, 1999), 2; "Interview with Peter Ackroyd," *Twentieth-Century Literature* 42.2 (1996), 218. Jeremy Gibson and Julian Wolfreys attempt to disassociate Ackroyd from the conservative sentiments of *English Music* by arguing that they represent an elaborate pastiche of cultural attitudes associated with 1980s conservatism, reproduced as ironic mimicry through the narrative voice of Timothy Harcombe. See Gibson and Wolfreys, *Peter Ackroyd: The Ludic and Labyrinthine Text*, Peter Nicholls (foreword) (New York: St. Martin's Press, 2000), 140, 143.
35 Ackroyd has shifted considerably both his definitions of postmodernism and his relationship to it. Perhaps his most revealing and useful definition appears in a 1986 review of Timothy Mo's *An Insular Possession*, where he declares: "If 'post-modernism' means anything, it is in its disavowal both of conventional realism and self-conscious experimentalism, and this is precisely the area where historical fiction has come into its own" (*Collection*, 191).
36 Gibson and Wolfreys, *Peter Ackroyd: The Ludic and Labyrinthine Text*, 143.
37 Ackroyd, *Notes for a New Culture: An Essay on Modernism* (London: Vision, 1976), 49–50. Eliot's own use of the term "medium" to describe a creative writer can be found in *Selected Essays*, new edn. (New York: Harcourt, Brace & World, 1964), 9.
38 The notion that imitation or pastiche can facilitate an accurate historical reconstruction is also endorsed by A. S. Byatt, whose pastiche in *Possession: A Romance* (1990) has been taken to be one of the most remarkable works of postmodern fiction. In her essay "True Stories and the Facts in Fiction" (2000), Byatt asserts: "I do believe that if I read *enough*, and carefully enough, I shall have some sense of what words meant in the past, and how they related to other words in the past, and be able to use them in a modern text so that they do not lose their relations to other words in the interconnected web of their own vocabulary." See Byatt, *On Histories and Stories: Selected Essays* (London: Chatto & Windus, 2000), 177. Byatt later qualifies this assertion (197), and in her essay "Forefathers" she faults

Ackroyd's biography on Charles Dickens for combining factual research with imagined dialogues between himself and his subject. See John J. Su, "Fantasies of (Re)collection: Collecting and Imagination in A. S. Byatt's *Possession: A Romance*," *Contemporary Literature* 45.4 (2004), 684–712.

39 Lewis, *My Words Echo Thus*, 38, 46.

40 De Man, *Blindness and Insight: Essays in the Rhetoric of Contemporary Criticism*, 2nd revised edn. (Minneapolis: University of Minnesota Press, 1983), 239.

41 Ackroyd, *Chatterton* (New York: Grove Press, 1987), 231.

42 Ibid., 228.

43 Ackroyd, *First Light* (New York: Ballantine, 1989), 323.

44 Ibid., 325.

45 Ackroyd, *English Music*, 1992 (New York: Ballantine, 1994), 392. Subsequent references are given in the text.

46 Ackroyd, *First Light*, 3.

47 Ibid., 7.

48 Ibid., 102.

49 Lawrence Buell, *The Environmental Imagination: Thoreau, Nature Writing, and the Formation of American Culture* (Cambridge, MA: Belknap Press, 1995), 32.

50 Quoted by Lewis, *My Words Echo Thus*, 186.

51 Ackroyd opens his biography of William Blake with the declaration: "In the visionary imagination of William Blake there is no birth and no death, no beginning and no end, only the perpetual pilgrimage within time towards eternity." See Ackroyd, *Blake* (London: Sinclair-Stevenson, 1995), 17.

52 Eliot, *Selected Essays*, 4.

53 William Empson, *Some Versions of Pastoral* (London, Chatto & Windus, 1950), 6.

54 This is not to say that the history of the pastoral prior to its usage within the English novel provides no useful information or shape to its usage within the novel. But the focus on the representative anecdote that Paul Alpers identifies with pastoral poetry might not be as relevant within novelistic traditions. Alpers draws the basis of his definition of the representative anecdote from Kenneth Burke. According to Alpers, the representative anecdote is so important for analyzing the pastoral because "pastoral makes explicit a certain disproportion between its fictions, conspicuously modest and selective, and the meanings they bear or imply: there is always a suggestion that 'more is meant than meets the ear.'" See Alpers, *What Is Pastoral?* (University of Chicago Press, 1996), 16. By focusing on the representative anecdote, Alpers establishes a much more restrictive definition of pastoral than Annabel Patterson, Lawrence Buell, Andrew V. Ettin, William Empson, and others who have argued that the pastoral has historically demonstrated a plasticity that defies efforts at rigid definition. However, his point that the pastoral appears more conventional than other forms because its conventions focus on community is very useful. The pastoral's focus on community sits

well with Eliot's conception of the writer as a medium rather than an individual personality at the same time that it acknowledges the possibility for individual imagination that is so important to Ackroyd, and that distinguishes Ackroyd from Eliot. Indeed, imagination appears again and again as an issue in *English Music*, and the idea of an English imagination is at the heart of Ackroyd's notion of tradition. As Thomas K. Hubbard suggests, the pastoral's focus on intertextuality has always meant that it provided a space for evoking and revising tradition, for proclaiming one's originality on the basis of knowledge of tradition. He writes: "The core texts of the pastoral tradition are thus preeminently poems about literary tradition and the quest for a new and independent voice that can stand up to the cumulative weight of tradition." See Hubbard, *The Pipes of Pan: Intertextuality and Literary Filiation in the Pastoral Tradition from Theocritus to Milton* (Ann Arbor: University of Michigan Press, 1998), 6. Hence, portrayals of old masters teaching their songs to young men and women is a paradigmatic narrative feature of the pastoral.

55 For further analysis of Waugh's nostalgia, see my *Ethics and Nostalgia in the Contemporary Novel* (Cambridge University Press, 2005), 119–30.

56 David Dabydeen, *Disappearance* (London: Martin Secker & Warburg, 1993), 178.

57 Iain Chambers, *Migrancy, Culture, Identity* (London: Routledge, 1994), 27.

58 Dabydeen, *Disappearance*, 131.

59 Barnes, *England, England* (New York: Alfred A. Knopf, 1999), 41. Subsequent references are given in the text.

60 Head, *The Cambridge Introduction to Modern British Fiction, 1950–2000* (Cambridge University Press, 2002), 120. Julian Murphet reads *England, England* as paradigmatic of a "potent ideological wish under the cool surfaces of the Postmodern UK." See Murphet, "Fiction and Postmodernity," in *The Cambridge History of Twentieth Century English Literature*, ed. Laura Marcus and Peter Nicholls (Cambridge University Press, 2004), 720. The pastoral worlds created by the novel represent, according to this argument, an English reaction to global postmodernism – positing the existence of worlds unravaged by capitalism, yet recognizing that the very act of doing so has become a cliché in the wake of Romanticism.

61 Barnes, *Flaubert's Parrot*, 1984 (New York: McGraw-Hill, 1985), 216.

62 Barnes, *A History of the World in 10½ Chapters* (New York: Alfred A. Knopf, 1989), 243–44.

63 Sara Henstra, "The McReal Thing: Personal/National Identity in Julian Barnes's *England, England*," in *British Fiction of the 1990s*, ed. Nick Bentley (London: Routledge, 2005), 105.

64 James Wood similarly notes that Englishness has been repeatedly characterized as undefinable in literary texts; in contrast to Paxman, however, Wood finds this to be a fault rather than a virtue. Indeed, Wood argues that "We need to mobilise Englishness as an activity rather than an attribute," as something that can be changed or even dissolved. See

Wood, "An Activity Not an Attribute: Mobilising Englishness," in *The Revision of Englishness*, ed. David Rogers and John McLeod (Manchester University Press, 2004), 64.

65 Barnes, *Letters from London* (New York: Vintage International, 1995), 27.

66 McKeon, "The Pastoral Revolution," 267.

67 Radhakrishnan, *Theory in an Uneven World* (Malden: Blackwell, 2003), x.

4 HYBRIDITY, ENTERPRISE CULTURE, AND THE FICTION OF MULTICULTURAL BRITAIN

1 The creation of a national "enterprise culture" was one of the central projects of Prime Minister Margaret Thatcher in the 1980s. Seen as an alternative to the postwar "culture of dependency," enterprise culture encouraged individuals to look to personal ingenuity and the marketplace rather than the government for solutions to economic and social issues. For further discussion of enterprise culture and its effects on British society, see John Corner and Sylvia Harvey (eds.), *Enterprise and Heritage: Crosscurrents of National Culture* (London: Routledge, 1991) and Robert Hewison, *Culture and Consensus: England, Art and Politics since 1940* (London: Methuen, 1995).

2 Kureishi, *My Beautiful Laundrette and Other Writings* (London: Faber & Faber, 1996), 77.

3 Ibid., 48.

4 The introductions to Pnina Werbner and Tariq Modood's *Debating Cultural Hybridity: Multi-Cultural Identities and the Politics of Anti-Racism* (London: Zed, 1997) and Avtar Brah and Annie E. Coombs's *Hybridity and Its Discontents: Politics, Science, Culture* (London: Routledge, 2000) provide useful summaries of the debates surrounding conceptions of cultural hybridity. Influential critiques of Homi Bhabha's conception by Aijaz Ahmad, Arif Dirlik, and Benita Parry have shaped much of the subsequent debate. All three of these critiques were grounded in materialist theories and faulted Bhabha's representation of the colonial encounter as "a complicit relationship" rather than an antagonistic one (Parry, 67); his tendency to "replace all historicity with mere contingency" (Ahmad, 17); and his "reduction of social and political problems to psychological ones" (Dirlik, 333). Other critiques have focused on the "implicit politics of heterosexuality" associated with hybridity as a cultural description (Young, 25) and the tendency of theories of hybridity to promote a sense that colonial violence was inevitable (Afzal-Khan, 27). See Parry, *Postcolonial Studies: A Materialist Critique* (London: Routledge, 2004), 67; Ahmad, "The Politics of Literary Postcoloniality," *Race & Class* (1995), 17; Dirlik, "The Postcolonial Aura: Third World Criticism in the Age of Global Capitalism," *Critical Inquiry* 20.2 (1994), 333; Robert Young, *Colonial Desire: Hybridity in Theory, Culture and Race* (London: Routledge, 1995), 25; Afzal-Khan, "At the Margins of Postcolonial Studies: Part 2," in *The Pre-Occupation of Postcolonial Studies*, ed. Fawzia Afzal-Khan and Kalpana Seshadri-Crooks (Durham: Duke University Press, 2000), 27.

5 For a broad survey of different conceptions of hybridity in contemporary British fiction, see Philip Tew, *The Contemporary British Novel* (London: Continuum, 2004), 150–79.

6 Ashley Dawson, *Mongrel Nation: Diasporic Culture and the Making of Postcolonial Britain* (Ann Arbor: University of Michigan Press, 2007), 14, 26.

7 See, for example, Homi K. Bhabha, *The Location of Culture* (London: Routledge, 1994), 167, 225–26; Kenneth C. Kaleta, *Hanif Kureishi: Postcolonial Storyteller* (Austin: University of Texas Press, 1998); and Dominic Head, "Zadie Smith's *White Teeth*," in *Contemporary British Fiction*, ed. Richard J. Lane, Rod Mengham, and Philip Tew (Cambridge: Polity, 2003).

8 See Bhabha, "The Third Space: Interview with Homi Bhabha," in *Identity: Community, Culture, Difference*, ed. Jonathan Rutherford (London: Lawrence and Wishart, 1990), 208, and *The Location of Culture* (London: Routledge, 1994), 34.

9 Bhabha, "The Third Space," 211.

10 The discomfort with Bhabha's spatial metaphors is particularly apparent in a conversation with Bhabha, Rashid Araeen, Susheila Nasta, and Patrick Wright recorded in the journal *Wasafiri*. For Araeen, spatial metaphors imply that identity is static, and theories that employ them tend to endorse identity politics and to neglect works of authors who cannot be easily identified with a specific group. See Wright, "Reinventing Britain: Interview with Homi Bhabha, Susheila Nasta, and Rashid Araeen," *Wasafiri* 29 (1999), 41. Nasta also asserts that spatial metaphors have been used to valorize migrancy in ways that discount histories of resistance associated with particular locations (42).

11 Bhabha's writings on hybridity continue to be cast as the definitive statement even in recent studies committed to moving beyond the language of hybridity, such as Ashley Dawson's *Mongrel Nation* (see, e.g., 160).

12 In Bhabha's usage, hybridity has at least two distinct though not incompatible meanings. Hybridity refers to both a *condition* that results from encounters between individuals of different cultures and a *strategy* for appropriating imperial social codes and ideas in order to challenge their authority. Bhabha has consistently asserted that all cultures are engaged in an ongoing process of hybridizing ("The Third Space," 211; see also Young, *Colonial Desire*, 23). Bhabha also discusses numerous instances of colonized populations employing the "powers of hybridity" as a strategy for challenging colonial power by appearing to submit to its authority (*The Location of Culture*, 118). In one of his most well-known examples, Bhabha discusses how Indians in the early nineteenth century requested that Bibles be translated into local languages, a request that threatened to disrupt the authority of the British colonial administration by breaking the "God–Englishman equivalence" that was one of the central pillars of colonial power (see 102–22).

13 Bhabha, "The Third Space," 211.

14 Selvon, *The Lonely Londoners*, 1956 (New York: Longman, 1985), 140.

15 Bhabha, *The Location of Culture*, 86.

16 Selvon, *Moses Ascending*, 1975 (London: Heinemann, 1984), 4.

17 Naipaul, *The Mimic Men*, 1967 (New York: Vintage International, 2001), 24.

18 Ibid., 300.

19 Ibid., 26.

20 Ibid., 300–1.

21 Phillips, *The Final Passage* (London: Faber & Faber, 1985), 198.

22 For a succinct history of the term *hybridity* and its usage within discourses on British national identity, see Young, *Colonial Desire*, 6–19.

23 Phillips, *Cambridge*, 1991 (New York: Vintage International, 1993), 52.

24 Ibid., 76.

25 Phillips's 2003 novel *A Distant Shore* represents a partial exception to his tendency to portray intercultural dialogues as failures. The male protagonist of the novel, an African who enters England illegally to escape certain death in his home country, is eventually befriended by an Irish lorry driver named Mike and the elderly couple he lives with, Mr. and Mrs. Anderson. Solomon, the protagonist's assumed name, demonstrates profound gratitude to Mike and the Andersons for giving him a home in England, yet he is subsequently beaten, kidnapped, and murdered by a group of racist teenagers.

26 Parry, *Postcolonial Studies*, 65.

27 Ibid., 67.

28 Bhabha appears to see the psychoanalytic characterization of history as an extension of Ernest Renan's seminal argument that nationalism depends on forgetting as much as remembering. Bhabha argues: "It is the process of remembering-to-forget that gives the national culture its deep psychological hold and its political legitimacy." See Bhabha, "A Question of Survival: Nations and Psychic States," in *Psychoanalysis and Cultural Theory: Thresholds*, ed. James Donald (New York: St. Martin's Press, 1991), 93.

29 Bhabha himself argues that postwar immigration to Britain from its former colonies represents the "material legacy of this repressed history" ("Third Space," 218).

30 For detailed explorations of the relationship between portrayals of the English country house and national identity, see chapter 4 of my *Ethics and Nostalgia in the Contemporary Novel* (Cambridge University Press, 2005) and chapter 5 of Ian Baucom's *Out of Place: Englishness, Empire, and the Locations of Identity* (Princeton University Press, 1999).

31 Ishiguro, *The Remains of the Day* (New York: Vintage Books, 1989), 123.

32 Ibid., 124.

33 Robert Hewison, *Culture and Consensus: England, Art and Politics since 1940* (London: Methuen, 1995), 212.

34 E. San Juan Jr., *Beyond Postcolonial Theory* (New York: St. Martin's Press, 1998), 166.

35 Steven Connor argues that there was a disturbing "critical unanimity" among early reviews of Ishiguro's novel that it was focused on questions of Japanese identity rather than British (107).

36 Parry, *Postcolonial Studies*, 63.

37 Rushdie, *Midnight's Children* (New York: Avon Books, 1980), 306.

38 Rushdie, *Imaginary Homelands: Essays and Criticism 1981–1991* (London: Granta Books, 1991), 137.

39 Ibid., 394.

40 Gikandi, *Maps of Englishness*, 213.

41 Rushdie, *The Satanic Verses*, 1988 (Dover: Consortium, 1992), 5. Subsequent references are given in the text.

42 My argument here corresponds in large degree with Judith Butler's revised theory of performativity presented in *Bodies that Matter: On the Discursive Limits of "Sex."* Responding to critics of her conception of "gender performativity," in *Gender Trouble* and other early works, Butler argues against the conflation of *performativity* and *performance*. Conflating the two terms makes it difficult to reconcile the fact that gender identities are not costumes that an individual may choose or discard at will and yet they are produced and modified over time through reiterated descriptions of women. Thus, for Butler, performance involves a deliberate fabrication in which the performer chooses a certain role, and "works to conceal, if not disavow, what remains opaque, unconscious, unperformable." See Butler, *Bodies that Matter: On the Discursive Limits of "Sex"* (London: Routledge, 1993), 234. Performativity, in contrast, "must be understood not as a singular or deliberate 'act,' but, rather, as the reiterative and citational practice by which discourse produces the effects that it names" (2). This definition of performativity is complex and idiosyncratic, given that it appropriates Jacques Derrida's revision of J. L. Austin's term and places it within a Foucauldian discourse of power. But the central point it enables Butler to make is that any given attempt to redefine gender must confront an entire history of how the term has been used within a culture. As a result, gender identities are highly stable not because of biology but because of a history of repeated usage, and even efforts to subvert historical usage tend to have limited effectiveness because they reinvoke the very history they seek to escape.

43 Bhabha, "The Third Space," 213; see also Wright, "Reinventing Britain: Interview with Homi Bhabha, Susheila Nasta, and Rashid Araeen," 42.

44 The problem with using Rushdie as an example of Bhabha's cultural hybridity becomes apparent in Susheila Nasta's criticism of hybridity. For Nasta, Bhabha's conception of hybridity is equated with what she terms "Rushdie's migrants floating upwards from history" ("Reinventing Britain," 42). Indeed, Rushdie reveals a more general problem associated with Bhabha's thinking; according to Nasta: "The danger with a lot of postmodern and postcolonial theorising of the migrant figure is that paradoxically the migrant

is not traveling as light as might sometimes appear." Bhabha, in contrast, has focused on migrancy as a metaphor rather than on characters who are migrants. In his reading of *The Satanic Verses* in "The Third Space," for example, Bhabha argues: "To think of migration as metaphor suggests that the very language of the novel, its form and rhetoric, must be open to meanings that are ambivalent, doubling, and dissembling. Metaphor produces hybrid realities by yoking together unlikely traditions of thought. *The Satanic Verses* is, in this sense, structured around the metaphor of migrancy" (212).

45 Bhabha, *The Location of Culture*, 27.

46 Ibid., 39.

47 Graham Huggan makes a similar argument, claiming that Chamcha's mimicry lacks the disruptiveness Bhabha claims for it. Indeed, Huggan asserts that Chamcha's mimicry functions "more as a symptom of his subjection to a vast, metropolitan-based image-making industry." See Huggan, *The Postcolonial Exotic: Marketing the Margins* (London: Routledge, 2001), 93.

48 Rushdie, *Shame*, 90.

49 Martin Corner, "Beyond Revisions: Rushdie, Newness and the End of Authenticity," in *The Revision of Englishness*, ed. David Rogers and John McLeod (Manchester University Press, 2004), 160.

50 Daniel Pipes, *The Rushdie Affair: The Novel, the Ayatollah, and the West* (New York: Birch Lane Press, 1990), 241.

51 Rushdie, *Imaginary Homelands*, 394. The sad irony is that, throughout the 1980s, Rushdie took pains to underscore the heterogeneity of Islam, and to criticize the implicit racism in most Western portrayals of the religion. In his 1985 essay "In God We Trust," for example, Rushdie declares: "What 'Islam' now means in the West is an idea that is not merely medieval, barbarous, repressive and hostile to Western civilization, but also united, unified, homogeneous, and therefore dangerous" (*Imaginary Homelands*, 382). In the defense of *The Satanic Verses*, however, Rushdie asserted that the novel "tells us there are no rules. It hands down no commandments," implying that his critics were primarily concerned with preserving eternal and unchanging religious purity (423).

52 Kureishi, *The Black Album*, 1995 (New York: Scribner, 1996), 255. Subsequent references are given in the text.

53 Kureishi, *The Buddha of Suburbia*, 1990 (New York: Penguin, 1991), 3.

54 Sukhdev Sandhu, "Pop Goes the Center: Hanif Kureishi's London," in *Postcolonial Theory and Criticism*, ed. Laura Chrisman and Benita Parry (Cambridge: D. S. Brewer, 2000), 142. Jago Morrison makes a similar argument, suggesting that Kureishi is attempting to move "beyond race," concentrating instead on the problems of conformism and consumerism. See Morrison, *Contemporary Fiction* (London: Routledge, 2003), 183.

55 Kureishi, *The Buddha of Suburbia*, 213.

56 In a sly reference to Rushdie, Kureishi portrays Shahid "betraying" Al-Hussain by rewriting his poetry. In one of the most inflammatory

scenes of *The Satanic Verses*, a character named Salman the Persian is portrayed as modifying the verses Mahound receives from the angel Gibreel.

57 Bart Moore-Gilbert, "*The Black Album*: Hanif Kureishi's Revisions of 'Englishness'," in *The Revision of Englishness*, ed. David Rogers and John McLeod (Manchester University Press, 2004), 143.

58 Bhabha in Wright, "Reinventing Britain," 42.

59 In the introduction to his screenplay *My Son the Fanatic* (1997), Kureishi identifies a similar opposition between fundamentalism and writers. The problem with fundamentalism, according to Kureishi, is that it offers just "one story" in which truth is fixed and unchangeable; writers, in contrast, provide many stories with many different purposes, linked only by their capacity to grant "pleasure of different kinds." See Kureishi, *Collected Screenplays* (London: Faber and Faber, 2002), 221.

60 Ali, *Brick Lane* (New York: Scribner, 2003), 56.

61 Ibid., 172.

62 Ibid., 400.

63 Ibid., 415.

64 While it is beyond the scope of this chapter, a fuller account of shifting attitudes toward cultural hybridity would also explore how part of the retreat from expansive claims about the future of multicultural Britain since the mid-1990s should be attributed to a shift in perception about the importance of Englishness. Perhaps the most stunning example of this shift can be found in David Dabydeen's *Disappearance* (London: Martin Secker & Warburg, 1993). In this novel, the protagonist – an engineer from Guyana working to shore up Dunsmere Cliffs on the Kent coast from erosion – ultimately dismisses England as a nostalgic and decaying monument. "To smash up England would be no more than going berserk in a waxwork museum," he declares. "It would be a waste of action" (179). Immigrants from former colonies more figuratively shore up the imperial center in Meera Syal's *Anita and Me* (London: Flamingo, 1996), which portrays Indian immigrants purchasing the "Big House" of Tollington village and its failing coal mine, which had supported the local economy (13).

65 Laura Moss, "The Politics of Everyday Hybridity: Zadie Smith's *White Teeth*," *Wasafiri* 39 (2003), 14.

66 Smith, *White Teeth* (New York: Vintage International, 2000), 271. Subsequent references are given in the text.

67 Dominic Head, "Zadie Smith's *White Teeth*," in *Contemporary British Fiction*, ed. Richard J. Lane, Rod Mengham, and Philip Tew (Cambridge: Polity, 2003), 114.

68 Peter Childs, *Contemporary Novelists: British Fiction since 1970* (New York: Palgrave Macmillan, 2005), 203.

69 Paul Gilroy, *Against Race: Imagining Popular Culture beyond the Color Line* (Cambridge, MA: Belknap Press, 2000), 117.

70 Ibid., 356.

5 GHOSTS OF ESSENTIALISM: RACIAL MEMORY
AS EPISTEMOLOGICAL CLAIM

1 This definition of essence traces back to Aristotle's *Metaphysics*, although precedents can be found in Plato. See Christine Battersby, *The Phenomenal Woman: Feminist Metaphysics and the Patterns of Identity* (Cambridge: Polity Press, 1998), 25. Less rigid conceptions of essence can be found in John Locke and Henri Bergson, but critiques of essentialism almost invariably focus on the Aristotelian conception.

2 For a succinct discussion of the recent "thaw" toward essentialism, see Linda Martín Alcoff, *Visible Identities: Race, Gender, and the Self* (New York: Oxford University Press, 2006), 14–15.

3 Stephen Heath, "Difference," *Screen* 19 (Autumn 1978), 99.

4 Gayatri Chakravorty Spivak, "In a Word. Interview," *differences* 1 (Summer 1989), 129.

5 Diana Fuss, *Essentially Speaking: Feminism, Nature & Difference* (New York: Routledge, 1989), 4.

6 Linda Martín Alcoff, "Who's Afraid of Identity Politics?" In *Reclaiming Identity: Realist Theory and the Predicament of Postmodernism*, ed. Paula M. L. Moya and Michael R. Hames-García (Berkeley: University of California Press, 2000), 322.

7 Walter Benn Michaels, "Race into Culture: A Critical Genealogy of Cultural Identity," *Critical Inquiry* 18 (Summer 1992), 684–85. A recent formulation of his argument appears in *The Trouble with Diversity: How We Learned to Love Identity and Ignore Inequality* (New York: Metropolitan Books, 2006). Here, Michaels argues that the "American love affair with race" is motivated by a widespread desire to avoid confronting class inequalities (7).

8 In their 1994 response to Michaels, Avery Gordon and Christopher Newfield characterize his work as symptomatic of a burgeoning movement of "post-civil rights liberalism" that identifies the elimination of the concept of race as a realistic and necessary ideal for America. See "White Philosophy," *Critical Inquiry* 20 (Summer 1994), 738. A renewed critique of racial identity and ethnic studies programs has also been made by scholars influenced by Marxian theories, and it is apparent in a number of recent studies including Paul Gilroy's *Against Race: Imagining Popular Culture beyond the Color Line* (Cambridge, MA: Belknap Press, 2000); E. San Juan Jr.'s *Racism and Cultural Studies: Critiques of Multiculturalist Ideology and Politics of Difference* (Durham: Duke University Press, 2002); Antonia Darder and Rodolfo D. Torres's *After Race: Racism after Multiculturalism* (New York University Press, 2004); and, to a lesser extent, Terry Eagleton's *After Theory* (New York: Basic Books, 2003). My chapter provides an indirect response to these studies, as they do not couch their critique in terms of the issue of essence. These studies share a sense that the preoccupation with race and racial identity in ethnic studies programs occludes more basic class exploitation, and prevents the formation of broadly based alliances that might resist multinational

corporations. The vision of multiculturalism promoted by ethnic studies programs, San Juan argues, thereby serves the interests of multinational capitalism by recasting foundational inequalities in terms of "difference." "Multiculturalism, as long as it is conceived within the existing framework of the racial polity, of a hegemonic order founded on class inequality, cannot offer the means to realize justice, fairness, and the recognition of peoples' singular identities and worth" (8).

9 Fuss, *Essentially Speaking*, 4.

10 Stuart Hall, "New Ethnicities," in *Black Film, British Cinema* (London: Institute of Contemporary Arts, 1988), 30.

11 N. Scott Momaday, "Personal Reflections," in *The American Indian and the Problem of History*, ed. Calvin Martin (New York: Oxford University Press, 1987), 156.

12 Ibid.

13 Arnold Krupat, *The Voice in the Margin: Native American Literature and the Canon* (Berkeley: University of California Press, 1989), 14. In *The Turn to the Native* (Lincoln: University of Nebraska Press, 1996), Krupat offers a somewhat modified assessment in the context of his reading of Gerald Vizenor's *Heirs of Columbus*. Here, Krupat suggests that Momaday's conception of racial memory may be motivated by very laudable goals, but it nonetheless promotes "politically retrograde" thinking (62). Krupat favors what he perceives as Vizenor's more self-conscious, postmodern strategy of invoking blood memory as a trope, yet he still concludes that it represents a "troubling locution" (60).

14 Satya P. Mohanty, *Literary Theory and the Claims of History: Postmodernism, Objectivity, Multicultural Politics* (Ithaca: Cornell University Press, 1997), 216.

15 I use the term *ethnic American author* advisedly. A number of scholars of Native American literature and culture including Simon Ortiz, Robert Warrior, Jace Weaver, Craig S. Womack, and Sean Teuton have argued for the importance of reading authors such as Momaday with respect to a tribal, nationalist framework rather than an ethnic one. Weaver asserts: "Such incorporation denies Native literature recognition of its own distinct existence, specific differences, and independent status as literary production and, as [Louis] Owens contends, retards consideration of Native works in their own cultural contexts." See *That the People Might Live: Native American Literatures and Native American Community* (Oxford University Press, 1997), 23. This argument is further developed in Jace Weaver, Craig S. Womack, and Robert Warrior's *American Indian Literary Nationalism* (Albuquerque: University of New Mexico Press, 2006) and Sean Teuton's *Red Land, Red Power: Grounding Knowledge in the American Indian Novel* (Durham: Duke University Press, 2008). My intention is to complement such scholarship; I use the term *ethnic American author* to emphasize that my primary focus is reading Momaday's work in relation to other writers in the United States whose cultural traditions and life experiences have been similarly marginalized.

16 N. Scott Momaday, "The Man Made of Words," in *Literature of the American Indians: Views and Interpretations*, ed. Abraham Chapman (New York: Meridian, 1975), 97; my emphasis. Subsequent references are given in the text.

17 See Matthias Schubnell, *N. Scott Momaday: The Cultural and Literary Background* (Norman: University of Oklahoma Press, 1985); Susan Scarberry-García, *Landmarks of Healing: A Study of House Made of Dawn* (Albuquerque: University of New Mexico Press, 1990); Louis Owens, *Other Destinies: Understanding the American Indian Novel* (Norman: University of Oklahoma Press, 1992); and Chadwick Allen, *Blood Narrative: Indigenous Identity and American Indian and Maori Literary and Activist Texts* (Durham: Duke University Press, 2002).

18 Joan Scott, "Experience," in *Feminists Theorize the Political*, ed. Judith Butler and Joan Scott (New York: Routledge, 1992), 34.

19 See, for example, Jace Weaver, *That the People Might Live: Native American Literatures and Native American Community* (New York: Oxford University Press, 1997), 7, and Craig S. Womack, *Red on Red: Native American Literary Separatism* (Minneapolis: University of Minnesota Press, 1999), 26.

20 Rey Chow, *Writing Diaspora: Tactics of Intervention in Contemporary Cultural Studies* (Bloomington: Indiana University Press, 1993), 38.

21 Gayatri Chakravorty Spivak, *In Other Worlds: Essays in Cultural Politics* (New York: Routledge, 1988), 205. Spivak has distanced herself from strategic essentialism, although the term continues to enjoy widespread usage. See "In a Word. Interview," 127.

22 Mohanty shares Spivak's sense that identities are necessary for political activism; he differs from Spivak, however, in his belief that political goals and philosophical commitments are mutually constitutive. Indeed, for Mohanty, questions of identity are inseparable from questions of how individuals or collectives should act. "[T]he possibility of accurately interpreting our world fundamentally depends on our coming to know what it would take to change it," Mohanty argues, "on our identifying the central relations of power and privilege which sustain it and make the world what it is" (*Literary Theory*, 214). To accomplish this end, individuals must draw on their personal experiences, as Michaels would insist, but Mohanty's theory recognizes the partial validity of the poststructuralist critique of experience made most famously by Joan Scott. Because an individual's conception of his or her own experience is not self-evident but the result of reflection and interpretation, experience can often be a source of distortion and mystification as much as knowledge. To minimize mystification and arrive at more objective knowledge about themselves and their experiences, individuals must continually explore how their various experiences might be better understood in relation to broader social forces that position individuals in categories of relative privilege or want. Such explorations will necessarily involve drawing upon experiences in which individuals did not personally participate. Thus, Mohanty would presumably be sympathetic to Michaels's

assertion that slavery and the Holocaust should not *inherently* be central dimensions of an African American or Jewish cultural identity; however, these events would be relevant if they help to explain why people who are identified with these groups currently face economic inequalities or discriminatory policies.

23 N. Scott Momaday, *The Ancient Child* (New York: Doubleday, 1989), 45.

24 Ibid., 312.

25 Ibid., 315.

26 Chadwick Allen, "Blood (and) Memory," *American Literature* 71.1 (March 1999), 94.

27 Kwame Anthony Appiah, *The Ethics of Identity* (Princeton University Press, 2005), 66.

28 A similar argument can be found in Terry Eagleton's *After Theory*. Eagleton asserts that the idea that cultural identities are easily malleable has been one of the central errors of postmodern thinking. "Living as [postmodernists] apparently do in a pre-Darwinist, pre-technological world," he writes, "they fail to see that Nature is in some ways much more pliable stuff than culture. It has proved a lot easier to level mountains than to change patriarchal values ... Cultural beliefs, not least the fundamentalist variety which are bound up with fears for one's identity, are far harder to uproot than forests." See *After Theory* (New York: Basic Books, 2003), 50.

29 Frank Chin, *Donald Duk* (Minneapolis: Coffee House Press, 1991), 42. Subsequent references are given in the text.

30 Christine Battersby, *The Phenomenal Woman: Feminist Metaphysics and the Patterns of Identity* (Cambridge: Polity Press, 1998), 16.

31 Frank Chin, "Come All Ye Asian American Writers of the Real and the Fake," in *The Big Aiiieeeee!: An Anthology of Chinese American and Japanese American Literature*, ed. Jeffrey Paul Chan et al. (New York: Meridian, 1991), 1–92.

32 Jinqi Ling, *Narrating Nationalisms: Ideology and Form in Asian American Literature* (New York: Oxford University Press, 1998), 14.

33 Lisa Lowe, *Immigrant Acts: On Asian American Cultural Politics* (Durham: Duke University Press, 1996), 64.

34 Frank Chin, *The Chickencoop Chinaman and The Year of the Dragon: Two Plays*, intro. Dorothy Ritsuko McDonald (Seattle: University of Washington Press, 1981), 6.

35 Frank Chin et al. (eds.), *Aiiieeeee! An Anthology of Asian-American Writers* (Washington, DC: Howard University Press, 1974), xlvii.

36 Chin, "Come All Ye Asian American Writers," 140.

37 Efforts by David Leiwei Li to rehabilitate Chin's work by invoking Spivak's notion of strategic essentialism have failed because Chin provides no indication that his conception of identity is provisional, "a stage in the ultimate transcendence of racisms." See David Leiwei Li, *Imagining the Nation: Asian American Literature and Cultural Consent* (Stanford University Press, 1998), 122.

38 Avery F. Gordon, *Ghostly Matters: Haunting and the Sociological Imagination* (Minneapolis: University of Minnesota Press, 1997), 16.

39 Sonia Kruks, *Retrieving Experience: Subjectivity and Recognition in Feminist Politics* (Ithaca: Cornell University Press, 2001), 85.

40 Linda Martín Alcoff, *Real Knowing: New Versions of the Coherence Theory* (Ithaca: Cornell University Press, 1996), 221.

41 According to Allen, "orthodox postcolonial critics often fail to understand how discourses that intersect with the controversial blood/land/memory complex, including the discourse of treaties, might appear cogent for indigenous activists and writers." See *Blood Narrative: Indigenous Identity in American Indian and Maori Literary and Activist Texts* (Durham: Duke University Press, 2002), 30. For further discussion of the relationship between land and memory in Momaday's work, see chapter 3 of my *Ethics and Nostalgia in the Contemporary Novel* (Cambridge University Press, 2005).

42 N. Scott Momaday, "Confronting Columbus Again," in *Native American Testimony: A Chronicle of Indian-White Relations from Prophecy to the Present, 1492–2000*, ed. Peter Nabokov (New York: Penguin, 1999), 440.

43 Quoted by Matthias Schubnell (ed.), *Conversations with N. Scott Momaday* (Jackson: University Press of Mississippi, 1997), 3.

44 Ibid., 6.

45 N. Scott Momaday, *The Way to Rainy Mountain* (Albuquerque: University of New Mexico Press, 1969), 4.

46 N. Scott Momaday, *The Names: A Memoir* (Tucson: University of Arizona Press, 1976), 22.

47 San Juan, *Racism and Cultural Studies*, 160.

48 Mohanty, *Literary Theory*, 232–33. See also Paula M. L. Moya, *Learning from Experience: Minority Identities, Multicultural Struggles* (Berkeley: University of California Press, 2002), 38.

6 AMITAV GHOSH AND THE AESTHETIC TURN IN POSTCOLONIAL STUDIES

1 Deepika Bahri, *Native Intelligence: Aesthetics, Politics, and Postcolonial Literature* (Minneapolis: University of Minnesota Press, 2003), 1.

2 This tendency is apparent even in Graham Huggan's remarkable *The Postcolonial Exotic: Marketing the Margins* (London: Routledge, 2001), which argues that aesthetics provides the means for exploiting cultural differences through the production of a notion of the exotic. Exoticism, according to Huggan, is an "aestheticising process through which the cultural other is translated, relayed back through the familiar" (ix). Aesthetics, for Huggan, is a mechanism of decontextualizing cultural practices and traditions in order to render them for consumption by metropolitan audiences. Intriguingly, Huggan holds out the possibility that exoticism in postcolonial writing has the potential to "unsettle metropolitan expectations" and to critique

"differential relations of power" (ix, x), but aesthetics is not understood to play a part.

3 Robert J. C. Young, "Ideologies of the Postcolonial," *Interventions: International Journal of Postcolonial Studies* 1.1 (1998), 7. The curious neglect of aesthetics is apparent in many of the seminal works of postcolonial studies. Aesthetics does not even appear in the index of Edward Said's *Orientalism* or Homi Bhabha's *The Location of Culture*; in Gayatri Chakravorty Spivak's *A Critique of Postcolonial Reason*, "aesthetic judgment" and "Hegel's *Aesthetics*" each receives a single page reference. Yet Spivak opens her work with a critical reading of Kant's *Critique of Judgment*, which, according to her argument, inaugurates a tradition within European thinking of constructing the *native informant* as "needed and foreclosed" in order to construct Europeans as the universal human norm. See Spivak, *A Critique of Postcolonial Reason: Toward a History of the Vanishing Present* (Cambridge, MA: Harvard University Press, 1999), 6. Said similarly locates the rise of modern Orientalism in the late eighteenth century, though he makes no explicit connection to the concurrent rise of modern notions of aesthetics. He does indicate that the aesthetic plays a role in the formation of an imperialist tradition, but only in passing, such as when he asks: "What other sorts of intellectual, aesthetic, scholarly, and cultural energies went into the making of an imperialist tradition like the Orientalist one?" See Said, *Orientalism* (New York: Vintage, 1979), 15.

4 See, for example, Laura Chrisman, *Postcolonial Contraventions: Cultural Readings of Race, Imperialism, and Transnationalism* (Manchester University Press, 2003), 1.

5 Bahri, *Native Intelligence*, 9.

6 Brown, *Utopian Generations: The Political Horizon of Twentieth-Century Literature* (Princeton University Press, 2005), 22–23.

7 Chakrabarty has been criticized for creating a monolithic, worldwide notion of modernity. Partha Chatterjee provides a useful caution in the context of a critique of Benedict Anderson's thesis on nationalism, arguing that the evidence of "anticolonial nationalism" belies a notion that postcolonial nations are necessarily limited to certain "modular" forms already made available to them by Europe. To accept too readily such arguments about nationalism would risk reducing the postcolonial world to "perpetual consumers of modernity." See Chatterjee, *The Nation and Its Fragments: Colonial and Postcolonial Histories* (Princeton University Press, 1993), 5.

8 Gikandi argues: "It is this utopian possibility, the dream that the work of art might actually be separated from the slave economy that sustained it, that made the aesthetic central to the slave's attempt to claim the central categories of bourgeois culture, including freedom, morality, and subjectivity. It is one of the great ironies of modern culture that the people excluded from the realm of artistic genius and aesthetic judgments were the ones who valued the aesthetic the most." See Gikandi, "Race and the Idea of the Aesthetic," *Michigan Quarterly Review* 40.2 (2001), 344.

9 Herbert Marcuse, *The Aesthetic Dimension: Toward a Critique of Marxist Aesthetics* (Boston: Beacon Press, 1978), 62.

10 "No concept is more fundamental to modernity than the aesthetic," Harpham argues, "that radiant globe of material objects and attitudes ideally independent of politics, rationality, economics, desire, religion, or ethics." See Harpham, "Aesthetics and the Fundamentals of Modernity," in *Aesthetics and Ideology*, ed. George Levine (New Brunswick: Rutgers University Press, 1994), 124. Eagleton similarly argues: "The construction of the modern notion of the aesthetic artefact is thus inseparable from the construction of the dominant ideological forms of modern class-society, and indeed from a whole new form of human subjectivity appropriate to that social order." See Eagleton, *The Ideology of the Aesthetic* (Oxford: Blackwell, 1990), 3.

11 See Kant, *The Critique of Judgment*, 1790, trans. James Creed Meredith (Oxford: Clarendon press, 1952), §20–22.

12 Tobin Siebers, "Kant and the Politics of Beauty," *Philosophy and Literature* 22.1 (1998), 32. It is precisely this notion of communicability that is lost in Adorno's thought, as Hans Robert Jauss recognized more than twenty years ago. Jauss argues: "The strength and indispensability of Adorno's aesthetic theory ... has been purchased at the price of a derogation of all communicative functions." See Jauss, *Aesthetic Experience and Literary Hermeneutics*, trans. Michael Shaw, ed. Wlad Godzich (Minneapolis: University of Minnesota Press, 1982), 19. For Jauss, the importance Adorno ascribes to negativity in the experience of art does not necessarily require surrendering the possibility of what he terms the "communicative identification with a developing social norm and lifestyle" (18), and the literature of courtly love provides him a crucial example. Such literature, Jauss suggests, involves both a negation of ecclesiastical norms governing marriage and an emancipation of forms of communication between the sexes.

13 For R. Radhakrishnan, Ghosh develops a "strategy of polyvocality and heteroglossia that is much more multi-historical than the kind of metropolitan ventriloquism one finds in the works of Salman Rushdie." See Radhakrishnan, "Postmodernism and the Rest of the World," in *The Pre-Occupation of Postcolonial Studies*, ed. Fawzia Afzal-Khan and Kalpana Seshadri-Crooks (Durham: Duke University Press, 2000), 61.

14 In an interview with Claire Chambers, for example, Ghosh declares that he owes Naipaul an "enormous, enormous debt" as a pioneering Indian writer, although he "disagree[s] with almost everything that Naipaul says." See Chambers, "A Discussion with Amitav Ghosh," *Journal of Postcolonial Writing* 41.1 (2005), 35.

15 Frederick Luis Aldama, "An Interview with Amitav Ghosh," *World Literature Today* 76.2 (2002), 87, 89.

16 Ghosh, *The Glass Palace* (New York: Random House, 2001), 438. Subsequent references are given in the text.

17 Nonidentitarian aesthetics, like so many Adornean concepts, defies easy definition. In *Negative Dialectics*, Adorno defines identity as "the correspondence of the thing-in-itself to its concept." See Adorno, *Negative Dialectics*, trans. E. B. Ashton (New York: Seabury, 1973), 149. What this

means in practical terms is less obvious, however, because Adorno's critique of identitarian thinking appears to grow out of several sources. Susan Buck-Morss notes that Adorno was responding to the tradition of German idealism, and specifically Hegel; she also notes that it was apparently a response to Heidegger and Benjamin. See Buck-Morss, *The Origin of Negative Dialectics: Theodor W. Adorno, Walter Benjamin, and the Frankfurt Institute* (New York: The Free Press, 1977), 43–62, 232–33 n.1. Simon Jarvis insists that Adorno's theory is heavily indebted to Marx's theory of commodity fetishism. See Jarvis, *Adorno: A Critical Introduction* (Cambridge: Polity Press, 1998), 167. The implication is that capitalism represents an extreme form of an inherent human tendency to render the world comprehensible by means of classifying objects in terms of linguistic categories. In chapter 3 of her *Native Intelligence*, Bahri provides an excellent discussion of Adorno in light of postcolonial theory.

18 Adorno, *Aesthetic Theory*, trans. Robert Hullot-Kentor, ed. Gretal Adorno and Rolf Tiedemann (Minneapolis: University of Minnesota Press, 1997), 52.

19 Adorno emphasized in his final essay that the conscientious artist or intellectual "neither superscribes his conscience nor permits himself to be terrorized into action," recognizing that the refusal to engage in political praxis is itself the most radical form of dissent. Quoted by Said, "Adorno As Lateness Itself," in *Adorno: A Critical Reader*, ed. Nigel Gibson and Andrew Rubin (Malden: Blackwell, 2002), 202.

20 Ghosh: *Incendiary Circumstances: A Chronicle of the Turmoil of Our Times* (Boston: Houghton Mifflin Company, 2005), 136. Subsequent references are given in the text.

21 Adorno, *Aesthetic Theory*, 70, 62.

22 Ibid., 73.

23 Kant offers his most concise definition of beauty in §22 of *The Critique of Judgment*: "The beautiful is that which, apart from a concept, is cognized as object of a *necessary* delight" (85).

24 Tobin Siebers argues for a politics of beauty that develops Kant's argument in *The Critique of Judgment* that judgments of the beautiful involve not a private feeling but a "public sense" (84). For Siebers, aesthetic judgment thereby provides an analogy for political judgment: "It offers the experience of a free political space, a space of intersubjectivity, in which a multitude of thinking people are dedicated to an open discussion – unbound by previously existing prejudices – and committed to reaching an agreement acceptable to all. Beauty is, in short, politics' idea of utopia, and although it be utopian, a wonderful idea it sometimes is" ("Kant and the Politics of Beauty," 48).

25 In interviews, Ghosh has repeatedly emphasized over the years his efforts to blend and mix genres. In an interview with Frederick Luis Aldama, Ghosh declares: "I know that the institutional structure of our world presses us to think of fiction and nonfiction as being absolutely separate … But I think the techniques one brings to bear upon nonfiction, certainly the techniques

I've brought to bear on nonfiction, essentially come from my fiction." See Aldama, "An Interview with Amitav Ghosh," 86. Similarly, in conversation with T. Vijay Kumar, Ghosh declares: "See, for me the novel is *the* form that synthesizes all kinds of expression … So this is why I write novels, because I think novels can synthesize geology, history, personal relationships, emotion, everything." See Kumar, "'Postcolonial' Describes You As a Negative," *Interventions: International Journal of Postcolonial Studies* 9.1 (2007), 103.

26 In "The Fundamentalist Challenge," Ghosh's call for reimagining spaces of "creative dissent" of the kind that Dinu models is motivated not simply by the desire to find an effective response to the market ideal but also by the anxiety that religious extremism will increasingly become the dominant mode of expressing dissent against it (*Incendiary Circumstances*, 137). Religion, in Adorno's *Aesthetic Theory*, is dismissed as a pathetic and anachronistic fantasy, "those Sunday institutions that provide solace" (2). In this, he follows Marx in seeing religion primarily as a means of shoring up capitalism by providing promises of eternal, if delayed, gratification for submitting to the yoke of this world. Growing up in postindependence India, Ghosh, in contrast, saw firsthand the capacity of religion to provide a powerful source of identity and political mobilization that is frequently not contained by dominant institutions of power, though religious groups certainly maintain strategic alliances with them. Thus, for Ghosh, the question is not whether artworks have the capacity to express dissent or not; as will become more apparent later, dissent is an inevitable byproduct of capitalism itself. The question is rather what form dissent will take. In the absence of aesthetic spaces, Ghosh concludes that "the misdirected and ugly energies of religious extremism will only continue to flourish and grow" (*Incendiary Circumstances*, 137).

27 Chakrabarty argues that modern European political thought has been consistently guided by historicist assumptions that fail to account for the importance of the supernatural and religious beliefs. Chakrabarty argues: "We need to move away from two of the ontological assumptions entailed in secular conceptions of the political and the social. The first is that the human exists in a frame of a single and secular historical time that envelops all other kinds of time … The second assumption running through modern European political thought and the social sciences is that the human is ontologically singular, that gods and spirits are in the end 'social facts,' that the social somehow exists prior to them." See Chakrabarty, *Provincializing Europe*, 15–16.

28 Lambert Zuidervaart provides a compelling case for reading Adorno's approach as a "crucial counterweight" to prevailing assumptions about the social significance of the arts, even while acknowledging that since his death new social movements, the emergence of postmodernism, and transformations in institutions cast significant doubt on some of Adorno's central premises and arguments. See Zuidervaart, "Introduction," in *The Semblance of Subjectivity: Essays in Adorno's Aesthetic Theory*, ed. Tom Huhn and Lambert Zuidervaart (Cambridge, MA: MIT Press, 1997), 5.

29 Yumna Siddiqi follows Partha Chatterjee's seminal argument that nationalism is inextricably tied to Enlightenment rationality, hence the importance of exploring the possibility of separating emancipatory from coercive elements of reason. Siddiqi notes that while the novel does present a number of utopian scenarios, they tend to occur outside of the "bounded and closely regulated territory of the nation." See Siddiqi, "Police and Postcolonial Rationality and Amitav Ghosh's *The Circle of Reason*," *Cultural Critique* 50 (2002), 193. In so doing, Ghosh signals the unlikelihood of establishing a noncoercive reason; at best, he can mark the limits of Enlightenment reason and its guarantee of "epistemological transparency" through the character of Alu, whose opaqueness and unknowability continually defy the efforts of other characters or readers to interpret his reasoning.

30 Ghosh, *The Circle of Reason*, 1986 (New York: Mariner Books, 2005), 54. Subsequent references are given in the text.

31 In the midst of a conversation with Dr. Verma, Alu discovers a passage in *The Life of Pasteur* declaring that germs are an inevitable part of human life, further undercutting the idea of the "pure" aesthetic utopia.

32 Marc Redfield, *The Politics of Aesthetics: Nationalism, Gender, Romanticism* (Stanford University Press, 2003), 22.

33 Siebers, "Kant and the Politics of Beauty," 43–44.

34 Kant declares in §20: "The judgment of taste, therefore, depends on our presupposing the existence of a common sense. (But this is not to be taken to mean some external sense, but the effect arising from the free play of our powers of cognition)" (83). Indeed, Kant's anxiety about the actual existence of such a sense is apparent in the distinction he introduces between *sensus communis* and "common understanding" (*gemeine Verstand*). Common sense, he writes, "differs essentially from common understanding, which is also sometimes called common sense (*sensus communis*): for the judgment of the latter is not one by feeling, but always one by concepts, though usually only in the shape of obscurely represented principles" (82–83). Henry E. Allison's chapter "The Modality of Taste and the *sensus communis*," in *Kant's Theory of Taste: A Reading of the Critique of Aesthetic Judgment* (Cambridge University Press, 2001), provides a very useful discussion of the difference between the two terms.

35 In interviews and essays, Ghosh has argued that the heteroglossia characterizing Indian culture denies the possibility of a unitary or pregiven coherence to national identity. See Ghosh, "The Diaspora in Indian Culture," *Public Culture* 2.1 (1989), 75, 78; see also Patricia Sharmani Gabriel, "The Heteroglossia of Home: Re-'routing' the Boundaries of National Identity in Amitav Ghosh's *The Shadow Lines*," *Journal of Postcolonial Writing* 41.1 (2005), 40, 43, and Kumar, " 'Postcolonial' Describes You As a Negative," 104.

36 In an interview with T. Vijay Kumar, Ghosh declares that heteroglossia is a defining characteristic of India:

> We live in a society where heteroglossia is commonplace. It's a society where, if you seek to represent that society in a single language, no matter what that language is, you are in some profound way distorting the reality of that society.

See Kumar, "'Postcolonial' Describes You As a Negative," 104. Even under the most ideal and altruistic conditions, no single language can encompass all experiences, particularly in societies in which multiple languages coexist. In interviews and essays such as "The Diaspora in Indian Culture," Ghosh has argued that the heteroglossia characterizing Indian culture denies the possibility of a unitary or pregiven coherence to national identity (75, 78; see also Gabriel, "The Heteroglossia of Home," 40, 43).

37 Jonathan Loesberg proposes a return to aesthetics that involves not only redefining concepts such as autonomous form, disinterest, and symbolic embodiment but also revisiting the history of aesthetics itself: "aesthetics was not the companion to Enlightenment ideas about reason and objective justice, but was rather the model prior to reason and objectivity from which the Enlightenment attempted to give those concepts value." See Loesberg, *A Return to Aesthetics: Autonomy, Indifference, and Postmodernism* (Stanford University Press, 2005), 3.

38 In interviews, Ghosh has explicitly taken on Jameson's controversial thesis that Third World literature is focused on creating allegories of nationhood. For Ghosh, in contrast, families often represent a more crucial unit of identity than the nation, and represent the central focus of his work. Rejecting the notion that families represent a "mirror of nation" in his writing, Ghosh states that Jameson's thesis is "just a load of rubbish. Many of my books, if not all of my books, have really been centered on families ... And I think it is not just me. I think the reason why you see so many Indian books essentially centered on the family is precisely because the nation is not, as it were, the central imaginative unit. So I think Jameson and Bhabha and all the others are completely wrong about this" (Aldama, "An Interview with Amitav Ghosh," 89). In an extended e-mail dialogue with Dipesh Chakrabarty, Ghosh draws out his argument that the family rather than the nation represents the center of his literary works. The dialogue is transcribed in "A Correspondence on *Provincializing Europe*," *Radical History Review* 83 (2002), 146–72.

39 Ghosh, *The Shadow Lines*, 1988 (New York: Mariner Books, 2005), 221. Subsequent references are given in the text.

40 Ghosh, *In an Antique Land: History in the Guise of a Traveler's Tale*, 1992 (New York: Vintage Archers, 1994), 288. Subsequent references are given in the text.

41 James Clifford opens his *Routes: Travel and Translation in the Late Twentieth Century* (Cambridge, MA: Harvard University Press, 1997) with a discussion of Ghosh's "The Imam and the Indian," which appears in revised form in *In an Antique Land*. Clifford declares that the Egyptian village Ghosh describes represents a central "figure for postmodernity, the New World order of mobility" (1). Nor were the accolades for Ghosh's work limited to anthropologists. Theo D'Haen argued that the transgressive appropriations of European colonial literatures in *In an Antique Land* model a notion of "bound intertextuality" that should be central to a renewed form

of Comparative Literature studies. See D'Haen, "Antique Lands, New Worlds? Comparative Literature, Intertextuality, Translation," *Forum for Modern Language Studies* 43.2 (2007), 108. For a useful summary of the academic reception of *In an Antique Land*, see Gaurav Desai's "Old World Orders: Amitav Ghosh and the Writing of Nostalgia," *Representations* 85 (2004), 125–48.

42 Ghosh's efforts to articulate a non-Western form of cosmopolitanism have been one of the central topics of Ghosh scholarship. Inderpal Grewal, for example, argues that Ghosh reconstructs a romanticized notion of the precolonial in order to envision a cosmopolitanism distinct from "diasporic consciousness" popularized by postmodernism and postcolonial scholars influenced by it, such as Homi Bhabha. See Grewal, "Amitav Ghosh: Cosmopolitanisms, Literature, Transnationalisms," in *The Postcolonial and the Global*, ed. Revathi Krishnaswamy and John C. Hawley (Minneapolis: University of Minnesota Press, 2008), 180. Shameem Black points out that Ghosh's vision of cosmopolitanism does not come at the expense of loyalty to family or nation, as it has often been characterized as doing historically. Indeed, Black's analysis of Tridib in *The Shadow Lines* suggests that he was willing to risk his life on behalf of a family member only because of his cosmopolitanism. See Black, "Cosmopolitanism at Home: Amitav Ghosh's *The Shadow Lines*," *The Journal of Commonwealth Literature* 41 (2006), 61. Yet the risks of such a romanticized portrait of the past have sparked a number of critical commentaries from Desai, Gabriel, Grewal, and others. Desai is perhaps most noteworthy of these commentators, arguing that Ghosh's nostalgia may be important to countering a sense of melancholia and helplessness felt by former colonized populations but it nonetheless unwittingly participates in "more contemporary polarizing politics" (132).

43 Adorno, *Aesthetic Theory*, 132.

44 Ghosh, *The Calcutta Chromosome: A Novel of Fevers, Delirium & Discovery*, 1995 (New York: Perennial, 2001), 104.

45 Ibid., 105.

46 Ibid., 311.

47 Particularly for Hayden White and F. R. Ankersmit, the preference for the sublime over the beautiful represents a key element in the effort to formulate an alternative, non-Kantian historiography. White famously argued that Western historiography emerged out of eighteenth-century aesthetics and its preoccupation with the category of the beautiful, so that historical narratives become preoccupied with form, order, and meaningful teleology through which the historian can provide readers with clear and unambiguous reasons for why events occurred as they did. White argues:

> For insofar as the disciplinization of history entailed regulation, not only of what could count as a proper object of historical study but also of what could count as a proper representation of that object in a discourse, discipline consisted in subordinating written history to the categories of the "beautiful" suppressing those of the "sublime."

See White, *The Content of the Form: Narrative Discourse and Historical Representation* (Baltimore: Johns Hopkins University Press, 1987), 66–67. In other words, Western historical writing has consistently attempted to appropriate or domesticate all events within a narrative framework. Extending White's argument about the discipline of history and its obsession with the category of the beautiful, Ankersmit argues that history is so tied to its Kantian roots that we cannot see an alternative to a transcendental theory of knowledge, what he calls sublime historical experience. For Ankersmit, experiences tend to resist efforts at appropriation by historians. In stark contrast to Kant and much modern and postmodern philosophy, Ankersmit argues that language should not be seen as the principal condition for the possibility of knowledge and meaningful thinking. Ankersmit argues that language is used in order to avoid experience and the fears and terrors it typically provokes. See Ankersmit, *Sublime Historical Experience* (Stanford University Press, 2005), 11. Theoretically, at least, the point of honoring sublime historical experiences and making them a part of the discipline of history is to dissolve the absolute boundaries between the past and present, and thereby to achieve the opposite of appropriation. In Ankersmit's words, representations of the past do not make the alien familiar but actually defamiliarize the familiar, making us strangers to ourselves. See Ankersmit, *History and Tropology: The Rise and Fall of Metaphor* (Berkeley: University of California Press, 1994), 27. For a contrasting viewpoint, see Isobel Armstrong's *The Radical Aesthetic*. Armstrong argues that the fascination with the sublime, exemplified by Lyotard and Paul de Man, has been a disastrous choice politically: "But the sublime is a discourse of the past. The radical aesthetic cannot return to the point of no return. It must live in the present and the future." See Armstrong, *The Radical Aesthetic* (Oxford: Blackwell, 2000), 21.

48 Chakrabarty argues that the poetry of Rabindranath Tagore resists the idea that any one understanding of the political is sufficient. Chakrabarty writes: "This, it seems to me, is the heterogeneity in the very constitution of the political that the nationalist in Tagore articulated in proposing to his compatriots that the nationalist eye needed to possess two radically contradictory modes of vision. One was charged with the responsibility to locate the political in historical time; the other created a political that resisted historicization." See Chakrabarty, *Provincializing Europe*, 178–79.

49 While Eagleton insists that the aesthetic should neither be celebrated nor condemned uncritically, his own conclusions tend to be relatively pessimistic. In the introduction to *The Ideology of the Aesthetic*, for example, he declares: "If it offers a generous utopian image of reconciliation between men and women at present divided from one another, it also blocks and mystifies the real political movement towards such historical community" (9).

50 Gikandi, "Race and the Idea of the Aesthetic," 347.

CONCLUSION: IMAGINING TOGETHER?

1 Ian Baucom, "Afterword: States of Time," *Contemporary Literature* 49.4 (2008), 713; Rita Barnard, "Tsotsis: On Law, the Outlaw, and the Postcolonial State," *Contemporary Literature* 49.4 (2008), 543.

2 In the *Leviathan*, Hobbes characterizes the imagination as a "decaying sense." See Hobbes, *Leviathan*, 1651, ed. Richard E. Flathman and David Johnston (New York: W. W. Norton & Company, 1997), 16. Yet, as James Engell notes, Hobbes uses the imagination in a much more expansive sense later in his work (see Engell, *Creative Imagination*, 14).

3 Coleridge himself did not explicitly criticize fancy, though his characterization of its dependence on memory implies its relatively limited autonomy. See Douglas Hedley, "Imagination Amended: From Coleridge to Collingwood," in *Coleridge's Afterlives*, ed. James Vigus and Jane Wright (Houndmills: Palgrave Macmillan, 2008), 212.

4 The distinction between the imagination and fancy comes on the final page of the first volume; See Coleridge, *Biographia Literaria*, 1817, ed. J. Shawcross (London: Oxford University Press, 1907), 202:

> The IMAGINATION then I consider either as primary, or secondary. The primary IMAGINATION I hold to be the living Power and prime Agent of all human Perception, and as a repetition in the finite mind of the eternal act of creation in the infinite I AM. The secondary Imagination I consider as an echo of the former, co-existing with the conscious will, yet still as identical with the primary in the *kind* of its agency, and differing only in *degree*, and in the *mode* of its operation. It dissolves, diffuses, dissipates, in order to re-create; or where this process is rendered impossible, yet still at all events it struggles to idealize and to unify. It is essentially *vital*, even as all objects (as objects) are essentially fixed and dead.
>
> FANCY, on the contrary, has no other counters to play with, but fixities and definites. The Fancy is indeed no other than a mode of Memory emancipated from the order of time and space; while it is blended with, and modified by that empirical phenomenon of the will, which we express by the word CHOICE. But equally with the ordinary memory the Fancy must receive all its materials ready made from the law of association.

5 Coleridge, *Biographia Literaria*, 61.

6 Appadurai, *Modernity at Large*, 31.

7 Coleridge, *Biographia Literaria*, 202.

8 Ibid., 202; Appadurai, *Modernity at Large*, 7. Coleridge envisioned much the same possibility for the imagination: to provide the basis for the English nation to grow as a worldwide power without collapsing into the terror of the French Revolution. Beginning in the 1790s, Coleridge articulated a theory of the "One Life," according to which political and spiritual authorities were united, and the hierarchies produced by the state and the emergence of capitalism would be replaced by a unified nation. Yet, as Nigel Leask notes, the radicalism of Coleridge's writings and lectures during the 1790s was gradually replaced by more conservative, elitest notions regarding the imagination

and culture. His tortured apologetics regarding his earlier radicalism and his opposition to parliamentary legislative acts including the Corn Laws, the Catholic Relief Bill, and the Reform Bill led him to reproduce the binary between political and aesthetic realms that he sought to overcome earlier in his career. As Leask describes it, the institutionalization of the imagination meant that it was increasingly removed from the social and political domain. It might provide an alternative to the political ideologies of the day, but it was confined to the realm of art.

9 Dorothy Hale, "Aesthetics and Ethics: Theorizing the Novel in the Twenty-First Century," *PMLA* 124.3 (2009), 899.

10 Ibid., 901.

Bibliography

Achebe, Chinua. *Hopes and Impediments: Selected Essays.* 1988. New York: Doubleday, 1989.

Things Fall Apart. 1958. New York: Fawcett Crest, 1969.

The Trouble with Nigeria. London: Heinemann, 1984.

Acheson, James, and Sarah C. E. Ross, eds. *The Contemporary British Novel.* Edinburgh University Press, 2005.

Ackroyd, Peter. *Albion: The Origins of the English Imagination.* London: Chatto & Windus, 2002.

Blake. London: Sinclair-Stevenson, 1996.

Chatterton. New York: Grove Press, 1987.

The Collection. Ed. and with an Introduction by Thomas Wright. London: Chatto & Windus, 2001.

Dan Leno & the Limehouse Golem. 1994. London: Minerva, 1995.

Dickens. New York: HarperCollins, 1990.

English Music. 1992. New York: Ballantine, 1994.

First Light. New York: Ballantine, 1989.

Hawksmoor. 1985. New York: Perennial, 1987.

Notes for a New Culture: An Essay on Modernism. London: Vision, 1976.

T. S. Eliot: A Life. New York: Simon and Schuster, 1984.

Adorno, Theodor W. *Aesthetic Theory.* 1970. Trans. Robert Hullot-Kentor. Ed. Gretal Adorno and Rolf Tiedemann. Minneapolis: University of Minnesota Press, 1997.

Negative Dialectics. 1966. Trans. E. B. Ashton. New York: Seabury, 1973.

Prisms. 1967. Trans. Samuel and Shierry Weber. Cambridge, MA: MIT Press, 1981.

Afzal-Khan, Fawzia. "At the Margins of Postcolonial Studies: Part 2." *The Pre-Occupation of Postcolonial Studies.* Ed. Fawzia Afzal-Khan and Kalpana Seshadri-Crooks. Durham: Duke University Press, 2000. 24–34.

Ahmad, Aijaz. "The Politics of Literary Postcoloniality." *Race & Class* (1995): 1–20.

Alcoff, Linda Martín. *Real Knowing: New Versions of the Coherence Theory.* Ithaca: Cornell University Press, 1996.

Visible Identities: Race, Gender, and the Self. New York: Oxford University Press, 2006.

"Who's Afraid of Identity Politics?" *Reclaiming Identity: Realistic Theory and the Predicament of Postmodernism*. Ed. Paula M. L. Moya and Michael R. Hames-García. Berkeley: University of California Press, 2000. 312–44.

Aldama, Frederick Luis. "An Interview with Amitav Ghosh." *World Literature Today* 76.2 (2002): 84–90.

Ali, Monica. *Brick Lane*. New York: Scribner, 2003.

Allen, Chadwick. "Blood (and) Memory." *American Literature* 71.1 (1999): 93–116.

Blood Narrative: Indigenous Identity in American Indian and Maori Literary and Activist Texts. Durham: Duke University Press, 2002.

Allison, Henry E. *Kant's Theory of Taste: A Reading of the Critique of Aesthetic Judgment*. Cambridge University Press, 2001.

Alpers, Paul. *What is Pastoral?* University of Chicago Press, 1996.

Alter, Robert. "*Daniel Martin* and the Mimetic Task." *Critical Essays on John Fowles*. Ed. Ellen Pifer. Boston: G. K. Hall & Co., 1986. 150–62.

Anderson, Perry. *The Origins of Postmodernity*. London: Verso, 1998.

Anger, Suzy, ed. *Knowing the Past: Victorian Literature and Culture*. Ithaca: Cornell University Press, 2001.

Ankersmit, F. R. "In Praise of Subjectivity." *The Ethics of History*. Ed. David Carr, Thomas R. Flynn, and Rudolf A. Makkreel. Evanston: Northwestern University Press, 2004. 3–27.

History and Tropology: The Rise and Fall of Metaphor. Berkeley: University of California Press, 1994.

Sublime Historical Experience. Stanford University Press, 2005.

Appadurai, Arjun. *Modernity at Large: Cultural Dimensions of Globalization*. Minneapolis: University of Minnesota Press, 1996.

Appiah, Kwame Anthony. *The Ethics of Identity*. Princeton University Press, 2005.

"Liberalism, Individuality, and Identity." *Critical Inquiry* 27 (2001): 305–32.

Armstrong, Isobel. *The Radical Aesthetic*. Oxford: Blackwell, 2000.

Attridge, Derek. *J. M. Coetzee & the Ethics of Reading*. University of Chicago Press, 2004.

Attridge, Derek, and Rosemary Jolly, eds. *Writing South Africa: Literature, Apartheid, and Democracy, 1970–1995*. Cambridge University Press, 1998.

Attwell, David. *J. M. Coetzee: South Africa and the Politics of Writing*. Berkeley: University of California Press, 1993.

Bahri, Deepika. *Native Intelligence: Aesthetics, Politics, and Postcolonial Literature*. Minneapolis: University of Minnesota Press, 2003.

Baker, Stephen. *The Fiction of Postmodernity*. Edinburgh University Press, 2000.

Barnard, Rita. *Apartheid and Beyond: South African Writers and the Politics of Place*. Oxford University Press, 2007.

"Of Riots and Rainbows: South Africa, the US, and the Pitfalls of Comparison." *American Literary History* 17.2 (2005): 399–416.

"The Place of Beauty: Reflections on Elaine Scarry and Zakes Mda." *Beautiful/ Ugly: African and Diaspora Aesthetics*. Ed. Sarah Nuttall. Durham: Duke University Press, 2006. 102–21.

"Tsotsis: On Law, the Outlaw, and the Postcolonial State." *Contemporary Literature* 49.4 (2008): 541–72.

Barnes, Julian. *England, England*. 1998. New York: Alfred A. Knopf, 1999.

Flaubert's Parrot. 1984. New York: McGraw-Hill, 1985.

A History of the World in 10½ Chapters. New York: Alfred A. Knopf, 1989.

Letters from London. New York: Vintage International, 1995.

Battersby, Christine. *The Phenomenal Woman: Feminist Metaphysics and the Patterns of Identity*. Cambridge: Polity Press, 1998.

Baucom, Ian. "Afterword: States of Time." *Contemporary Literature* 49.4 (2008): 712–18.

Out of Place: Englishness, Empire, and the Locations of Identity. Princeton University Press, 1999.

Bazin, Nancy Topping and Marilyn Dallman Seymour, eds. *Conversations with Nadine Gordimer*. Jackson: University Press of Mississippi, 1990.

Beaumont, Matthew, ed. *Adventures in Realism*. Malden: Blackwell, 2007.

Beckett, Samuel. *Proust*. New York: Grove Press, 1931.

Benhabib, Seyla. *Situating the Self: Gender, Community, and Postmodernism in Contemporary Ethics*. New York: Routledge, 1992.

Bentley, Nick, ed. *British Fiction of the 1990s*. London: Routledge, 2005.

Bhabha, Homi K. *The Location of Culture*. London: Routledge, 1994.

"The Third Space: Interview with Homi Bhabha." *Identity: Community, Culture, Difference*. Ed. Jonathan Rutherford. London: Lawrence and Wishart, 1990. 207–21.

Black, Shameem. "Cosmopolitanism at Home: Amitav Ghosh's *The Shadow Lines*." *Journal of Commonwealth Literature* 41 (2006): 45–65.

Boehmer, Elleke. "Endings and New Beginning: South African Fiction in Transition." *Writing South Africa: Literature, Apartheid, and Democracy, 1970–1995*. Ed. Derek Attridge and Rosemary Jolly. Cambridge University Press, 1998. 43–56.

Brah, Avtar, and Annie E. Coombs, eds. *Hybridity and Its Discontents: Politics, Science, Culture*. London: Routledge, 2000.

Brann, Eva T. H. *The World of the Imagination: Sum and Substance*. Savage, MD: Rowman & Littlefield, 1991.

Brannigan, John. *Orwell to the Present: Literature in England, 1945–2000*. New York: Palgrave Macmillan, 2003.

Brink, André. *A Dry White Season*. London: W. H. Allen, 1979.

Imaginings of Sand. San Diego: Harvest Books, 1996.

The Novel: Language and Narrative from Cervantes to Calvino. New York University Press, 1998.

On the Contrary. London: Secker and Warburg, 1993.

Reinventing a Continent: Writing and Politics in South Africa 1982–1995. London: Secker and Warburg, 1996.

"South Africa: Postmodernism in Afrikaans and English Literature." *International Postmodernism: Theory and Literary Practice*. Ed. Hans Bertens. Amsterdam: John Benjamins Publishing Company, 1997. 483–90.

States of Emergency. New York: Summit Books, 1988.

"Stories of History: Reimagining the Past in Post-Apartheid Narrative." *Negotiating the Past: The Making of Memory in South Africa*. Ed. Sarah Nuttall and Carli Coetzee. Cape Town: Oxford University Press, 1998. 29–42.

Writing in a State of Siege: Essays on Politics and Literature. New York: Summit Books, 1983.

Brown, Nicholas. *Utopian Generations: The Political Horizon of Twentieth-Century Literature*. Princeton University Press, 2005.

Buck-Morss, Susan. *The Origin of Negative Dialectics: Theodor W. Adorno, Walter Benjamin, and the Frankfurt Institute*. New York: The Free Press, 1977.

Buell, Lawrence. *The Environmental Imagination: Thoreau, Nature Writing, and the Formation of American Culture*. Cambridge, MA: Belknap Press, 1995.

Butler, Judith. *Bodies That Matter: On the Discursive Limits of "Sex."* New York: Routledge, 1993.

Byatt, A. S. Byatt, *On Histories and Stories: Selected Essays*. London: Chatto & Windus, 2000.

Casey, Edward S. *Imagining: A Phenomenological Study*. Revised edn. Bloomington: Indiana University Press, 2000.

Castoriadis, Cornelius. *World in Fragments: Writings on Politics, Society, Psychoanalysis, and the Imagination*. Ed. and translated by David Ames Curtis. Stanford University Press, 1997.

Chait, Sandra. "Mythology, Magic Realism, and White Writing after Apartheid." *Research in African Literatures* 31.2 (2000): 17–28.

Chakrabarty, Dipesh. *Provincializing Europe: Postcolonial Thought and Historical Difference*. Princeton University Press, 2000.

Chambers, Claire. "'The Absolute Essentialness of Conversations': A Discussion with Amitav Ghosh." *Journal of Postcolonial Writing* 41.1 (2005): 26–39.

Chambers, Iain. *Migrancy, Culture, Identity*. London: Routledge, 1994.

Chapman, Michael. *South African Literatures*. London: Longman, 1996.

Chatterjee, Partha. *The Nation and Its Fragments: Colonial and Postcolonial Histories*. Princeton University Press, 1993.

Nationalist Thought and the Colonial World: A Derivative Discourse? Minneapolis: University of Minnesota Press, 1986.

Childs, Peter. *Contemporary Novelists: British Fiction since 1970*. New York: Palgrave Macmillan, 2005.

Chin, Frank. *Donald Duk*. Minneapolis: Coffee House Press, 1991.

Chow, Rey. *Writing Diaspora: Tactics of Intervention in Contemporary Cultural Studies*. Bloomington: Indiana University Press, 1993.

Chrisman, Laura. *Postcolonial Contraventions: Cultural Readings of Race, Imperialism and Transnationalism*. Manchester University Press, 2003.

Chytry, Josef. *The Aesthetic State: A Quest in Modern German Thought*. Berkeley: University of California Press, 1989.

Clifford, James. *Routes: Travel and Translation in the Late Twentieth Century.* Cambridge, MA: Harvard University Press, 1997.

Clingman, Stephen. *The Novels of Nadine Gordimer: History from the Inside.* London: Allen & Unwin, 1986.

Coetzee, J. M. *Age of Iron.* 1990. New York: Penguin, 1998.

"André Brink and the Censor." *Research in African Literatures* 21.3 (1990): 59–74.

Doubling the Point: Essays and Interviews. Ed. David Attwell. Cambridge, MA: Harvard University Press, 1992.

Dusklands. 1974. New York: Penguin, 1996.

Elizabeth Costello. New York: Viking, 2003.

Foe. 1986. London: Penguin Books, 1987.

In the Heart of the Country. 1977. New York: Penguin, 1982.

Life & Times of Michael K. 1983. London: Penguin, 1985.

The Master of Petersburg. 1994. New York: Penguin, 1995.

Waiting for the Barbarians. 1980. New York: Penguin, 1982.

White Writing: On the Culture of Letters in South Africa. New Haven: Yale University Press, 1988.

Coleridge, Samuel Taylor. *Biographia Literaria.* 1817. Ed. J. Shawcross. Two volumes. London: Oxford University Press, 1907.

Connor, Steven, ed. *The Cambridge Companion to Postmodernism.* Cambridge University Press, 2004.

Conradi, Peter. *John Fowles.* London: Methuen, 1982.

Cooke, John. *The Novels of Nadine Gordimer: Private Lives/Public Landscapes.* Baton Rouge: Louisiana State University Press, 1985.

Corner, John, and Sylvia Harvey, eds. *Enterprise and Heritage: Crosscurrents of National Culture.* London: Routledge, 1991.

Corner, Martin. "Beyond Revisions: Rushdie, Newness and the End of Authenticity." *The Revision of Englishness.* Ed. David Rogers and John McLeod. Manchester University Press, 2004. 154–68.

Dabydeen, David. *Disappearance.* London: Martin Secker & Warburg, 1993.

Danto, Arthur C. *Narration and Knowledge.* New York: Columbia University Press, 1985.

Darder, Antonia, and Rodolfo D. Torres. *After Race: Racism after Multiculturalism.* New York University Press, 2004.

Dawson, Ashley. *Mongrel Nation: Diasporic Culture and the Making of Postcolonial Britain.* Ann Arbor: University of Michigan Press, 2007.

De Man, Paul. *Blindness and Insight: Essays in the Rhetoric of Contemporary Criticism.* 2nd revised edn. Minneapolis: University of Minnesota Press, 1983.

Deleuze, Gilles, and Félix Guattari. *Anti-Oedipus: Capitalism and Schizophrenia.* Trans. Robert Hurley, Mark Seem, and Helen R. Lane. Minneapolis: University of Minnesota Press, 1983.

Derrida, Jacques. "Racism's Last Word." Trans. Peggy Kamuf. *"Race," Writing, and Difference.* Ed. Henry Louis Gates Jr. University of Chicago Press, 1986. 329–38.

Specters of Marx: The State of the Debt, the Work of Mourning, and the New International. Trans. Peggy Kamuf. Ed. with an introduction by Bernd Magnus and Stephen Cullenberg. New York: Routledge, 1994.

Desai, Gaurav. "Old World Orders: Amitav Ghosh and the Writing of Nostalgia." *Representations* 85 (2004): 125–48.

Subject to Colonialism: African Self-Fashioning and the Colonial Library. Durham: Duke University Press, 2001.

D'Haen, Theo. "Antique Lands, New Worlds? Comparative Literature, Intertextuality, Translation." *Forum for Modern Language Studies* 43.2 (2007): 107–20.

Diala, Isadore. "Nadine Gordimer, J. M. Coetzee, and André Brink: Guilt, Expiation, and the Reconciliation Process in Post-Apartheid South Africa." *Journal of Modern Literature* 25.2 (2001/2002): 50–68.

Dirlik, Arif. "The Postcolonial Aura: Third World Criticism in the Age of Global Capitalism." *Critical Inquiry* 20.2 (1994): 328–56.

Donadio, Rachel. "Post-Apartheid Fiction." *New York Times* December 3, 2006. Online.

Durrant, Sam. "J. M. Coetzee, Elizabeth Costello, and the Limits of the Sympathetic Imagination." *J. M. Coetzee and the Idea of the Public Intellectual.* Ed. Jane Poyner. Athens: Ohio University Press, 2006. 118–34.

Eagleton, Terry. *After Theory.* New York: Basic Books, 2003.

The Ideology of the Aesthetic. Oxford: Blackwell, 1990.

The Illusions of Postmodernism. Oxford: Blackwell, 1996.

Elias, Amy J. *Sublime Desire: History and Post-1960s Fiction.* Baltimore: Johns Hopkins University Press, 2001.

Eliot, T. S. "Building up the Christian World." *The Listener* April 6, 1932: 501–02.

Selected Essays. New edn. New York: Harcourt, Brace & World, 1964.

Empson, William. *Some Versions of Pastoral.* London, Chatto & Windus, 1950.

Engell, James. *The Creative Imagination: Enlightenment to Romanticism.* Cambridge, MA: Harvard University Press, 1981.

Ettin, Andrew V. *Literature and the Pastoral.* New Haven: Yale University Press, 1984.

Betrayals of the Body Politic: The Literary Commitments of Nadine Gordimer. Charlottesville: University Press of Virginia, 1993.

Fowles, John. *The Aristos: A Self-Portrait in Ideas.* Boston: Little, Brown and Company, 1964.

Daniel Martin. 1977. New York: Signet, 1978.

The French Lieutenant's Woman. 1969. New York: Signet, 1970.

Wormholes: Essays and Occasional Writings. Ed. Jan Relf. New York: Henry Holt and Company, 1998.

Fukuyama, Francis. "The End of History?" *National Interest* 16 (1989): 3–18.

The End of History and the Last Man. New York: Free Press, 1992.

Fuss, Diana. *Essentially Speaking: Feminism, Nature & Difference.* New York: Routledge, 1989.

Gabriel, Sharmani Patricia. "The Heteroglossia of Home: Re-'routing' the Boundaries of National Identity in Amitav Ghosh's *The Shadow Lines*." *Journal of Postcolonial Writing* 41.1 (2005): 40–53.

Gadamer, Hans-Georg. *The Relevance of the Beautiful and Other Essays*. Trans. Nicholas Walker. Ed. Robert Bernasconi. Cambridge University Press, 1986.

    Truth and Method. Trans. Joel Weinsheimer and Donald G. Marshall. 2nd revised edn. New York: Continuum, 1999.

Gąsiorek, Andrzej. *Post-War British Fiction: Realism and After*. London: Edward Arnold, 1995.

Geertz, Clifford. "A Passage to India." *New Republic* 209 (August 23–30, 1993): 38, 40–41.

Gergen, Kenneth J. *The Saturated Self: Dilemmas of Identity in Contemporary Life*. New York: Basic Books, 1991.

Gervais, David. *Literary Englands: Versions of "Englishness" in Modern Writing*. Cambridge University Press, 1993.

Ghosh, Amitav. *The Calcutta Chromosome: A Novel of Fevers, Delirium & Discovery*. 1995. New York: Perennial, 2001.

    The Circle of Reason. 1986. New York: Mariner Books, 2005.

    "The Diaspora in Indian Culture." *Public Culture* 2.1 (1989): 73–78.

    The Glass Palace. New York: Random House, 2001.

    In an Antique Land: History in the Guise of a Traveler's Tale. 1992. New York: Vintage Departures, 1994.

    Incendiary Circumstances: A Chronicle of the Turmoil of Our Times. Boston: Houghton Mifflin Company, 2005.

    The Shadow Lines. 1988. New York: Mariner Books, 2005.

Ghosh, Amitav, and Dipesh Chakrabarty. "A Correspondence on *Provincializing Europe*." *Radical History Review* 83 (2002): 146–72.

Gibson, Jeremy, and Julian Wolfreys. *Peter Ackroyd: The Ludic and Labyrinthine Text*. Forword by Peter Nicholls. New York: St. Martin's Press, 2000.

Gikandi, Simon. *Maps of Englishness: Writing Identity in the Culture of Colonialism*. New York: Columbia University Press, 1996.

    "Race and the Idea of the Aesthetic." *Michigan Quarterly Review* 40.2 (2001): 318–50.

Gifford, Terry. *Pastoral*. London: Routledge, 1999.

Gilpin, George H. *The Art of Contemporary English Culture*. Houndmills: Macmillan, 1991.

Gilroy, Paul. *Against Race: Imagining Popular Culture beyond the Color Line*. Cambridge, MA: Belknap Press, 2000.

    Postcolonial Melancholia. New York: Columbia University Press, 2005.

Gordimer, Nadine. *Burger's Daughter*. 1979. Harmondsworth: Penguin Books, 1980.

    The Conservationist. 1974. Harmondsworth: Penguin, 1978.

    The Essential Gesture: Writing, Politics and Places. Ed. and introduced by Stephen Clingman. London: Jonathan Cape, 1988.

The House Gun. New York: Farrar, Straus and Giroux, 1998.

"The Idea of Gardening: *Life and Times of Michael K.* by J. M. Coetzee." *Critical Essays on J. M. Coetzee.* Ed. Sue Kossew. New York: G. K. Hall & Co., 1998. 139–44.

July's People. 1981. New York: Penguin, 1982.

Living in Hope and History: Notes from Our Century. New York: Farrar, Straus and Giroux, 1999.

My Son's Story. New York: Farrar, Straus and Giroux, 1990.

"Preface." *Critical Perspectives on J. M. Coetzee.* Ed. Graham Huggan and Stephen Watson. Houndmills: Macmillan, 1996. vii–xii.

A Sport of Nature. 1987. New York: Penguin, 1988.

Writing and Being. Cambridge, MA: Harvard University Press, 1995.

Gordon, Avery F. *Ghostly Matters: Haunting and the Sociological Imagination.* Minneapolis: University of Minnesota Press, 1997.

Gordon, Avery, and Christopher Newfield. "White Philosophy." *Critical Inquiry* 20 (1994): 737–57.

Gorra, Michael. "Response to *Identities*." *Identities.* Ed. Kwame Anthony Appiah and Henry Louis Gates Jr. University of Chicago Press, 1995. 434–38.

Grewal, Inderpal. "Amitav Ghosh: Cosmopolitanisms, Literature, Transnationalisms." *The Postcolonial and the Global.* Ed. Revathi Krishnaswamy and John C. Hawley. Minneapolis: University of Minnesota Press, 2008. 178–90.

Hale, Dorothy J. "Aesthetics and the New Ethics: Theorizing the Novel in the Twenty-First Century." *PMLA* 124.3 (2009): 896–905.

Hall, Stuart. "New Ethnicities." *Black Film, British Cinema.* London: Institute of Contemporary Arts, 1988.

Halperin, David M. *Before Pastoral: Theocritus and the Ancient Tradition of Bucolic Poetry.* New Haven: Yale University Press, 1983.

Haraway, Donna. "Situated Knowledges: The Science Question in Feminism and the Privilege of Partial Perspective." *Feminist Studies* 14.3 (1988): 575–99.

Harding, Sandra. *Is Science Multicultural? Postcolonialisms, Feminisms, and Epistemologies.* Bloomington: Indiana University Press, 1998.

Hardy, Thomas. *The Woodlanders.* Ed. Patricia Ingham. London: Penguin, 1998.

Harpham, Geoffrey Galt. "Aesthetics and the Fundamentals of Modernity." *Aesthetics and Ideology.* Ed. George Levine. New Brunswick: Rutgers University Press, 1994. 124–52.

Shadows of Ethics: Criticism and the Just Society. Durham: Duke University Press, 1999.

Harvey, David. *The Condition of Postmodernity: An Enquiry into the Origins of Cultural Change.* Cambridge, MA: Blackwell, 1990.

Head, Dominic. *The Cambridge Introduction to Modern British Fiction, 1950–2000.* Cambridge University Press, 2002.

J. M. Coetzee. Cambridge University Press, 1997.

Nadine Gordimer. Cambridge University Press, 1994.

"Zadie Smith's *White Teeth.*" *Contemporary British Fiction.* Ed. Richard J. Lane, Rod Mengham, and Philip Tew. Cambridge: Polity, 2003. 106–19.

Heath, Stephen. "Difference." *Screen* 19.3 (1978): 50–112.

Hedley, Douglas. "Imagination Amended: from Coleridge to Collingwood." *Coleridge's Afterlives.* Ed. James Vigus and Jane Wright. Houndmills: Palgrave Macmillan, 2008. 210–23.

Henstra, Sarah. "The McReal Thing: Personal/National Identity in Julian Barnes's *England, England.*" *British Fiction of the 1990s.* Ed. Nick Bentley. London: Routledge, 2005. 95–107.

Hewison, Robert. *Culture and Consensus: England, Art and Politics since 1940.* London: Methuen, 1995.

Heywood, Christopher. *A History of South African Literature.* Cambridge University Press, 2004.

Hobbes, Thomas. *Leviathan.* 1651. Ed. Richard E. Flathman and David Johnston. New York: W. W. Norton & Company, 1997.

Hubbard, Thomas K. *The Pipes of Pan: Intertextuality and Literary Filiation in the Pastoral Tradition from Theocritus to Milton.* Ann Arbor: *University of Michigan Press*, 1998.

Huggan, Graham. *The Postcolonial Exotic: Marketing the Margins.* London: Routledge, 2001.

Huggan, Graham, and Stephen Watson, eds. *Critical Perspectives on J. M. Coetzee.* Houndmills: Macmillan Press, 1996.

Hutcheon, Linda. *A Poetics of Postmodernism: History, Theory, Fiction.* New York: Routledge, 1988.

The Politics of Postmodernism. 2nd edn. London: Routledge, 2002.

Irele, Abiola. "The African Imagination." *Research in African Literatures* 21.1 (1990): 49–67.

Jacoby, Russell. *Picture Imperfect: Utopian Thought for an Anti-Utopian Age.* New York: Columbia University Press, 2005.

Jameson, Fredric. *Postmodernism, or, The Cultural Logic of Late Capitalism.* Durham: Duke University Press, 1991.

JanMohamed, Abdul R. *Manichean Aesthetics: The Politics of Literature in Colonial Africa.* Amherst: University of Massachusetts Press, 1983.

Jarvis, Simon. *Adorno: A Critical Introduction.* Cambridge: Polity Press, 1998.

Jauss, Hans Robert. *Aesthetic Experience and Literary Hermeneutics.* Trans. Michael Shaw. Ed. Wlad Godzich. Minneapolis: University of Minnesota Press, 1982.

Jencks, Charles. *What is Post-Modernism?* New York: St. Martin's Press, 1986.

Jolly, Rosemary Jane. *Colonization, Violence, and Narration in White South African Writing: André Brink, Breyten Breytenbach, and J. M. Coetzee.* Athens: Ohio University Press, 1996.

Kaleta, Kenneth C. *Hanif Kureishi: Postcolonial Storyteller.* Austin: University of Texas Press, 1998.

Kant, Immanuel. *The Critique of Judgment.* 1790. Trans. James Creed Meredith. Oxford: Clarendon Press, 1952.

Kearney, Richard. *Poetics of Imagining: Modern to Post-modern.* New York: Fordham University Press, 1998.

The Wake of Imagination: Toward a Postmodern Culture. Minneapolis: University of Minnesota Press, 1988.

Kossew, Sue. "Introduction." *Critical Essays on J. M. Coetzee.* Ed. Sue Kossew. New York: G. K. Hall & Co., 1998. 1–17.

Kruks, Sonia. *Retrieving Experience: Subjectivity and Recognition in Feminist Politics.* Ithaca: Cornell University Press, 2001.

Krupat, Arnold. *The Voice in the Margin: Native American Literature and the Canon.* Berkeley: University of California Press, 1989.

Kumar, Krishan. *The Making of English National Identity.* Cambridge University Press, 2003.

Kumar, T. Vijay. "'Postcolonial' Describes You As a Negative." *Interventions: International Journal of Postcolonial Studies* 9.1 (2007): 99–105.

Kureishi, Hanif. *My Beautiful Laundrette and Other Writings.* London: Faber & Faber, 1996.

The Black Album. 1995. New York: Scribner, 1996.

The Buddha of Suburbia. 1990. New York: Penguin, 1991.

Lane, Richard J., Rob Mengham, and Philip Tew, eds. *Contemporary British Fiction.* Cambridge: Polity Press, 2003.

Lawrence, D. H. *The Rainbow.* Ed. with an Introduction and notes by John Worthen. London: Penguin, 1989.

Leask, Nigel. *The Politics of Imagination in Coleridge's Critical Thought.* Basingstoke, Macmillan: 1988.

Leavis, F. R. *The Great Tradition: George Eliot, Henry James, Joseph Conrad.* 1948. New York: New York University Press, 1960.

Lee, A. Robert, ed. *Other Britain, Other British: Contemporary Multicultural Fiction.* London: Pluto Press, 1995.

Lee, Alison. *Realism and Power: Postmodern British Fiction.* London: Routledge, 1990.

Levine, George. "*Daniel Deronda*: A New Epistemology." *Knowing the Past: Victorian Literature and Culture.* Ed. Suzy Anger. Ithaca: Cornell University Press, 2001.

"Introduction: Reclaiming the Aesthetic." *Aesthetics and Ideology.* Ed. George Levine. New Brunswick: Rutgers University Press, 1994. 1–30.

Lewis, Barry. *My Words Echo Thus: Possessing the Past in Peter Ackroyd.* Columbia: University of South Carolina Press, 2007.

Little, Daniel. *Microfoundations, Method, and Causation.* New Brunswick: Transaction Publishers, 1998.

Loesberg, Jonathan. *A Return to Aesthetics: Autonomy, and Difference, and Postmodernism.* Stanford University Press, 2005.

Lowe, Lisa. *Immigrant Acts: On Asian American Cultural Politics.* Durham: Duke University Press, 1996.

Lukács, Georg. *The Historical Novel.* 1937. Trans. Hannah and Stanley Mitchell. London: Merlin Press, 1962.

History and Class Consciousness. 1923. Trans. R. Livingstone. London: Merlin Press, 1990.

Makdisi, Saree. *Romantic Imperialism: Universal Empire and the Culture of Modernity*. Cambridge University Press, 1998.

Marais, Michael. "From the Standpoint of Redemption: Aesthetic Autonomy and Social Engagement in J. M. Coetzee's Fiction of the Late Apartheid Period." *Journal of Narrative Theory* 38.2 (2008): 229–48.

"J. M. Coetzee's *Disgrace* and the Task of the Imagination." *Journal of Modern Literature* 53.4 (2006): 75–93.

Marcuse, Herbert. *The Aesthetic Dimension: Toward a Critique of Marxist Aesthetics*. Boston: Beacon Press, 1978.

One-Dimensional Man: Studies in the Ideology of Advanced Industrial Society. Ed. Douglas Kellner. Boston: Beacon Press, 1991.

Marinelli, Peter V. *Pastoral*. London: Methuen, 1971.

Matless, David. *Landscape and Englishness*. London: Reaktion Books, 1998.

McClintock, Anne, and Rob Nixon. "No Names Apart: The Separation of Word and History in Derrida's 'Le Dernier Mot du Racisme.'" *"Race," Writing, and Difference*. Ed. Henry Louis Gates Jr. University of Chicago Press, 1986. 339–53.

McGann, Jerome J. *The Romantic Ideology: A Critical Investigation*. University of Chicago Press, 1983.

McHale, Brian. *Postmodernist Fiction*. New York: Methuen, 1987.

McKeon, Michael. "The Pastoral Revolution." *Refiguring Revolutions: Aesthetics and Politics from the English Revolution to the Romantic Revolution*. Ed. Kevin Sharpe and Stephen N. Zwicker. Berkeley: University of California Press, 1998. 267–89.

Meffan, James, and Kim L. Worthington. "Ethics before Politics: J. M. Coetzee's *Disgrace*." *Mapping the Ethical Turn: A Reader in Ethics, Culture, and Literary Theory*. Ed. Todd F. Davis and Kenneth Womack. Charlottesville: University of Virginia Press, 2001. 131–50.

Mengham, Rod, ed. *An Introduction to Contemporary Fiction: International Writing in English since 1970*. Cambridge: Polity Press, 1999.

Michaels, Walter Benn. "The No-Drop Rule." *Critical Inquiry* 20 (1994): 758–69.

Our America: Nativism, Modernism, and Pluralism. Durham: Duke University Press, 1995.

"Race into Culture: A Critical Genealogy of Cultural Identity." *Critical Inquiry* 18 (1992): 655–85.

The Shape of the Signifier: 1967 to the End of History. Princeton University Press, 2004.

"'You Who Never Was There': Slavery and the New Historicism, Deconstruction and the Holocaust." *Narrative* 4.1 (1996): 1–16.

Middleton, Peter, and Tim Woods. *Literatures of Memory: History, Time and Space in Postwar Writing*. Manchester University Press, 2000.

Mishra, Vijay, and Bob Hodge. "What Was Postcolonialism?" *New Literary History* 36 (2005): 375–402.

Mohanty, Satya P. "Can Our Values be Objective? On Ethics, Aesthetics, and Progressive Politics." *New Literary History* 32 (2001): 803–33.

Literary Theory and the Claims of History: Postmodernism, Objectivity, Multicultural Politics. Ithaca: Cornell University Press, 1997.

Momaday, N. Scott. "Confronting Columbus Again." *Native American Testimony: A Chronicle of Indian-White Relations from Prophecy to the Present, 1492–2000.* Ed. Peter Nabokov. New York: Penguin Books, 1999. 437–40.

House Made of Dawn. New York: Harper & Row, 1968.

"The Man Made of Words." *Literature of the American Indians: Views and Interpretations.* Ed. Abraham Chapman. New York: Meridian, 1975. 96–110.

The Names: A Memoir. Tucson: University of Arizona Press, 1976.

"Personal Reflections." *The American Indian and the Problem of History.* Ed. Calvin Martin. New York: Oxford University Press, 1987. 156–61.

The Way to Rainy Mountain: University of New Mexico Press, 1969.

Moore-Gilbert, Bart. "*The Black Album*: Hanif Kureishi's Revisions of 'Englishness.'" *The Revision of Englishness.* Ed. David Rogers and John McLeod. Manchester University Press, 2004. 138–53.

Morris, Rosalind C. "Imperial Pastoral: The Politics and Aesthetics of Translation in British Malaya." *Representations* 99 (2007): 159–93.

Morrison, Jago. *Contemporary Fiction.* London: Routledge, 2003.

Morrison, Toni. *Beloved.* New York: Plume, 1987.

Moseley, Merritt. *Understanding Julian Barnes.* Columbia: University of South Carolina Press, 1997.

Moss, Laura. "The Politics of Everyday Hybridity: Zadie Smith's *White Teeth.*" *Wasafiri* 39 (2003): 11–17.

Moya, Paula M. L. *Learning from Experience: Minority Identities, Multicultural Struggles.* Berkeley: University of California Press, 2002.

Mudimbe, V. Y. *The Invention of Africa: Gnosis, Philosophy, and the Order of Knowledge.* Bloomington: Indiana University Press, 1988.

Murphet, Julian. "Fiction and Postmodernity." *The Cambridge History of Twentieth-Century English Literature.* Ed. Laura Marcus and Peter Nicholls. Cambridge University Press, 2004. 716–35.

Naipaul, V. S. *The Enigma of Arrival.* New York: Vintage, 1988.

The Mimic Men. 1967. New York: Vintage International, 2001.

Ndebele, Njabulo S. *South African Literature and Culture: Rediscovery of the Ordinary.* Manchester University Press, 1994.

Ngũgĩ wa Thiong'o. *Decolonising the Mind: The Politics of Language in African Literature.* London: James Currey, 1986.

Devil on the Cross. London: Heinemann Educational Books, 1982 (Gikũyũ version 1980).

Homecoming: Essays on African and Caribbean Literature, Culture and Politics. London: Heinemann, 1972.

Penpoints, Gunpoints, and Dreams: Towards a Critical Theory of the Arts and the State in Africa. Oxford: Clarendon Press, 1998.

Nicholsen, Shierry Weber. *Exact Imagination, Late Work: On Adorno's Aesthetics*. Cambridge, MA: MIT Press, 1997.

Nixon, Rob. *Homelands, Harlem and Hollywood: South African Culture and the World Beyond*. New York: Routledge, 1994.

Norris, Christopher. *The Truth about Postmodernism*. Oxford: Blackwell, 1993.

Nuttall, Sarah, ed. *Beautiful/Ugly: African and Diaspora Aesthetics*. Durham: Duke University Press, 2006.

Onega, Susana. "Interview with Peter Ackroyd," *Twentieth-Century Literature* 42.2 (1996): 202–20.

   Metafiction and Myth in the Novels of Peter Ackroyd. Columbia, SC: Camden House, 1999.

Parry, Benita. *Postcolonial Studies: A Materialist Critique*. London: Routledge, 2004.

   "Speech and Silence in the Fictions of J. M. Coetzee." *Critical Perspectives on J. M. Coetzee*. Ed. Graham Huggan and Stephen Watson. Houndmills: Macmillan, 1996. 37–65.

Pateman, Matthew. *Julian Barnes*. Horndon: Northcote House, 2002.

Paxman, Jeremy. *The English: A Portrait of a People*. Woodstock: Overlook Press, 2000.

Peck, Richard. *A Morbid Fascination: White Prose and Politics in Apartheid South Africa*. Westport: Greenwood Press, 1997.

   "What's a Poor White to Do? White South African Option in *A Sport of Nature*." *Critical Essays on Nadine Gordimer*. Ed. Rowland Smith. Boston: G. K. Hall & Co., 1990. 153–66.

Penner, Dick. *Countries of the Mind: The Fiction of J. M. Coetzee*. New York: Greenwood Press, 1989.

Phillips, Caryl. *Cambridge*. 1991. New York: Vintage International, 1993.

   A Distant Shore. New York: Alfred A. Knopf, 2003.

   The Final Passage. London: Faber & Faber, 1985.

Phillips, James, and James Morley, eds. *Imagination and Its Pathologies*. Cambridge, MA: MIT Press, 2003.

Pifer, Ellen, ed. *Critical Essays on John Fowles*. Boston: G. K. Hall & Co., 1986.

Pipes, Daniel. *The Rushdie Affair: The Novel, the Ayatollah, and the West*. New York: Birch Lane Press, 1990.

Poggioli, Renato. *The Oaten Flute: Essays on Pastoral Poetry and the Pastoral Ideal*. Cambridge, MA: Harvard University Press, 1975.

Poyner, Jane. "Introduction." *J. M. Coetzee and the Idea of the Public Intellectual*. Ed. Jane Poyner. Athens: Ohio University Press, 2006.

Pyle, Forest. *The Ideology of Imagination: Subject and Society in the Discourse of Romanticism*. Stanford University Press, 1995.

Quayson, Ato. *Aesthetic Nervousness: Disability and the Crisis of Representation*. New York: Columbia University Press, 2007.

Radhakrishnan, R. "Postmodernism and the Rest of the World." *The Preoccupation of Postcolonial Studies*. Ed. Fawzia Afzal-Khan and Kalpana Seshadri-Crooks. Durham: Duke University Press, 2000. 37–70.

Theory in an Uneven World. Malden: Blackwell, 2003.

Redfield, Marc. *The Politics of Aesthetics: Nationalism, Gender, Romanticism.* Stanford University Press, 2003.

Rhys, Jean. *Voyage in the Dark.* 1934. New York: W. W. Norton & Company, 1982.

Rich, Paul. "Tradition and Revolt in South African Fiction." *Journal of Southern African Studies* 9.1 (1982): 54–72.

Ricoeur, Paul. "Imagination in Discourse and in Action." *Rethinking Imagination: Culture and Creativity.* Ed. Gillian Robinson and John Rundell. London: Routledge, 1994. 118–35.

Rogers, David, and John McLeod, eds. *The Revision of Englishness.* Manchester University Press, 2004.

Rorty, Richard. *Philosophy and The Mirror of Nature.* Princeton University Press, 1979.

Rundell, John. "Creativity and Judgment: Kant on Reason and Imagination." *Rethinking Imagination: Culture and Creativity.* Ed. Gillian Robinson and John Rundell. London: Routledge, 1994.

Rushdie, Salman. *Imaginary Homelands: Essays and Criticism 1981–1991.* London: Granta Books, 1991.

Midnight's Children. New York: Avon Books, 1980.

"A Novel that Leaves us Blindfolded among History's Rubble." *The Independent* (London) May 7, 2000.

The Satanic Verses. 1988. Dover: Consortium, 1992.

Shame. 1983. New York: Vintage International, 1989.

Ryle, Gilbert. *The Concept of Mind.* New York: Barnes & Noble, 1949.

Sachs, Albie. "Preparing Ourselves for Freedom." *Writing South Africa: Literature, Apartheid, and Democracy, 1970–1995.* Ed. Derek Attridge and Rosemary Jolly. Cambridge University Press, 1998.

Said, Edward W. "Adorno as Lateness Itself." *Adorno: A Critical Reader.* Ed. Nigel Gibson and Andrew Rubin. Malden: Blackwell, 2002. 193–208.

Orientalism. New York: Vintage, 1979.

Salami, Mahmoud. *John Fowles's Fiction and the Poetics of Postmodernism.* Rutherford: Fairleigh Dickinson University Press, 1992.

San Juan Jr., E. *Beyond Postcolonial Theory.* New York: St. Martin's Press, 1998.

Racism and Cultural Studies: Critiques of Multiculturalist Ideology and Politics of Difference. Durham: Duke University Press, 2002.

Sanders, Mark. *Complicities: The Intellectual and Apartheid.* Durham: Duke University Press, 2002.

Sandhu, Sukhdev. "Pop Goes the Centre: Hanif Kureishi's London." *Postcolonial Theory and Criticism.* Ed. Laura Chrisman and Benita Parry. Cambridge: D. S. Brewer, 2000. 133–54.

Schiller, Friedrich. *On the Aesthetic Education of Man: In a Series of Letters.* Trans. Reginald Snell. New York: Frederick Ungar Publishing Co., 1965.

Schor, Naomi. "Introduction." *The Essential Difference.* Ed. Naomi Schor and Elizabeth Weed. Bloomington: Indiana University Press, 1994. vii–xix.

Schubnell, Matthias, ed. *Conversations with N. Scott Momaday.* Jackson: University Press of Mississippi, 1997.

Scott, Joan. "Experience." *Feminists Theorize the Political.* Ed. Judith Butler and Joan Scott. New York: Routledge, 1992. 22–40.

Scruton, Roger. *England: An Elegy.* London: Chatto & Windus, 2000.

Segall, Kimberly Wedeven. "Pursuing Ghosts: The Traumatic Sublime in J. M. Coetzee's *Disgrace.*" *Research in African Literatures* 36.4 (2005): 40–54.

Selvon, Sam. *The Lonely Londoners.* 1956. New York: Longman, 1985.

Moses Ascending. 1975. London: Heinemann, 1984.

Shaw, Harry E. *Narrating Reality: Austen, Scott, Eliot.* Ithaca: Cornell University Press, 1999.

Siddiqi, Yumna. "Police and Postcolonial Rationality in Amitav Ghosh's *The Circle of Reason.*" *Cultural Critique* 50 (2002): 175–211.

Siebers, Tobin. "Kant and the Politics of Beauty." *Philosophy and Literature* 22.1 (1998): 31–50.

Skoie, Mathilde, and Sonia Bjørnstad Velázquez, eds. *Pastoral and the Humanities: Arcadia Re-inscribed.* Exeter: Bristol Phoenix Press, 2006.

Smith, Adam. *The Theory of Moral Sentiments.* 1759. Ed. Knud Haakonssen. Cambridge University Press, 2002.

Smith, Rowland. "Masters and Servants: Nadine Gordimer's *July's People* and the Themes of Her Fiction." *Critical Essays on Nadine Gordimer.* Ed. Rowland Smith. Boston: G. K. Hall & Co., 1990. 140–52.

Smith, Zadie. *White Teeth.* New York: Vintage International, 2000.

Spargo, R. Clifton. *The Ethics of Mourning: Grief and Responsibility in Elegiac Literature.* Baltimore: Johns Hopkins University Press, 2004.

Spivak, Gayatri Chakravorty. *A Critique of Postcolonial Reason: Toward a History of the Vanishing Present.* Cambridge, MA: Harvard University Press, 1999.

"In a Word. Interview." *differences* 1.2 (1989): 124–54.

Su, John J. *Ethics and Nostalgia in the Contemporary Novel.* Cambridge University Press, 2005.

"Fantasies of (Re)collection: Collecting and Imagination in A. S. Byatt's *Possession: A Romance.*" *Contemporary Literature* 45.4 (2004): 684–712.

Syal, Meera. *Anita and Me.* London: Flamingo, 1996.

Tarbox, Katherine. *The Art of John Fowles.* Athens: University of Georgia Press, 1988.

Tew, Philip. *The Contemporary British Novel.* London: Continuum, 2004.

Tolliver, Harold E. *Pastoral: Forms and Attitudes.* Berkeley: University of California Press, 1971.

van der Kolk, B. A., and Onno van der Hart. "The Intrusive Past: the Flexibility of Memory and the Engraving of Trauma." *American Imago* 48.4 (1991): 425–54.

Vaughan, Michael. "Literature and Politics: Currents in South African Writing in the Seventies." *Critical Essays on J. M. Coetzee.* Ed. Sue Kossew. New York: G. K. Hall & Co., 1998. 50–65.

Vipond, Dianne L., ed. *Conversations with John Fowles.* Jackson: University of Mississippi Press, 1999.

Werbner, Pnina, and Tariq Modood, eds. *Debating Cultural Hybridity: Multi-Cultural Identities and the Politics of Anti-Racism*. London: Zed, 1997.

Whale, John. *Imagination under Pressure, 1789–1832: Aesthetics, Politics and Utility*. Cambridge University Press, 2000.

White, Deborah Elise. *Romantic Returns: Superstition, Imagination, History*. Stanford University Press, 2000.

White, Hayden. *The Content of the Form: Narrative Discourse and Historical Representation*. Baltimore: Johns Hopkins University Press, 1987.

   "Historical Emplotment and the Problem of Truth." *Probing the Limits of Representation: Nazism and the "Final Solution"*. Ed. Saul Friedlander. Cambridge, MA: Harvard University Press, 1992. 37–53.

Williams, Raymond. *The Country and the City*. New York: Oxford University Press, 1975.

Wood, Felicity. "Interview with André Brink." *English Academy Review* 18 (2001): 112–21.

Wood, James. "An Activity Not an Attribute: Mobilising Englishness." *The Revision of Englishness*. Ed. David Rogers and John McLeod. Manchester University Press, 2004. 55–64.

Woodard, Charles L. *Ancestral Voice: Conversations with N. Scott Momaday*. Lincoln: University of Nebraska Press, 1989.

Wright, Patrick. "Reinventing Britain: Interview with Homi Bhabha, Susheila Nasta, and Rashid Araeen." *Wasafiri* 29 (1999): 39–43.

Young, Robert J. C. *Colonial Desire: Hybridity in Theory, Culture and Race*. London: Routledge, 1995.

   "Ideologies of the Postcolonial." *Interventions: International Journal of Postcolonial Studies* 1.1 (1998): 4–8.

Zuidervaart, Lambert. "Introduction." *The Semblance of Subjectivity: Essays in Adorno's Aesthetic Theory*. Ed. Tom Huhn and Lambert Zuidervaart. Cambridge, MA: MIT Press, 1997. 1–28.

Index

11117726R00131

Made in the USA
San Bernardino, CA
06 May 2014